C000198162

Qualitative Rese
for Development

Praise for the book

'This book is a practical and informative addition to the existing text books on qualitative methods. The authors show the scope of qualitative research and the value of the approach to international development. Having a foot in both academia and development has enabled them to produce a valuable guide which addresses many of the questions raised by development organizations about how you do qualitative research, analyse and write up. I am delighted to see this valuable book!'

Janet Seeley, Professor of Anthropology and Health,
London School of Hygiene & Tropical Medicine

'Is there a need for yet another textbook on qualitative methods? At first sight, perhaps not, but after having read this volume there are good reasons to rethink that 'gut response'. The debate between qualitative and quantitative methods is old and might be coming to an end. The understanding – and lack of understanding – of qualitative methods varies over time, and hence each period of time needs its own explanation of qualitative methods. The current volume sets the discussion squarely in current discussions around evidence, learning, rigour and performance management. While it is mainly directed at practitioners of qualitative research, I hope many others study its contents: project and programme managers, those who take decisions on the design and funding of research and evaluation, and in particular all who use research findings and who have opinions on whether a particular research process can be considered as 'rigorous evidence'.

Kim Forss, Swedish Expert Committee on Aid Analysis and Evaluation

Qualitative Research for Development

A guide for practitioners

Morten Skovdal and Flora Cornish

PRACTICAL ACTION
Publishing

Practical Action Publishing Ltd
Rugby, Warwickshire, UK
www.practicalactionpublishing.org

© Save the Children Fund, 2015
Reprinted 2017

The right of the authors to be identified as authors of this work has been asserted
under sections 77 and 78 of the Copyright Designs and Patents Act 1988.

All rights reserved. No part of this publication may be reprinted or reproduced or
utilized in any form or by any electronic, mechanical, or other means, now known
or hereafter invented, including photocopying and recording, or in any information
storage or retrieval system, without the written permission of the publishers.

Product or corporate names may be trademarks or registered trademarks, and are used
only for identification and explanation without intent to infringe.

A catalogue record for this book is available from the British Library.

A catalogue record for this book has been requested from the Library of Congress.

ISBN 9781853398537 Hardback
ISBN 9781853398544 Paperback
ISBN 9781780448534 Library Ebook
ISBN 9781780448541 Ebook

Citation: Skovdal, M., and Cornish, F., (2015) Qualitative Research for Development,
Rugby, UK: Practical Action Publishing, <http://dx.doi.org/10.3362/9781780448534>

Since 1974, Practical Action Publishing has published and disseminated books and
information in support of international development work throughout the world.
Practical Action Publishing is a trading name of Practical Action Publishing Ltd
(Company Reg. No. 1159018), the wholly owned publishing company of Practical
Action. Practical Action Publishing trades only in support of its parent charity
objectives and any profits are covenanted back to Practical Action (Charity Reg. No.
247257, Group VAT Registration No. 880 9924 76).

The views and opinions in this publication are those of the authors and do not
represent those of Practical Action Publishing Ltd or its parent charity Practical Action.
Reasonable efforts have been made to publish reliable data and information, but the
authors and publisher cannot assume responsibility for the validity of all materials or
for the consequences of their use.

Cover design by Mercer Design
Typeset by Allzone Digital Services
Printed by 4Edge Limited, UK

Printed on FSC accredited paper

Contents

List of figures, tables, boxes, and activities   viii

About the authors   xi

Preface   xiii

Acknowledgements   xvi

1   **Improving programme impact and accountability through qualitative research**   1
   Towards a 'research approach' in monitoring and evaluation   2
   Qualitative research   4
     What is qualitative research?   4
     What are some of the limitations of qualitative research?   7
   Qualitative research for development   8
     Beneficiary engagement, relevance, and empowerment   9
     Accountability   10
     Impact, innovation and evidence   12
     Value for money   14
     Scalability and replicability   14
     Advocacy, campaigning, and social change   15
   Embedding qualitative research within a project
   and programme cycle   16
     Situational analysis and needs assessment   16
     Local context analysis   16
     Barriers to and facilitators of programme progress analysis   20
     'Stories of change' analysis   21
     'Programme strengths and limitations analysis'   22
     Other options for analysis   22

2   **Designing and planning a qualitative study**   27
   Why plan a qualitative study?   27
   Contextualizing the need for the study   30
   Being clear about your research motivations   32
   Carrying out a literature review   33
   Developing a research question and study objectives   35

http://dx.doi.org/10.3362/9781780448534.000

Qualitative study design   37
Selecting a study approach   37
Setting up a study team   39
Identifying a location and selecting study participants   40
Choosing qualitative research methods   42
Overcoming socio-ethical dilemmas   44
Data analysis   47
Cost and timescale   49
Conflicts of interest   51
Quality criteria of qualitative research   51

3 **Interviews and focus group discussions**   55
What are interviews and focus group discussions?   56
Why conduct interviews and focus groups?   57
Interviews or focus groups? How to choose   60
Designing an interview or focus group study   61
Checklist: A good topic guide   70
Typical challenges and possible responses   71

4 **Participant observation**   75
What is participant observation?   77
Why use participant observation?   78
Designing a participant observation study   83
Justify the choice of participant observation   83
The role and varying uses of participant observation   83
Participant observer roles and degrees of involvement   85
Case selection and sampling within the case   87
Data collection   88
Challenges and responses   92
Access and acceptability   93
Researcher bias   93
Ethical issues   94

5 **Participatory data collection methods**   99
Introduction to participatory research   100
Participatory data collection methods   102
Problem tree   104
Body mapping   107
Stories of change   111
Daily diagrams   112
History profiles   114
Preference ranking   115

Community mapping 117
Spidergram 120
Common pitfalls in using participatory data collection methods 122
Complexity of community 122
Power relations 123
Participation 123
Capacity building 124
Time commitments 124
How to be a good facilitator 124
Data capture and management 127

6 **Photovoice: methodology and use** 131
Introduction to Photovoice 131
Photovoice in the programme cycle 134
Planning and design 135
Questions to consider 135
Specifying the aim of your project 137
Setting up a team 138
Selecting participants and a setting 139
Ethical considerations 139
Workshop facilitation 142
Delivering and facilitating Photovoice: 10 steps 143

7 **Analysing qualitative data** 157
Getting started with qualitative data analysis 159
Qualitative data analysis strategies 163
Thematic analysis 164
Case study analysis 172
Computer-assisted qualitative data analysis software 177
Information management 177
Code and retrieve 177
Exploring patterns 179
What CAQDAS progam should you use? 179

8 **Writing a research report** 183
Structuring a development research report 184
Writing for the public 195
Writing for a peer-reviewed publication 196

Glossary 203

List of figures, tables, boxes, and activities

Figures

1.1	Iterative process of combining qualitative and quantitative methods in research	8
1.2	Qualitative research for development	9
1.3	Opportunities for qualitative research within the programme cycle	17
1.4	Children practising taking pictures	18
2.1	Working street children	31
5.1	An example of a problem tree	106
5.2	Example of how body parts can be used as metaphors to spark dialogue	108
5.3	An 'H' assessment	110
5.4	Daily diagrams drawn by a 14-year-old girl in Kenya	113
5.5	Example of a history profile by a 13-year-old girl from Kenya	115
5.6	Community map created by caregiving children in western Kenya	119
5.7	Spidergram for assessing community participation	120
5.8	Body map illustrating the characteristics of a good or poor participatory research facilitator	130
6.1	Bangladeshi children participating in a Photovoice project	141
7.1	Extract of a transcript	161
7.2	Picture taken by a study participant	165
7.3	Primary and secondary themes taken from NVivo's sample project	178

Tables

1.1	Summary of the key differences between qualitative and quantitative research	6
2.1	Electronic search engines for identifying research papers	34
2.2	Example of what a qualitative research timetable might look like	50
2.3	Example of what a qualitative research budget might look like	51
3.1	Should I use interviews or focus groups?	60
3.2	Steps in interview and focus group research design	61
3.3	Types of interview question	64

5.1	Methods matrix	105
5.2	Example of pairwise voting on community problems	116
5.3	Example of preference ranking through pairwise voting	116
7.1	Steps and guidelines to prepare a transcript	160
7.2	Five steps to develop a thematic network from codes or primary themes	167
7.3	Example of a case study comparison chart	175
8.1	Comparing different types of research output	183
8.2	How to structure a development research report	184

Boxes

1.1	Key aspects of a 'research approach'	3
1.2	Children using participatory methods to assess local needs	18
1.3	Children participating in a context analysis in West Africa	20
2.1	Working street children in Karachi, Pakistan – a case study	31
2.2	Possible structure and headings for a study protocol	32
2.3	Examples of how a qualitative research question can be formulated	36
3.1	Examples of research questions for interview or focus group studies	62
3.2	The sample in a large-scale qualitative domestic violence study	64
3.3	A brief topic guide for a focus group exploring the situation regarding domestic violence in a community	68
4.1	Example of participant observation data	78
4.2	Topics to cover in a methods section	83
4.3	Three different uses of participant observation data in a study	84
4.4	Three different roles for the participant observer	85
4.5	Field notes template	90
5.1	Selected resources freely available online	102
6.1	Example of accountability and transparency in a Photovoice project	141
7.1	Example of how a thematic network can guide the structure of your presentation of findings	171
8.1	Reporting findings on stigma among people living with HIV in Khartoum	191
8.2	Alternative means of communicating research to the public	194
8.3	Is my research suitable for peer-reviewed publication?	195
8.4	'What this study adds'	196

Activities

2.1	Planning for and responding to surprises	29
2.2	Motivational factors behind the study	33
2.3	Searching for literature	35

2.4	Deciding on a research question	36
2.5	Linking study interests and approaches	38
2.6	Consulting your gatekeepers	40
2.7	Choosing qualitative research methods	43
2.8	Potential conflicts of interest	51
3.1	Write research questions	62
3.2	Improve these topic guide questions	69
3.3	Creating a good interview dynamic	70
4.1	Design a participant observation study	89
4.2	Practise writing field notes	92
4.3	Distinguish between observation, interpretation, and reflexivity	92
5.1	Reflecting on the diversity of communities	123
5.2	What makes a good facilitator?	127
6.1	Ethical issues in a Photovoice project	142
7.1	Coding your data	165
8.1	Write an executive summary	186
8.2	'What this study adds'	196

About the authors

Morten Skovdal (PhD from London School of Economics and Political Science) is Associate Professor in the Department of Public Health at the University of Copenhagen, where he teaches qualitative research methods. He has 10 years of experience in conducting qualitative research in the field of development and global health. Before joining the University of Copenhagen, Morten worked as a Senior Advisor on Impact and Evidence at Save the Children UK. He is also a founding trustee of a UK trust supporting child welfare programmes in Kenya.

Flora Cornish (PhD from London School of Economics and Political Science) is Associate Professor in the Department of Methodology at the London School of Economics and Political Science, where she teaches qualitative research methods. She has 15 years of experience in conducting qualitative research in collaboration with small local NGOs, government health services, and large international charities.

Morten and Flora collectively have 25 years of experience in conducting qualitative research with development organizations. They have published over 140 academic articles, using qualitative methods to better understand health and development.

Preface

This book has grown out of our collective work on qualitative research in the context of development and global health over the past 15 years. During this time, we have had a foot in both academia and international development organizations, and have collaborated with many local NGOs. We feel extremely fortunate to have been able to combine our training as qualitative researchers and academics with *people-centred* development. Our research focuses on giving voice to some of the most marginalized members of society, highlighting injustices and opportunities for participatory decision making in the practice of development, social work, and global public health. But our engagement with development practitioners has also been challenging at times. This book is a culmination of some of the rich and challenging discussions we have had with colleagues working for development agencies. They kept us on our toes, and forced us to continually re-think and re-work our academic and qualitative research practice to fit with the realities and interests of development agencies. Nonetheless, our engagement and discussions spotlighted confusion and lack of clarity within development organizations pertaining to what qualitative inquiries are 'good for' in the context of development, and when they are 'good enough' to constitute qualitative evidence. We see this lack of clarity as a key obstacle to a more widespread application of qualitative research methods in the context of humanitarian responses and development programmes.

For a long time we struggled to explain what qualitative research is 'good for' in the context of international development work. This may seem a bit odd given our qualitative research experience. However, we quickly learned that it was not merely a matter of explaining what qualitative research is about and what it can be used for. We also learned that this was not a matter of convincing quantitatively trained monitoring and evaluation staff about what qualitative research can do. In fact, most of them know that qualitative research is about giving people a chance to communicate their perspectives in order to gain a more in-depth understanding of an issue. Instead, it became a matter of highlighting and identifying how qualitative research can feed into development practitioners' everyday work practice and support their efforts to develop impactful development programmes that reach a greater number of people with quality services. In other words, it became a matter of showcasing exactly how qualitative research can contribute in a concrete way to organizational targets, humanitarian responses, and development programmes. With support from a great number of colleagues working in the field of development, we hope that this book provides some pointers as to what qualitative research can do in a concrete way for development practice.

The question about when a qualitative inquiry is 'good enough' to constitute evidence is less straightforward. For a long time, development practitioners have used qualitative investigations in their work, without necessarily considering these activities as evidence-generating or research. However, with a growing push for development practitioners to design, implement, and take to scale evidence-informed programmes, they are increasingly encouraged to adopt more methodological practices in their qualitative investigations, aspiring to the more rigorous standards found in academic qualitative research. It is a push that is driven both externally (by funding agencies) and internally (motivated by development agencies' desire to do better), and it exposes the qualitative research capacity needs of organizations. It is a push that has opened up new problems and opportunities for specialists in monitoring and evaluation, particularly in relation to their qualitative research skills, and has raised questions about how methodological they will have to be in their qualitative investigations to generate information worthy of being called 'evidence'.

Tom Ling, former head of the Impact, Innovation and Evidence Team at Save the Children UK, once said to us that to get closer to answering the 'good enough' question, we need to consider 'good enough' for whom and reflect on the purpose and audience of qualitative investigations. This encourages us to distinguish between two forms of qualitative evidence. *Qualitative research* is key to building an evidence base that can be shared widely and drawn upon beyond the programme under study. In other words, its utility is to generate insights that can be used across space and time. Conducting rigorous qualitative research requires a degree of specialized skills and a methodological, often quite rigid, approach in line with international standards of solid qualitative research, adding to the cost and time of the inquiry. Rapid *qualitative appraisals*, on the other hand, are cheaper, more flexible, less methodological (and effectively less rigorous), and serve the purpose of providing real-time information from communities and beneficiaries, to enable the design of context-sensitive programmes, or to enable informed judgements of how to change and enhance a programme. In other words, their utility is to provide specific and local evidence to support real-time decision making.

Distinguishing between qualitative research and appraisal helps clarify the different purposes that guide qualitative investigations, enabling the appropriate management of expectations and resources. To determine whether a qualitative investigation is 'good enough' from a methodological perspective therefore partly depends on the type of evidence that is being generated: 1) qualitative appraisal evidence for real-time feedback and decision making; or 2) qualitative research evidence that is transferable to other contexts.

It is not surprising that many development practitioners feel apprehensive about conducting qualitative research, and keen to know what it is 'good for' and whether what they do is 'good enough' to constitute qualitative research evidence. We hope that this book can provide development practitioners with inspiration on how best to integrate qualitative investigations into programming (the 'good for') and with procedural clarity on how to produce good qualitative research evidence (towards 'good enough'). In other words, we hope that the book will provide development practitioners with the impetus, skills, and confidence to use qualitative research more actively in their important work.

Although the book is written with international development practitioners in mind, we believe the book is relevant to a much broader audience. Many of the challenges outlined above not only apply to the context of international development, but are faced by practitioners in many other fields. Using international development as an example, the book provides qualitative research guidance to practitioners in any intervention setting, whether it be in social development or public health, with adults or children, or in low-, middle- or high-income countries. Also students and aspiring researchers interested in intervention studies will find the book useful.

The book consists of eight chapters, taking readers through the entire research process. The first two chapters are about *getting started*, with Chapter 1 providing background to qualitative research and a framework for integrating qualitative methods into development programming. Chapter 2 provides details on how to plan and design a study, together with step-by-step guidance on how to produce a qualitative study protocol. The subsequent four chapters introduce different *methods for generating qualitative data*. Chapter 3 provides an understanding of the role of interviews and focus group discussions, and knowledge of each step to be taken in designing and carrying out an interview or focus group study. Chapter 4 equips readers with an understanding of the role of participant observation in development research, knowledge of key terms and design considerations, and skills for undertaking participant observation research. Chapter 5 introduces participatory data collection methods and discusses some of the many challenges and obstacles of using participatory methods. Chapter 6 introduces Photovoice as a research method and offers 10-step guidance in how to plan and design a Photovoice project. The remaining two chapters relate to the process of *identifying and reporting on findings*. Chapter 7 presents guiding principles for qualitative analysis and step-by-step guidance on two concrete and commonly used strategies for conducting qualitative data analysis. One strategy falls under the category of 'thematic analysis', and the other relates to the analysis and presentation of 'case studies'. Lastly, Chapter 8 sets out key concerns in writing up development research for a variety of different audiences, and provides practical tips for such writing. The chapter also outlines the structure of a research report and discusses the material that belongs in each section.

We hope that readers find the book accessible, in relation to organization, cost, language, and style.

Morten Skovdal and Flora Cornish
October 2015

Acknowledgements

We are grateful to many people who have been supportive in producing this book; many colleagues have helped shape the thinking behind it. First of all, we would like to thank the Impact, Innovation and Evidence Team at Save the Children UK for instigating and financially supporting this book. In particular, we would like to thank Tom Ling, Rachel Eager, and Mavis Owusu-Gyamfi for enthusiastically backing this project, and for valuable inputs along the way. Second, we would like to thank all the reviewers for their invaluable feedback and comments on particular chapters. These include Tom Ling, Rachel Eager, Ehtisham Ul Hassan, Sarah Lilley, Isabelle Risso-Gill, Nitika Tolani-Brown, Julie Newton, and Zoe Davidson from Save the Children. We also received valuable feedback from Kelley Bunkers and Nimesh Dhungana. Thanks to Jacques Schillings from Save the Children for facilitating the review process. We would also like to thank Diego Alburez-Gutierrez for expert searching of the grey literature to identify suitable examples.

Flora Cornish is particularly grateful to her colleagues in the Department of Methodology at the London School of Economics and Political Science, for providing an ideal environment in which to teach, learn, create, and critique research methods. In particular, teaching qualitative methods together with Martin Bauer, Aude Bicquelet, Elena Gonzalez-Polledo, Alasdair Jones, and Jen Tarr is an ongoing top-notch education in communicating qualitative methods clearly and designing effective skill-building exercises.

Morten Skovdal wishes to extend his gratitude to former colleagues in the Department of Programme Policy and Quality, Save the Children UK, for countless discussions about how to position and integrate qualitative research into the work of Save the Children. He would also like to thank colleagues and students within the Department of Public Health, University of Copenhagen, for continuing to make this such a conducive and enjoyable place to work.

We are both indebted to Catherine Campbell who has been instrumental in our research training.

Finally, at Practical Action Publishing we would like to thank Clare Tawney and Helen Wishart for their prompt and professional processing of the book. Also, thanks to Casper Nielsen from the Centre of Online and Blended Learning at the University of Copenhagen for expertly producing the illustrations featured in the book.

CHAPTER 1

Improving programme impact and accountability through qualitative research

Abstract

Qualitative research has much to offer to the practical work of humanitarian and development organizations. Growing recognition of the potential for qualitative research to enhance programme impact is putting pressure on development practitioners to adapt a 'research approach' in their monitoring, evaluation, accountability, and learning work. This introductory chapter starts off by outlining some of the ways in which qualitative research can be used to improve the impact, quality, and accountability of development projects and programmes. It will then introduce some basic principles of qualitative research and illustrate some of the ways in which qualitative research can be incorporated into various stages of the programme cycle.

Keywords: Qualitative research; research for development; monitoring and evaluation; programme impact; programme accountability; evidence

Learning objectives

After reading this chapter, you will be able to:

- outline the ways in which qualitative research can improve development programmes and their impact;
- describe the link between qualitative research and accountability;
- explain what qualitative research is, including its strengths and weaknesses; and
- identify ways of integrating qualitative research into a programme cycle.

Key terms (definitions)

- *Accountability*: The means by which people and organizations are held responsible for their actions by having to account for them to other people.
- *Evidence*: The available body of facts or information indicating whether a belief or proposition is true or valid.
- *Findings*: Summaries, impressions, or conclusions reached after an examination or investigation of data.

http://dx.doi.org/10.3362/9781780448534.001

- *Formative evaluation*: An early examination of an active programme with the aim of identifying areas for improvement in its design and performance.
- *Generalizability*: The ability to make statements and draw conclusions that can have a general application.
- *Programme cycle*: The process and sequence in which a programme develops from start to finish.
- *Qualitative research*: A method of inquiry that takes as a starting point the belief that there are benefits to exploring, unpacking, and describing social meanings and perceptions of an issue or a programme.
- *Research*: To study something systematically, gathering and reporting on detailed and accurate information.

Towards a 'research approach' in monitoring and evaluation

With an ever-growing emphasis on evidence-informed programming, there is a push for development practitioners to strengthen the quality of their monitoring, evaluation, accountability, and learning (MEAL) activities. For many development practitioners, evidence continues to be associated with quantitative evaluations of development initiatives. In fact, until recently, many people working in MEAL have been suspicious of qualitative methods and have had little incentive to develop a qualitative evidence capacity (Bamberger et al., 2010). While quantitative evidence is crucial for decision making and rightfully continues to play a key role in the development of evidence, there is growing recognition of the need for qualitative evidence.

This recognition is born out of the fact that development programmes have often been designed and implemented without sufficient qualitative evidence to understand the needs, wishes, and context of the target population. Too often, local perspectives have been neglected in the design, implementation, and evaluation of programmes, despite local voices containing crucial information that can help development practitioners understand pathways to programme success and failure (Chambers, 1983, 1997).

Qualitative research can systematize and formalize the process of generating qualitative evidence. Qualitative research can be used to understand the context of a programme better; it can provide us with insights to new issues and help us understand the complexity of connections and relationships between people, programmes, and organizations. It can provide beneficiaries with an opportunity to share their perspectives of an issue or a programme, which in turn can help us understand the nuances with regard to how different people experience a programme. Importantly, qualitative research can be used to ensure that development programmes resonate with local realities and expectations.

However, given the dominance of quantitative MEAL efforts, many development practitioners lack the skills and confidence to authoritatively produce qualitative evidence. In particular, there continues to be confusion and lack of clarity within development organizations about what qualitative evidence looks like and how best to conduct rigorous qualitative studies.

Although we welcome a drive for more rigorous qualitative research, we also recognize that in a 'development organization' context, there is a tension between achieving rigour, what is feasible, and what is considered useful.

We accept that some development practitioners are likely to face significant constraints in adapting some of the practices we describe in this book. We are therefore not looking to turn you into an 'academic researcher'; rather, we aim to introduce you to the 'rules of the game' for conducting rigorous qualitative research at all stages of a development project cycle. We want to encourage and equip you with the knowledge and skills required to adopt a 'research approach' (see Box 1.1) in your MEAL and development activities (Laws et al., 2013).

We believe that it is important for development practitioners to engage with qualitative research and adapt a 'research approach' in the generation of qualitative evidence for four main reasons.

- Development practitioners are at the frontline, responding to humanitarian and development needs, which makes them particularly well suited to **identifying issues** on which research is required and to taking an active role in facilitating research.
- Development practitioners can accelerate the **use of research** findings and translate them into programming and advocacy.
- With the turn to evidence-informed policy and practice, **interventions need to be based on systematic qualitative research** from the ground as well as on evidence from evaluations in other locations. Assessing value for money and taking programmes to scale cannot be based on anecdotes and impressions.
- Systematic qualitative research helps development practitioners **improve the quality, accountability, and impact of their programmes**.

Box 1.1 Key aspects of a 'research approach'

These include:

- being curious and having an interest in learning about the causes of things;
- being willing to learn from data, and change your mind about prior beliefs;
- having a concern to really understand what people say and the meanings behind their statements;
- having an awareness of how you, the researcher, may shape what is being said and the direction of the research;
- striving for analytical sophistication, identifying patterns that may not be immediately obvious;
- being systematic and keeping records of all the data;
- being interested in discussing findings in a broader context, for example in relation to previous experiences or the experiences of others.

Source: Laws et al. (2013: 14).

This book is designed to guide development practitioners through the process of planning, conducting, and reporting on qualitative research, while simultaneously showing how qualitative methods can support the work of development practitioners. In other words, we focus on the particular uses of qualitative research in the programme cycle and highlight the role of qualitative evidence in improving the impact, quality, and accountability of development programmes.

Our practical aim is to demystify the qualitative research process and provide development practitioners with the procedural clarity, skills, and confidence to use qualitative methods authoritatively and advocate for the need to embed qualitative research in the programme cycle, either on its own or together with quantitative studies.

Qualitative research

What is qualitative research? And how is it different from quantitative research?

Research involves collecting information, also referred to as data, in a systematic way in order to answer a question. However, your research question, and the methods you use to generate data that can answer that question, are likely to reflect one of two research approaches, or a mix.

One such approach refers to quantitative research. Quantitative research typically explores questions that examine the relationship between different events, or occurrences. In an evaluation context, this might include looking at how change can be linked or attributed to a particular intervention. Such a question might be: 'What impact did child-friendly spaces have on refugee children's psycho-social well-being?' To test the causality or link between 'child-friendly spaces', an intervention, and children's 'psycho-social well-being', researchers will have to try to maintain a level of control of the different factors, also called variables, that may influence the relationship between the events. They will also need to recruit research participants randomly. Quantitative data is often gathered through surveys and questionnaires that are carefully developed, structured, and administered to provide you with numerical data that can be explored statistically and yield a result that can be generalized to some larger population (Bauer et al., 2000).

Another approach, and the focus of this book, is qualitative research. Qualitative research seeks to explore personal and social experiences, meanings, and practices as well as the role of context in shaping these. Qualitative research thus takes as a starting point the belief that there are benefits to exploring, unpacking, and describing social meanings and perceptions of a phenomenon, or a programme (Flick, 2002). Not only can qualitative research give voice to people who are ordinarily silent or whose perceptions are rarely considered, it can help explain 'how', 'why', and 'under what circumstances' does a particular phenomenon, or programme, operate as it does.

As such, you can use qualitative research to obtain information about:

- local **knowledge** and understanding of a given issue or programme
- people's **perceptions** and **experiences** of an issue, their needs, or a programme;
- how people **act** and **engage** with a programme, each other, and organizations;
- local **responses** and the **acceptability** and **feasibility** of a programme;
- **meanings** people attach to certain experiences, relationships, or life events;
- **social processes** and **contextual factors** (for example, social norms, values, behaviours, and cultural practices) that marginalize a group of people or have an impact on a programme;
- local **agency** and responses in mitigating poverty and the marginalization of vulnerable populations.

As these examples of research areas suggest, you can use qualitative research to gain a better understanding of either an issue or a particular programme or intervention. Issue-focused research can help you develop a better understanding of an issue, or phenomenon, and how it affects a group of people. This may, for example, include the health risks facing children in a particular location, or the barriers that expectant mothers face in accessing maternal healthcare. Qualitative research is particularly good at investigating sensitive topics, whether it be sexual abuse or intimate partner violence. It could also include examining the care or living arrangements of hard-to-reach groups, such as children living or working on the street. Issue-focused research can provide information that better prepares you to advocate for a cause or develop and plan a programme that addresses some of the problems that the research identifies.

Intervention studies and programme-focused research look at stakeholders' interaction with a programme. This might include looking at some of the different ways in which a programme has an impact, community-level acceptability of a programme, or the factors enabling or hindering programme success. Programme-focused research could also involve examining how beneficiaries experience a programme. For example, a research question might read: 'What are children's experiences of spending time in child-friendly spaces?' To explore children's views of 'child-friendly spaces', researchers can use creative, flexible, semi- or unstructured methods that enable and capture children's views. Such methods may include individual or group interviews (see Chapter 3), participant observations (see Chapter 4), participatory methods (see Chapter 5), or Photovoice (see Chapter 6). The information generated through these methods can be used to map out and contextualize children's social experiences or to identify a range of minority, majority, or contradictory experiences or perceptions of child-friendly spaces.

Table 1.1 summarizes key differences between qualitative and quantitative research. Although the two approaches ask different questions and have different strengths, presenting them as distinct and opposite is not overly

Table 1.1 Summary of the key differences between qualitative and quantitative research

	Qualitative research approach	Quantitative research approach
Examples of research questions	How do cash transfers support the education of children?	What impact did cash transfers have on children's school performance?
	In what ways can a literacy boost programme affect children's education?	Does a literacy boost programme improve children's reading skills?
	What social factors influence women's access to healthcare?	Is socio-economic status correlated to women's health?
Type of knowledge	Subjective	Objective
Aim	Exploratory and observational	Generalizable and hypothesis-testing
Characteristics	Flexible	Fixed and controlled
	Contextual portrayal	Independent and dependent variables
	Dynamic, continuous view of change	Pre- and post-programme measurement of change
Sampling	Purposeful	Random
Data collection	Semi-structured or unstructured	Structured
Nature of data	Narratives, quotations, descriptions	Numbers, statistics
	Value uniqueness, particularity	Replication
Analysis	Thematic and interpretative	Statistical

helpful. In practice, they are often combined or draw on elements from each other (Bauer et al., 2000). For example, quantitative surveys often include open-ended questions. Similarly, qualitative responses can be quantified.

Qualitative and quantitative methods can also support each other, both through triangulation of findings and by building on each other. Triangulation is when you use different data sources and methods to shed light on an issue or programme. You can triangulate either by gathering data from different research participants or by examining an issue using different data collection methods. For example, you could compare the perspectives of teachers, students, and parents on the quality of schooling or gain an understanding of student perspectives through a questionnaire, interviews and participant observations. Why is it important to gather the perspectives of different stakeholders and/ or use different methods? Triangulation can either create confidence in the trustworthiness of your findings or highlight further complexity (Denzin, 1989; Gaskell and Bauer, 2000). If, for example, different stakeholders all share a similar concern, or if your data collection methods all lead to similar observations, you are a step closer to overcoming bias (an inclination to hold a particular view) either induced by a particular method, or by only considering the views of one group of research participants. However, through data and method triangulation, you may also uncover inconsistencies or contradictions, which will require you to further understand the origin of these complexities (Gaskell and Bauer, 2000). Either way, triangulation can strengthen your conclusions and identify areas for further work.

Qualitative and quantitative methods can also be used to build on each other in an iterative manner. MEAL activities typically draw on a mix of qualitative and quantitative methods. This is because one research approach (qualitative or quantitative) can rarely fully address the research questions that are posed or provide the information required for a log frame. The approach of drawing on both qualitative and quantitative methods has been referred to as mixed methods.

The weight given to qualitative or quantitative methods may differ, as can the sequence in which qualitative and quantitative data is collected (Creswell, 2002). For example, qualitative research can be used to develop and guide the questions in a survey, and ensure that they both include relevant indicators and ask appropriate questions. Equally, a statistical analysis of a survey may identify variances, trends, and patterns, which can then be explained and explored further through qualitative research (see Figure 1.1).

The iterative process illustrated in Figure 1.1 is typical. Other sequences include collecting both quantitative and qualitative data at the same time, or starting to collect either qualitative or quantitative data, which is then followed up with an alternative method. Depending on your research question, one method may carry more weight than another. For example, you may conduct a qualitative study but also gather a few descriptive statistics from your context. In this case, the weight lies with the qualitative research methodology. There is no right or wrong sequence or weight. The most important thing is that you choose a strategy that can best answer your research question.

What are some of the limitations of qualitative research?

There are some limitations to qualitative research. While qualitative research is ideally suited to understanding local knowledge and perspectives, the knowledge produced from such studies is not easily generalizable to other

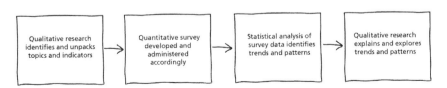

Figure 1.1 Iterative process of combining qualitative and quantitative methods in research
Source: Adapted from Bamberger et al. (2010).

people or other settings. One therefore has to be careful about making sweeping generalizations about the findings generated from qualitative research. Qualitative research embraces different views and perspectives, and is likely to unpack a variety of different experiences and perceptions; it is therefore rarely appropriate to test hypotheses using qualitative methods. Qualitative research can instead be used to generate hypotheses that can then be tested using quantitative methods.

All research is vulnerable to bias – and this includes quantitative research. However, qualitative research explicitly embraces subjectivity, which means that personal experiences, perceptions, and judgements are valued, whether they come from research participants or from the way in which researchers purposefully recruit participants to the study. Qualitative researchers also make observations and interpret data based on preconceived ideas about the topic. The background, experiences, and values of those researchers will therefore inevitably influence the generation of qualitative evidence. According to Madden (2010), this makes the researcher a key instrument and tool for the generation of qualitative evidence. It also means that qualitative findings are never objective truths; rather, they are carefully formed and shaped by the researcher. For sceptics of qualitative research, this raises questions about its rigour and the scientific value. However, precisely because of the subjectivity of qualitative research, it is important to use a set of quality criteria that are different from those of quantitative research: namely, reliability, validity, and generalizability (Gaskell and Bauer, 2000). In Chapter 2, we will describe different quality criteria of qualitative research, which help enhance its rigour and scientific value.

As a result of these limitations, people in positions of power often associate qualitative research with limited use and credibility. However, this is a grave misunderstanding of what systematic qualitative research has to offer. And it is a misunderstanding with real implications for the funding and support of the development of qualitative research capacity. As a consequence, there remains little procedural clarity or guidance on how to conduct good qualitative research in the development sector. While this is slowly changing, it reminds us that we all have a responsibility to maintain and further strengthen the quality and integrity of qualitative research.

By now, you probably have a good understanding of what qualitative research is and what it is not. To further explain the use and potential of such research to the work of development practitioners, we will now discuss some of the different ways in which qualitative research can improve and strengthen development processes.

Qualitative research for development

Development agencies are continually aiming to develop programmes that are optimal in relation to relevance, impact, cost, reach, and social change. Qualitative research can help development practitioners achieve each of these goals more fully. In this section, we will introduce six components of development and discuss the contribution of qualitative research to each one. As illustrated in Figure 1.2, the components we will be discussing are: 1) beneficiary engagement, relevance, and empowerment; 2) accountability; 3) impact, innovation, and evidence; 4) value for money; 5) scalability and replicability; 6) advocacy, campaigning, and social change.

Beneficiary engagement, relevance, and empowerment

Many development and humanitarian organizations have it within their mandate to empower the people they work to assist, and they often see participation as an essential strategy to achieve this. Qualitative research can facilitate participation. As a research approach, it actively encourages the use and development of creative and flexible methods that enable different voices to be heard (O'Kane, 2008). In fact, some qualitative research methods

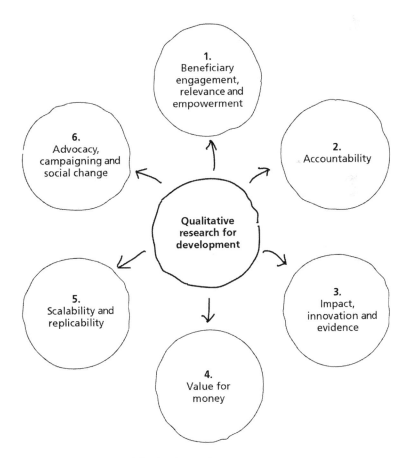

Figure 1.2 Qualitative research for development

have been developed with the specific purpose of enabling the people whom development agencies are looking to assist to participate in the planning of development programmes (Chambers, 1983; Rifkin and Pridmore, 2001). See Chapters 5 and 6 for more detail and examples of such qualitative and participatory research methods. Using qualitative research to facilitate participation is important for a number of reasons:

- Qualitative research can be used to **consult** a wide variety of local stakeholders. Often the least powerful and visible people of a community, such as children, struggle to have a voice in community and programme sensitization forums. Qualitative research can thus ensure that different groups of people are given an opportunity to voice their perspectives about an issue or a programme.
- In return, and to ensure **relevance**, development practitioners can use these perspectives to tailor the intervention to make it more aligned to the spectrum of views, expectations, and needs that exist in a programme context.
- If community members feel that the opinions and experiences they articulated through qualitative research have been taken into account, and have influenced decisions, they are more likely to stay positively engaged with the programme and have a sense of **ownership**.
- Some qualitative research methods (such as Photovoice; see Chapter 6) can actively facilitate **deliberation**, awareness raising, and critical thinking (Freire, 1973). Such analytical skills are essential for good community-level programme management and for developing relationships with external change agents.
- Related to this, the type of participation that qualitative research facilitates can be empowering. Participation and **empowerment** are deeply intertwined, reinforcing each other, both as means and ends. On the one hand, participation can lead to the development of new skills, feelings of control, and power over the participants' lives. On the other hand, participation in activities, and under conditions that do not enable change, can contribute to a sense of powerlessness and further discourage participation (Campbell and Jovchelovitch, 2000).

As these five examples suggest, qualitative research has the potential to facilitate beneficiary engagement, which not only ensures that programmes are relevant but can, as argued by Kilby (2006), help development organizations become effective agents of empowerment.

Accountability

Accountability broadly refers to the mechanisms that are in place within a development and humanitarian organization to ensure that it uses its position of power responsibly. It typically involves 'giving an account' to someone who has a stake in a development programme (Cornwall et al., 2000). More often than not, this involves demonstrating to a funding agency that a programme has been worth funding. Development practitioners are all too familiar with the process of generating data and information to demonstrate to their donors that their programmes are worthwhile. While being accountable to donors continues to be key in the delivery of aid and development programmes, the past few decades have witnessed a powerful movement to ensure that accountability is not limited to the funding agencies and donors, but also considers the responsibility of development organizations to be accountable to the people they seek to assist.

The Humanitarian Accountability Partnership (HAP) has been instrumental in promoting accountability to beneficiaries of humanitarian and development organizations. HAP has developed some standards, or benchmarks, of accountability (Darcy et al., 2013). These include the following:

- *Establishing and delivering on commitments:* the organization develops a plan that sets out its commitment to accountability.
- *Staff competency*: the organization ensures that its staff have the necessary competencies to deliver a plan of action for accountability.
- *Sharing information*: the organization ensures that all stakeholders, including its beneficiaries, have access to timely and relevant information about the organization and its activities.
- *Participation*: the organization gives voice to the people it aims to assist and incorporates their views into programming.
- *Handling complaints*: the organization puts in place mechanisms that enable all stakeholders, including beneficiaries, to safely deliver complaints and receive a reply that gives details about how the organization is responding to the complaint.
- *Learning and continual improvement*: the organization learns from its experience and applies learning to improve its performance.

These six benchmarks of accountability encourage us to think more holistically about accountability, shifting the focus away from auditing, which benefits donors, to implementing agencies' responsibility to be held accountable to their beneficiaries.

A quick glance at the six benchmarks suggests the relevance of qualitative research to accountability. As already discussed, qualitative research is fundamental to the benchmarks of participation and learning. However, the 'handling of complaints' benchmark can also be actioned through qualitative research to some extent. Qualitative research is not a complaints-handling procedure and should not substitute for more established complaints mechanisms that are geared towards handling and responding to a wide variety of issues. However, the feedback generated through qualitative research can expose grievances and criticisms about a programme, enabling development practitioners to make necessary changes.

While qualitative research can generate learning about programme outcomes, feeding into donor reports, it also offers a great opportunity for real-time feedback that development practitioners can act upon to improve programme performance (Featherstone, 2013). But qualitative research is not a magic bullet for accountability. Qualitative research per se does not ensure accountability. It merely seeks to generate learning from a variety of programme stakeholders. Accountability happens when development practitioners use this learning, ideally in collaboration with the beneficiaries, to improve their 'ways of working' with local communities and to enhance the performance of their programmes. In addition, there are many other more established ways for you to promote accountability, which qualitative research cannot and should not replace.

Save the Children has developed a *Programme Accountability Guidance Pack* (Munyas Ghadially, 2013) that offers guidance and tools in areas such as information sharing, participation, complaints handling, capacity building of staff, and monitoring of accountability measures. You can download the pack and watch videos developed to improve understanding and facilitate discussions on programme accountability at <www.savethechildren.org.uk/resources/online-library/programme-accountability-guidance-pack>.

Impact, innovation and evidence

Development practitioners have an interest in implementing impactful programmes that: 1) can be measured by monitoring and evaluation frameworks; 2) are highly valued by the people they seek to assist; 3) represent good value for the time and resources invested. The decision to implement one type of intervention over another often rests on the experience of development practitioners, the scant availability of evidence, and what can be measured to demonstrate impact. While tacit or common knowledge, however limited it may be, can contribute to the development of fantastic programmes, the question of whether or not another intervention could produce better outcomes is always present.

It is this curiosity about whether or not better and more impactful programmes could be implemented for the same amount of money and effort that leads to innovation and evidence building. It is also this type of curiosity that encourages development practitioners to go beyond demonstrating impact to donors, and to innovate and develop evidence that helps them establish programmes that are optimal in relation to relevance, impact, cost, reach, and social change.

Quantitative inquiries are key to the development of such evidence, both to determine programme outcomes and to compare different development approaches. However, qualitative research is equally important and can be used to generate knowledge and facilitate learning in a number of different ways that can help practitioners develop innovative and evidence-informed programmes. We will now describe three ways in which qualitative research can be used to further impact, innovation, and evidence.

First, qualitative research can help localize development programmes. Development programmes are most successful when they are embedded in a local context, reflect locally perceived needs, and draw on local assets (Moser,

1998). This is widely recognized and it is not uncommon for donor agencies, in their proposals, to ask for an account of how community members were involved in the development of the proposal and how they can be expected to participate in the planning and implementation of the programme. Participatory and qualitative research plays a key role in generating information and evidence to inform future programmes so that they are tailored to local realities.

The process of localizing development programmes can involve two steps. First is a needs assessment, where qualitative research can be used to map the local perceptions of needs, examine their nature and causes, and set priorities for future action. A second step can involve using qualitative research to chart the cultural context, local assets, and community resources. These contextual factors may well form part of local coping strategies to hardship and would be important to consider, both to align programmatic and local responses and to optimize the utilization of local and external resources. Qualitative research can help generate a better understanding of the issues that affect local community members and can identify realistic solutions that reflect local knowledge and assets.

Second, qualitative research can be used to explore local experiences of a programme – not only as a formative evaluation tool but also as part of the end-of-programme evaluation. Only by giving local people and service providers an opportunity to communicate what they perceive to be the strengths and weaknesses of a programme, and the way it was implemented, will we be in a position to make programmatic changes that can either strengthen current and active programmes or inform future programmes. Qualitative research is thus a major part of formative evaluation, allowing beneficiaries to express their reactions to an active programme so that development practitioners can make the necessary changes for the programme to progress in a more valued direction (in line with accountability, as described above). From an end-of-programme evaluation perspective, qualitative research can be used to unpack local understandings of impact. While log frames are typically developed to measure hypothesized programme impacts, primarily to show donors that programmes have achieved what they set out to do, these impacts are often limited and deliberately reduced to what we and our donors find relevant. Qualitative research – for example through an investigation of the 'most significant changes' (described more fully below) – can provide details on what the programme beneficiaries perceive the impact of the programme to be.

Third, qualitative research can help contextualize 'what happened'. Development programmes are not implemented in a vacuum, but interact with a host of social and contextual factors. These could include other development programmes, socio-cultural norms, and changes to the physical environment, as well as the personal skills, sensitivities, and characteristics of the people implementing the programme. Qualitative research can be used to unpack the contextual factors and processes that have contributed to either the success or failure of a programme. Such knowledge can help development practitioners mitigate potential risks to programme success and increase the chances of success and impact.

In summary, qualitative research can generate evidence that can be used to develop programmes that are tailored to local contexts. Qualitative research can also be used to determine improvements and changes to a programme. When acted upon, such evidence can optimize programme impact and satisfaction among the people the development programmes seek to assist.

Value for money

Development agencies are increasingly looking to deliver programmes that represent value for money. This is not about developing and implementing low-cost programmes, but about maximizing the impact of funds spent to improve poor people's lives. In other words, 'value for money' is about ensuring that development programmes have the greatest impact at the lowest cost. Qualitative research is not typically associated with the 'value for money' agenda. But, as alluded to above, qualitative research is vital to any process looking to make development programmes more efficient, effective, and equitable, which in turn makes programmes more economical. Qualitative research can explore ways to enhance programme impact and overcome unintended consequences, such as drawing on local resources and strengths, or to involve local stakeholders to address possible barriers to the programme's impact (for example, a cultural belief or detrimental gender constructions), all of which is likely to increase value for money. Moreover, it is notoriously difficult to document value for money. While solid and rigorous quantitative research designs are central to a 'value for money' analysis, it is increasingly recognized that a good analysis incorporates different sources of information, including qualitative evidence, to build a comprehensive picture of programme impact and value. This could, for example, include an outline of local perceptions of impact, above and beyond that stipulated by the logical framework guiding programme monitoring and evaluation.

Scalability and replicability

We have said it before: The ultimate aim of a development agency is to have a positive impact in the areas where they work. So far, impact has primarily been discussed in relation to developing programmes that are successful and create a positive change for the people they seek to assist. Impact, however, also refers to reach. A programme can be very successful yet reach only a small number of people. What is better is a programme that is equally successful but reaches a much larger number of people. Development agencies therefore have an interest in taking impactful programmes 'to scale'. This can involve taking a stand-alone programme to scale, or it can mean working through national stakeholders, such as local government departments, which can extend their activities to a greater number of people. Often it is a mix of the two.

Going to scale inevitably involves replicating activities in other locations and mainstreaming certain elements so that they can be implemented realistically by facilitators with varied skills and experience.

It cannot be assumed that, just because a programme has been successful in one context, it can be repeated in another context with equal success. Programmes are implemented by people with varied knowledge, skills, attitudes, and behaviours in contexts that are socially determined. Qualitative research plays an instrumental role in making sure that development agencies fully understand all the contributing factors to programme impact. Qualitative research, for example, can be used to unpack the many different contextual barriers and facilitators to programme impact and determine what elements of the programme need to be fostered further or where changes should be made in order to ensure that the programme has the flexibility to be tailored to different socio-economic or cultural contexts.

Advocacy, campaigning, and social change

Achieving social change requires action at many different levels. While development programmes can provide poor people with opportunities to escape poverty and live healthier lives, there are often limits in their scope to change the policy, legislation, and geopolitical processes that either leave people poor and vulnerable in the first place or fail to protect those who are most vulnerable. For that reason, many larger development agencies have staff, and sometimes an entire department, who are designated to advocacy. Save the Children define advocacy as 'a set of organised activities designed to influence the policies and actions of others to achieve positive changes for children's lives based on the experience and knowledge of working directly with children, their families and communities' (Gosling and Cohen, 2007: 12).

Qualitative research, by giving a voice to marginalized people, can help development practitioners develop knowledge about the experiences of the most vulnerable. These voices, and the knowledge they represent, can be used by development practitioners to reframe an issue and develop new ways of seeing (Laws et al., 2013). The perspectives gathered through qualitative research can also be used in campaign materials, extending the voices of local people to a global audience. Some qualitative research methods, such as Photovoice (see Chapter 6), were developed with the explicit purpose of gathering voices to advocate for structural change.

We have now offered six reasons why qualitative research is vital to the field of development. Qualitative research is not only key to the development and implementation of projects, but also to understanding the impact and reach of development programmes. We now proceed to discuss some of the different phases in a development programme cycle where qualitative methods can be employed to enhance programme impact, quality, and accountability.

Embedding qualitative research within a project and programme cycle

Qualitative research can be embedded in a development programme at many different points of its implementation cycle – serving different learning purposes. To demonstrate this, in this section we will describe five specific qualitative analyses in the programme cycle as well as highlighting some of the more general research, advocacy, and accountability opportunities that may shoot off at different points of the cycle (see Figure 1.3). These analyses are by no means exhaustive, but they offer concrete examples of how qualitative research can be embedded in a programme cycle with the aim of strengthening programme impact, quality, and accountability. We will discuss each of them in turn.

Situational analysis and needs assessment

Before a development programme is conceived, and a funding proposal written, there is a need to carry out a situational analysis and a needs assessment. This

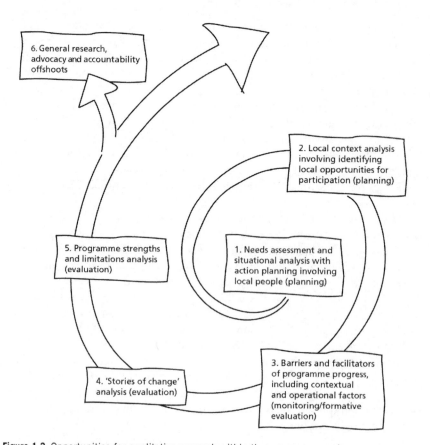

Figure 1.3 Opportunities for qualitative research within the programme cycle

is a process of identifying and understanding the specificities of a problem and the broader context in which a programme operates, and using this information to plan actions to address the problem.

A situational analysis offers development practitioners with an understanding of the internal and external environment in which a programme will operate. Internally, this could include an analysis of organizational capabilities, while externally, if the organization works with and for children, it could include a country-level child rights situational analysis (CRSA). For organizations working in fragile states, the situational analysis could also include a security assessment. While situational analyses often depend heavily on literature reviews, they also often draw on interviews with key stakeholders. Once a situational analysis has mapped out macro-environmental factors that may affect or guide organizational operations, the process of identifying and understanding the specificities of the problem and planning actions to address that problem can commence. This is also called a needs assessment.

Identifying a problem and assessing a need often involve an iterative process that considers the capabilities, principles, and values of a development organization, the national strategies of a country, and the perspectives of the people the programmes are intended to assist. Once a general problem area has been identified – in the area of education, health, or hunger and livelihoods, for instance – a systematic process that places the intended beneficiaries centre stage can begin to determine people's specific needs.

While surveys can be useful to determine the scale of a problem, the process of generating qualitative evidence pertaining to the views and perspectives of beneficiaries at a community level is key to determining what interventions will be most appropriate and successful in alleviating risks and hardships (Rossi and Lipsey, 2004). Individual and group interviews (see Chapter 3) as well as participatory learning and action (PLA) methods (see Chapters 5 and 6) are particularly well suited for needs assessments. Needs assessments that develop in a partnership between development practitioners and local people (Rifkin and Pridmore, 2001) can do the following:

- They can offer **critical reflection** and raise the consciousness of community members about the conditions that compromise their well-being.
- They can enable **diverse groups of people to participate**. This includes children and other marginalized groups who are ordinarily absent from community forums (see Box 1.2 for an example).
- They can identify key **barriers to change**, risks, and hazards facing local communities.
- They can identify **assets, capacities, and local resources** that can be used to address their needs.
- They can help community members **prioritize** and draw up action plans for development activities.

- They can support the **selection of indicators** that can be used to identify and measure the areas of change that a development programme expects to bring about.

A number of toolkits and guidance notes are available online to support development practitioners apply qualitative research methods in needs assessments. Examples include:

- the Vulnerability and Capacities Assessment (VCA) toolbox from the Red Cross (IFRC, 2007), available in English, French and Spanish at <www.ifrc.org>
- 'The short guide to rapid joint education needs assessments' from the Global Education Cluster, available in English and French at <www.savethechildren.org.uk/resources/online-library>
- 'Photovoice guidance: 10 simple steps to involve children in needs assessments' from Save the Children, available in English at <http://resourcecentre.savethechildren.se/>.

Local context analysis

Once a needs assessment has been carried out, and it is clear what problems or 'gaps' between current and desired conditions a development programme is looking to tackle, a more in-depth local context analysis can be undertaken. Local context analyses play an important role in the programme-planning process and seek to map the socio-economic, cultural, environmental, political,

---

Box 1.2 Children using participatory methods to assess local needs

Save the Children used participatory learning and action tools, including Photovoice (see Chapter 6), to involve children in a needs assessment for a programme tackling chronic malnutrition in south-west Bangladesh.

The aim was to give children the opportunity to voice their concerns and challenges with regards to food and nutrition and to use this information in the planning of a programme.

Figure 1.4 Children practising taking pictures
Source: Julie Newton/Save the Children.

and legislative conditions that may affect a programme (see Box 1.3 for an example). For example, a local context analysis may provide information regarding the factors listed below:

- When is it a good **time to start** implementing the programme? Religious holidays, local elections, or seasons when drought is likely or animals are prone to disease may delay a programme, or in a worst-case scenario they might stop it being implemented.
- What are the local **experiences and perceptions** of the phenomenon that leaves some people vulnerable and at risk? This will help you gain a clear picture of circumstances that compromise people's well-being as well as an understanding of the people who will be affected by the programme.
- Which local **norms and practices** play a role in responding to, or exacerbating, the social conditions that compromise people's well-being?
- Local **representations and understandings** may be in conflict with the values and principles of development organizations, requiring a sensitive approach. The work by Save the Children, for example, is guided by the Convention on the Rights of the Child, yet local communities, often determined by poverty, may place greater emphasis on children's responsibilities in sustaining household livelihoods.
- Can local **assets and capacities** be drawn upon to implement the programme in line with local responses and resources? This may include the experience and knowledge of some local people, infrastructures that can house training sessions and other events, communal land to host a borehole, and so forth.
- What **existing services** are there, and what are their roles and responsibilities in addressing issues relevant to the programme aim?

Using qualitative research methods, a local context analysis supplements the needs assessment and situational analysis by gathering more in-depth and contextual information about the specific problem that a development programme is looking to address. It also explores what opportunities might

---

Box 1.3 Children participating in a context analysis in West Africa

In 2013–14, the Child Protection Initiative of Save the Children conducted local context analyses into kinship care in communities across six countries in West and East Africa. The research was primarily qualitative, participatory, and exploratory, and was designed to enhance Save the Children's understanding of the factors that influence children's experience of kinship care, such as their kinship care arrangements and positive and negative experiences of kinship. Norms, practices, and understandings were gathered from different stakeholders, including children, caregivers, and local leaders. These local context analyses offered a foundation to strengthen programmes in the region that promote the prevention of family separation and family strengthening within a comprehensive care and protection system (Chukwudozie et al, 2015).

be available for local participation in the planning and implementation of the programme, both to overcome potential conflicts and to recognize and build on existing capacities. On occasion, organizations may conduct very thorough needs assessments and situational analyses, which encompass many of the components of a context analysis.

Given that development programmes are most likely to achieve buy-in and resonate with local needs and resources if they have been developed in partnership with local community members (Skovdal et al., 2013), it is increasingly seen as good practice to use qualitative research methods to engage prospective beneficiaries in needs assessments and local context analyses. This is demonstrated by the fact that many donor agencies ask in their proposals for an account of how community members were involved in the planning and development of a programme.

Barriers to and facilitators of programme progress analysis

Development programmes interact with a range of factors that can either facilitate or hinder progress and impact.

Therefore, once a development programme is up and running, it is important to monitor progress and carry out formative evaluations. Monitoring involves a continuous process of appraising programme progress and identifying strengths and weaknesses, with the aim of modifying and improving the programme (Gosling and Edwards, 2003). In the context of programme monitoring, Gosling and Edwards (2003) identify six types of monitoring:

- *Project inputs*: monitoring whether what is needed to implement the programme is readily available, and following budgetary and work plan schedules.
- *Project outputs*: monitoring what has been done, problems encountered, and changes to the environment or circumstances in which a programme is active.
- *Meeting objectives*: monitoring the applicability of programme objectives and whether the programme is working towards them.
- *Impact*: scoping intended and unintended consequences of the programme, highlighting positive and negative impacts.
- *Management*: monitoring the way in which a programme is being implemented, such as the management style of the implementing agency as well as the participation of local people.
- *Context*: monitoring the local context, being aware of socio-economic, political, and environmental developments that may affect the programme.

These are just a few areas where programme monitoring can take place. Some of them focus on process, while others look at impact or context. It is important to consider process, impact, and context monitoring as these are linked and can help us understand the pathways that lead to change. Qualitative research methods, such as individual interviews and focus group discussions (see Chapter 3), are ideal for conducting a formative evaluation, examining barriers and facilitators to programme progress. Local stakeholders – including a selection of beneficiaries, community members, and programme staff – can be interviewed at any stage during programme implementation. Interviews can follow a topic guide that examines barriers and facilitators to the six areas of monitoring mentioned above. Such interviews will reveal what has been achieved to date, as well as some of the operational processes and contextual factors that have either facilitated or hindered programme impact. Development practitioners can then use this feedback to modify the programme and capitalize on its strengths.

You can gather information from a variety of sources for the purpose of monitoring and formative evaluations (field visits, community meetings, field reports, records of activities, and so on). You may already do so as part of your job. Why should you then formalize the process and use qualitative research methods? Adopting a research approach, and gathering feedback systematically, can serve as a quality control and make sure that valuable learning is properly captured, stored, assimilated, and applied to development programmes in other areas or sectors.

'Stories of change' analysis

There are a number of different ways in which you can use qualitative methods to evaluate the impact of a programme. A 'stories of change' analysis allows you to investigate the most significant changes that the programme has brought about (Dart and Davies, 2003). It is important that these 'stories of change' are gathered in a participatory and inductive ('bottom-up') way and not guided by indicators of what you, as a practitioner, believe is important and constitutes significant change. A qualitative 'stories of change' analysis should effectively be done independently of the quantitative research. However, if the qualitative 'stories of change' resonate with the quantitative indicators, they would strengthen and complement each other well.

The 'stories of change' will hopefully elaborate on and give detail to the social processes and contextual factors that contributed to the most significant changes. If these are limited, and if time and resources permit, you can try to arrange short follow-up interviews with individual participants, asking them about the background to these perceived significant changes. A 'stories of change' analysis is likely to highlight both expected and unexpected outcomes. This makes the approach attractive both as a way of supplementing and expanding on a quantitative summative evaluation and for mapping out the breadth of programme impact (which is useful from a 'value for money' perspective). 'Stories of change' analyses can be implemented with any stakeholder, allowing for comparisons. Adults and children who have benefited from the programme can speak from personal experience, while non-benefiting community members can speak about the changes they have observed. Also, programme staff and key stakeholders may have a perspective on the changes the programme has brought about.

The 'stories of change' can be gathered in a number of different ways, ranging from interviews (see Chapter 3), to participatory learning and action tools (see Chapter 5), and to Photovoice (see Chapter 6). While it is useful to map out the spectrum of positive and negative changes a programme has initiated, it is also helpful to ask community members to reflect on the changes they have observed and to come to a consensus about their significance, for example through a ranking. This way, entire communities can tell you what they consider the 'most significant changes' of a programme to be. However, be aware that different segments of a community may have different perceptions of what the 'most significant change' is, and so it is advisable for you to gather 'most significant change' stories from each of these groupings (for example, according to age group, gender, ethnic or language group, level of poverty, or health status).

Guidance on how to facilitate a 'stories of change' analysis in the context of development programme evaluation has been developed by Davies and Dart (2005).[1]

Programme strengths and limitations analysis

In addition to exploring local perceptions of change and impact, much can be learned from local perceptions of the strengths or limitations of a programme. This is particularly relevant to development practitioners who need to draw on past experiences to develop new, better, and scalable programmes. This type of inquiry builds on what is often referred to as a strengths, weaknesses, opportunities, and threats (SWOT) analysis. SWOT analyses are commonly used in performance management, but they can provide communities targeted by a development programme with a useful platform to discuss the programme's strengths and limitations in detail. Programme strengths and limitations can also be explored through interview methods and with a mix of stakeholders. This type of analysis should be conducted in order to summarize key strengths and limitations as well as to discover lessons to be learned and recommendations for future programming.

Other options for analysis

These five different forms of analysis make use of qualitative methods within a development programme cycle. The list is by no means exhaustive. Many other general research, advocacy, and accountability activities can be facilitated. Research, whether operational or issue focused, can be conducted at any stage of the programme cycle, irrespective of the monitoring and evaluation framework that has been designed. The analysis can draw on data gathered at one specific point in time (also referred to as a cross-sectional study), or on information collected by following a small group of people throughout the programme cycle and interviewing them at different stages (also referred to as longitudinal case studies). It is also important to note that not all five opportunities are relevant to all programmes and that it may not be realistic to conduct all five types of study, considering costs, timing, and staff capacity.

If information is gathered from a number of different communities, a review can be used to generate evidence and key lessons for future programming and advocacy. This review can contrast and combine results from the different studies conducted during the programme (or between sister programmes in other contexts).

Summary

Qualitative research offers development practitioners an opportunity to understand local perspectives, needs, and context. By adopting a 'research approach' and by systematizing and formalizing their use of qualitative research methods, development practitioners can make a significant contribution to the creation of an evidence base. Qualitative evidence generated systematically is integral to the objectives of development practitioners. Qualitative research can be used to: 1) engage programme beneficiaries; 2) promote accountability; 3) contribute to impact, innovation, and evidence; 4) support the 'value for money' agenda; 5) facilitate the scalability and replicability of programmes; 6) provide material and opportunities for advocacy and campaigning.

Qualitative research can be integrated into the programme cycle in a number of different ways, from the development of situational analyses and needs assessments through to the monitoring and evaluation of programmes. Information gathered at the different steps of the programme cycle can be used to explore the feasibility and acceptability of a programme as well as to determine areas for improvement. If lessons and recommendations that emerge through systematic qualitative research are considered and contribute to programme changes, this can have immediate benefits to programme beneficiaries. In the next seven chapters, we will provide guidance on how you can generate and report on qualitative evidence, equipping you with the knowledge and skills required to adopt a 'research approach'.

Endnote

1. The full text is available at <www.mande.co.uk/docs/MSCGuide.pdf> [accessed 27 July 2015].

References

Bamberger, M., Rao, V. and Woolcock, M. (2010) *Using Mixed Methods in Monitoring and Evaluation*, pp. 1–30, Research Working Papers, Washington DC: World Bank.

Bauer, M. W., Gaskell, G. and Allum, N. C. (2000) 'Quality, quantity and knowledge interests: avoiding confusions', in M. W. Bauer and G. Gaskell (eds), *Qualitative Researching with Text, Image and Sound*, pp. 3–17, London: SAGE Publications.

Campbell, C. and Jovchelovitch, S. (2000) 'Health, community and development: towards a social psychology of participation', *Journal of Community and Applied Social Psychology* 10 (4): 255–70.

Chambers, R. (1983) *Rural Development: Putting the Last First*, London: Longman.

Chambers, R. (1997) *Whose Reality Counts?: Putting the First Last*, London: Intermediate Technology.

Chukwudozie, O. Feinstein, C. Jensen, C. O'kane, C. Pina, S. Skovdal, M & Smith, R. (2015) 'Applying community-based participatory research to better understand and improve kinship care practices: insights from DRC, Nigeria and Sierra Leone' *Family and Community Health*, vol 38, no. 1, pp. 108-119.

Cornwall, A., Lucas, H. and Pasteur, K. (2000) 'Introduction: accountability through participation: developing workable partnership models in the health sector', *IDS Bulletin* 31 (1): 1–13, doi: 10.1111/j.1759-5436.2000.mp31001001.x.

Creswell, J. W. (2002) *Educational Research: Planning, Conducting and Evaluating Quantitative and Qualitative Research*, Boston MA: Pearson Education.

Darcy, J., Alexander, J. and Kiani, M. (2013) *2013 Humanitarian Accountability Report*, Geneva: Humanitarian Accountability Partnership.

Dart, J. and Davies, R. (2003) 'A dialogical, story-based evaluation tool: the most significant change technique', *American Journal of Evaluation* 24 (2): 137–55, doi: 10.1177/109821400302400202.

Davies, R. and Dart, J. (2005) *The Most Significant Change (MSC) Technique: A Guide to its Use*, self-published, <www.mande.co.uk/docs/MSCGuide.pdf> [accessed 27 July 2015].

Denzin, N. K. (1989) *The Research Act*, 3rd edn, Englewood Cliffs NJ: Prentice Hall.

Featherstone, A. (2013) *Improving Impact: Do Accountability Mechanisms Deliver Results?*, London: Christian Aid, HAP International, and Save the Children.

Flick, U. (2002) *An Introduction to Qualitative Research*, 2nd edn, London: SAGE Publications.

Freire, P. (1973) *Education for Critical Consciousness*, New York NY: Seabury Press.

Gaskell, G. and Bauer, M. W. (2000) 'Towards public accountability: beyond sampling, reliability and validity', in M. W. Bauer and G. Gaskell (eds), *Qualitative Researching with Text, Image and Sound*, London: SAGE Publications.

Gosling, L. and Cohen, D. (2007) *Advocacy Matters: Helping Children Change Their World*, London: Save the Children, <www.savethechildren.org.uk/sites/default/files/docs/Advocacy-Matters-Participants-Manual.pdf> [accessed 27 July 2015].

Gosling, L. and Edwards, M. (2003) *Toolkits: A Practical Guide to Planning, Monitoring, Evaluation and Impact Assessment*, Volume 5, London: Save the Children.

IFRC (2007) *VCA Toolbox: With Reference Sheets*, Geneva: International Federation of Red Cross and Red Crescent Societies, <www.ifrc.org/Global/Publications/disasters/vca/vca-toolbox-en.pdf> [accessed 27 July 2015].

Kilby, P. (2006) 'Accountability for empowerment: dilemmas facing non-governmental organizations', *World Development* 34 (6): 951–63, doi: http://dx.doi.org/10.1016/j.worlddev.2005.11.009.

Laws, S., Harper, C., Jones, N. and Marcus, R. (2013) *Research for Development: A Practical Guide*, 2nd edn, London: SAGE Publications.

Madden, R. (2010) *Being Ethnographic: A Guide to the Theory and Practice of Ethnography*, London: SAGE Publications.

Moser, C. (1998) 'The asset vulnerability framework: reassessing urban poverty reduction strategies', *World Development* 26 (1): 1–19.

Munyas Ghadially, B. (2013) *Programme Accountability Guidance Pack: A Save the Children Resource*, London: Save the Children, <www.savethechildren.org.uk/resources/online-library/programme-accountability-guidance-pack> [accessed 27 July 2015].

O'Kane, C. (2008) 'The development of participatory techniques: facilitating children's views about decisions which affect them', in P. Christensen and A. James (eds), *Research With Children: Perspectives and Practice*, pp. 125–55, London: Routledge.

Rifkin, S. and Pridmore, P. (2001) *Partners in Planning: Information, Participation and Empowerment*, London: TALC and Macmillan Education.

Rossi, P. H. and Lipsey, M. W. (2004) *Evaluation: A Systematic Approach*, London: SAGE Publications.

Skovdal, M., Robertson, L., Mushati, P., Dumba, L., Sherr, L., Nyamukapa, C. and Gregson, S. (2013) 'Acceptability of conditions in a community-led cash transfer programme for orphaned and vulnerable children in Zimbabwe', *Health Policy and Planning* 29 (7): 809–17, doi: 10.1093/heapol/czt060.

CHAPTER 2
Designing and planning a qualitative study

Abstract

A qualitative study benefits immensely from careful and early planning. As you plan, your study design unfolds. This chapter takes you through some of the many considerations you need to be aware of in order to design and plan for effective qualitative research that is achievable, ethical, and of high quality. In the process of doing so, the chapter offers you concrete guidance on how to develop a qualitative study protocol, and argues that this exercise provides you with an opportunity to clearly define your research purpose and develop research questions and an appropriate study design. The chapter ends with a discussion of quality criteria in qualitative research, highlighting how early planning is key to good and systematic qualitative research.

Keywords: Qualitative research; study protocol; research design; ethics; quality criteria

Learning objectives

After reading this chapter, you will be able to:

- translate research ideas into research aims and objectives;
- argue for a study approach and recruitment strategy;
- identify and develop plans to mitigate any potential ethical dilemmas of a study;
- develop a qualitative study protocol;
- explain the quality criteria of rigorous qualitative research.

Key terms (definitions)

- *Study design*: The approach and methodological procedure adopted to explore a research question.
- *Study protocol*: A document that describes the study design and operating features of a study.
- *Research question*: The question that the research will answer.

Why plan a qualitative study?

Are you considering conducting a qualitative study? Are you feeling a little unsure about how to proceed and how to get started? This is perfectly normal.

http://dx.doi.org/10.3362/9781780448534.002

There are indeed many things to consider and think about before you start. Even the most experienced qualitative researchers feel overwhelmed by all the things they need to consider in order to plan and set up a study. This chapter offers guidance on some of the many aspects of qualitative research that you will need to consider and plan for before you start. These include, but are not limited to:

- deciding on a research focus and refining research questions;
- selecting an appropriate study design that can answer your research questions;
- thinking about a qualitative analysis strategy that can shed light on the topic under investigation;
- setting up a study team, including researchers and members for an advisory group;
- identifying suitable research methods;
- agreeing on who the study participants should be as well as how to select them;
- considering ethical implications for study participants;
- developing a plan for how best to communicate study findings to inform future programming; and
- considering what is possible within the limits of time, money, and staff competencies.

Whether you will be conducting the research yourself, writing 'terms of reference' for a consultant, or managing a qualitative study as part of your job, these are some of the things you will need to consider before you get started. Such planning is often done through the development of a study protocol. A study protocol is a document that describes the general design and operating features of your qualitative study. In other words, a study protocol makes explicit your plans and considerations for using qualitative research methods. A study protocol, however, is not merely a document that describes your planned research activities; it is an instrumental tool in the development of a study in that it encourages you to think carefully about how all the elements of your study fit together. It is a process that enables you to do the following:

- *Develop a coherent study design*: Use the process of writing a study protocol as an opportunity to develop and make explicit your study design. A study design links your motivations, whether personal or gaps in the literature, research questions, choice of research methods, and analytical strategy. A study protocol helps you plan activities that build on each other and ultimately enable you to answer your research questions in a systematic and convincing manner.
- *Guard against surprises*: While you cannot predict all the events that may affect the research process, you can draw on your own experience and that of others to anticipate possible events. A good study protocol combines a forecast of potential developments with the preparation of scenarios for how to react to them. The more you plan ahead, the better you can guard against surprises.

- *Mitigate against resource constraints*: You should never underestimate the cost of qualitative research. Through the development of a study protocol, it will become clear exactly what resources, in terms of time, money, and staff, will be required to execute the study. This can lead to a realization that you will need to apply for funding or negotiate access for more resources from within your organization.
- *Ensure quality*: All of the above contribute to good qualitative research. But also being aware of quality criteria in qualitative research can help you plan and put in place activities that help you ensure quality (this is discussed later in this chapter).

Research involves carrying out activities in a systematic way to generate new knowledge and understanding. But research, particularly qualitative research, does not happen in a vacuum. Qualitative research takes place in real-life settings, involves human beings at every step of the process, and requires the engagement of a number of different stakeholders. All this interaction makes the process inherently unpredictable and challenging to plan and implement systematically – and especially if you are working in cross-cultural contexts. It is therefore worth reiterating that you cannot plan all aspects of qualitative research, precisely because of its interest in engaging with human beings in their local context. There will be elements of surprise and there will be times when you have to abandon your plan and improvise. This is normal and, to a certain degree, expected. You cannot possibly plan a response to every inconceivable surprise. But what you can do is accept that unpredictable events will occur. Some events, such as conflict or natural disasters, may force you to abandon your study altogether. Other, more subtle events, such as unanticipated knowledge, attitudes, and behaviours, or the influx of new actors or technologies into a context, can take your research in a slightly different direction. As highlighted by Wisker (2007), it is important that the study protocol does not become a 'straitjacket', but that you embrace these new directions and adapt your study protocol accordingly, for example by tweaking your research question, selecting additional or other research participants, or using different research methods. Doing so 'on the go' can be difficult and calls for the involvement of more experienced researchers, for example in advisory groups.

Activity 2.1 Planning for and responding to surprises

Think of a programme or a research project you have recently been involved in. Consider a programme where circumstances encouraged you to deviate from your original plans. Take five minutes to write down reflections on the following questions:

1. What circumstances led to changes in the programme? Could these have been circumvented?
2. Could the programme or study have been more successfully implemented had more time been invested in planning activities? What should have been considered before the programme was implemented?

The fact that on some occasions you may have to adapt and change your study protocol halfway through a study does not negate the importance of planning ahead. On the contrary, it highlights the importance of forecasting and considering different possibilities within an overarching study design.

A qualitative study protocol can take many shapes and forms and contain varied amounts of detail. The more detail you include, the better prepared you will be. Time spent on early and careful planning is likely to save you time and trouble during the process. It is therefore recommended that you treat it as a major milestone in the research process and use it as a foundation to develop your ideas, and to consult and engage with different stakeholders. This will help you to both refine the study design and obtain the necessary buy-in and ownership from key stakeholders.

This chapter guides you through the process of planning an effective qualitative study that links research questions and study objectives with an appropriate study design. Occasionally referring to a case study (see Box 2.1), exercises will take you through some of the many thought processes that can aid your planning. While it is not mandatory to develop a study protocol, we frame the chapter around the different considerations you may include in one. See Box 2.2 for possible headings in a study protocol.

Contextualizing the need for the study

Your development work experience has probably sparked lots of ideas for issues to research. As discussed in Chapter 1, this curiosity to question and learn is integral to the delivery of quality programmes. But how do you move from having an interest in knowing more about a particular area through to developing a research question(s) and determining the right study design? The first step, and the focus of this section, is to contextualize the need for the study and define the specific purpose and scope of your study.

Qualitative research is not free of cost. It takes time away from you, your colleagues, and not least the study participants. It also costs money and may divert resources away from other activities. It is therefore important that you justify the need for the study. You can begin to contextualize the need for your study by considering the following questions (adapted from Wisker, 2007):

- What are the issues you are interested in?
- What do you want to investigate?
- What other evidence exists on the topic?
- How is your study going to contribute to the existing evidence base?
- What do you hope to change through the research?
- What difference will your research make? Why does it 'matter'?

Some of these questions you can answer quite easily, based on your experience and observations, and by reflecting on what motivated you to conduct a qualitative study in the first place. Other questions will require you to do a bit of investigative work, reviewing external literature from databases on the internet as well as internal documents available within your organization.

Box 2.1 Working street children in Karachi, Pakistan – a case study

Poverty is forcing more and more children to seek work on the streets of Karachi, enabling them to take an active role in sustaining themselves and their families. While most children live with family or relatives, some children live on the street with no adult supervision or care.

Children are typically employed as street vendors, car washers, and shoe-shiners, or as beggars and scavengers. Furthermore, large numbers of children are picked up on the street to do ad hoc domestic work, particularly girls, often performing physically demanding tasks in situations where they face the risk of abuse and exploitation inside the walls of private homes.

Regardless of the type of labour, working street children often miss out on regular schooling and on opportunities that would enable them to pursue their right to a 'normal' childhood and a dream of escaping poverty. They are often required to engage in risky, heavy, and age-inappropriate forms of labour, which, among other issues, can have serious consequences for their physical and emotional health.

Imagine your organization is looking to develop a programme to support working street children in Karachi. You decide that the first step is to conduct a study that examines the struggles and coping strategies of this group of children.

Figure 2.1 Working street children

Box 2.2 Possible structure and headings for a study protocol

1. Cover page
  1.1. Indicative title of study
    1.2. Name of investigators
    1.3. Contact details of primary investigator (PI)
2. Contextualizing the need for the study
  2.1. Research motivations
    2.2. Literature review
    2.3. Research question and study objectives
3. Qualitative study design
  3.1. Study approach
    3.2. Study team
      3.2.1. Collaborators
      3.2.2. Advisory board
    3.3. Study location and participants
      3.3.1. Study location justification
      3.3.2. Accessing the locale
      3.3.3. Participant selection and recruitment
    3.4. Data collection
      3.4.1. Methods
      3.4.2. Procedure
    3.5. Socio-ethical considerations
      3.5.1. Cultural and linguistic considerations
      3.5.2. Informed consent
      3.5.3. Risks and benefits
      3.5.4. Confidentiality and data storage
      3.5.5. Compensation
    3.6. Data analysis
      3.6.1. Data preparation
      3.6.2. Analysis procedure
    3.7. Cost and timescale
      3.7.1. Timescale
      3.7.2. Budget
    3.8. Conflicts of interest
    3.9. Appendices
      3.9.1. Research tools (e.g. topic guides, observation guide, survey)
      3.9.2. Information sheets
      3.9.3. Informed consent forms
      3.9.4. Permission and collaboration letters

Being clear about your research motivations

Qualitative research is an opportunity to know more about an issue or a process that relates to a development programme. Given the amount of work involved in setting up a qualitative study, there is likely to be some kind of motivation behind it, driving the planning and execution forward. A self-awareness and articulation of what exactly these motivations are can help you stay focused and act as a stimulus should you encounter difficulties or challenges in the process.

It is important that the study protocol includes a paragraph detailing what sparked this study as well as how these motivational factors may influence

---

Activity 2.2 Motivational factors behind the study

You are planning to conduct a study with working street children in Karachi (see Box 2.1). Write down what you think might be some of the motivational factors behind the study from the perspective of:

1. a local development practitioner working with vulnerable children in Karachi.
2. an international development practitioner working in a head office.

For each factor, also write down how this may either positively or negatively affect the study.

Feedback is available at the end of the chapter.

---

and guide the planned study. In making clear your research motivations, you also declare your interests and involvement in the study. As a development practitioner conducting research, perhaps in a programme you helped develop, you occupy a dual role; it is important to recognize and reflect upon this. This is essential for transparency purposes and helps you to be aware of how your interests guide the research in a specific direction. In particular, it can encourage you to think about how your motivations might influence the way the study is conducted as well as the results (in either a good or a bad way).

Carrying out a literature review

A good protocol also briefly outlines existing evidence on the topic, requiring you to do a bit of investigative work. This might involve talking to colleagues and inquiring about what existing research and monitoring and evaluation work might be available within your organization and relevant to your study interests. Your organization might have an intranet website and central database where reports and publications can be identified and retrieved. It is also important that you consult the wider evidence available, namely the experiences of other organizations as well as formally published research. There are a number of research databases on the internet that you can use to identify existing evidence on your topic (see Table 2.1 for examples).

Some search engines are specialized and focus on specific disciplines and thematic areas, while others are multidisciplinary. Some databases contain information only about formal and academic research, while others include information about grey literature, which is informally published written material (such as reports). Databases with grey literature often make the full texts available (for example, 'Save the Children Resource Centre' and 'Research for Development'). The more formal research databases do not always provide access to the full texts, but only summaries or abstracts. For many of the articles, only individuals and organizations who subscribe to the journals where they are published will be able to access the full texts. An exception is the Directory of Open Access Journals, which allows you to search research articles that are freely available. Books are rarely freely available on

Table 2.1 Electronic search engines for identifying research papers

Research database	Focus	Website	Access
Google Scholar	Multidisciplinary	<www.scholar.google.com>	Free
POPLINE	Family planning and reproductive health	<www.popline.org/>	Free
Pubmed	Public health and medicine	<www.ncbi.nlm.nih.gov/pubmed>	Free
PubPsych	Psychology	<www.pubpsych.eu/>	Free
ERIC	Education	<http://eric.ed.gov/>	Free
Research for Development	Development	<http://r4d.dfid.gov.uk/>	Free
ResearchGate	Multidisciplinary	<www.researchgate.com>	Free
Save the Children Resource Centre	Child protection	<http://resourcecentre.savethechildren.se>	Free
Directory of Open Access Journals	Multidisciplinary	<https://doaj.org/>	Free
Web of Science	Multidisciplinary	<http://wokinfo.com/>	Subscription
Scopus	Multidisciplinary	<www.elsevier.com/online-tools/scopus>	Subscription

the internet. If you have access to a library, they might be able to help you access books or journals.

There is, however, a growing trend to make academic research more freely accessible. Academics are increasingly self-archiving their research. So if a search on a research database generates details of studies that are of interest to you but inaccessible, do not give up. Enter the title of the article in an internet search engine, and browse through the results. There is a chance that the author has uploaded the article to a university depository, or on social networking sites such as ResearchGate or Academia.edu. You can also make contact to the author via email, who is very likely to respond with a copy of the article you are requesting.

Reviewing the literature is an endless task and it can eat up all your time. While you cannot possibly review all the literature available, you can engage with some of the related work that has been produced and let it guide your next steps. You can identify a relevant field of study and take inspiration and ideas from these studies in order to finalize the design of your own research.

Reviewing the existing literature, whether internal or external, also helps ensure that you do not replicate work that has already been done. If your

---

Activity 2.3 Searching for literature

This exercise gives you an opportunity to try searching for and accessing literature. Imagine you want to conduct research that investigates the health of street children and you are interested to know what research already exists.

1. Go to the research database PubMed: <www.ncbi.nlm.nih.gov/pubmed>.
2. Conduct a search using the terms 'health' and 'street children'.
3. In the results list, you will find a selection of articles that may be more or less relevant to your proposed study. You will find that some of the articles are listed as free articles. This means that you can access the full text of these articles.
4. If you are interested only in freely accessible articles, you can click 'Free full text' under 'Text availability' in the top left-hand menu.
5. Play around with the research database using other search terms.

---

review of the existing literature provides you with clarity and answers to the issues you wanted to study, there may no longer be a need to conduct the study you had in mind. If, however, the review enabled you to raise more specific questions than answers about the issue, you can use the review to underpin the need for your study.

As a literature review can be used to define the investigation, set boundaries, and provide some level of direction, it is an important first step in taking your thoughts and ideas and translating them into a study focus and the development of a research question.

In practice, try to include a subheading in your study protocol entitled 'Literature review'. Write a brief overview, based on your reading, of existing evidence related to your study, and in the process clearly state what evidence is available and point out key knowledge gaps. Follow up the written overview with a problem statement that highlights a problem in current practice or evidence gaps. Conclude the literature overview by clarifying how your study is going to build on existing evidence as well as fill the evidence gaps – ultimately seeking to solve the problem that you describe above.

Developing a research question and study objectives

A good research question defines the investigation, sets boundaries, and provides direction (O'Leary, 2004). Developing a research question is an iterative process where you consider observations and motivations from your work, the literature you have read (as explained above), and what is feasible given your research skills or supervision available, time, and resources. Only when you have a clear understanding of what is needed and feasible can you begin to formulate a question that can guide your research.

A good qualitative research question determines what the researcher will be looking at, where, and with whom. A good qualitative research question therefore contains details about the issue being studied and its location as well as the participants. The research question should also specify what you are interested in investigating. You might be interested in NGO workers'

perceptions of working street children, the **factors** that leave the children vulnerable and at risk, the **functions** of particular variables, such as NGO or peer support, in mitigating the risk of working or living on the street, or the **relationships** between working street children, and so on. Box 2.3 lists a few examples of how you can begin to formulate a qualitative research question depending on your interests.

Box 2.3 Examples of how a qualitative research question can be formulated

What is the nature of...?
How do...differ...?
What are the functions of...?
How do...perceive...?
What factors affect...?
What strategies are used...?
How do...respond...?

How do...affect...?
What are the effects of...?
How are...defined?
Under what conditions do...?
What is the relationship between...?
What are the mechanisms by which...?

Activity 2.4 Deciding on a research question

Consider the three qualitative research questions below and decide which one you think is best formulated for the study outlined in Box 2.1.

1. What is life like for working street children?
2. What factors affect the struggles and coping strategies of working street children in Karachi?
3. How can Save the Children best support working street children in Karachi?

Feedback is available at the end of the chapter.

In the process of developing a research question, you are likely to think of a number of related research questions. It is useful to continually evaluate these questions, as this will help you refine and decide on your final question. You could ask the following, for example:

- Is there a good fit between your interests (personal and organizational motivations), the literature review, and the research question?
- Is the research question focused, clear, and well-articulated?
- Can the research question be answered? Is it feasible – given time, resource, and staff constraints?

If you find yourself with a list of research questions, try to identify one overarching question and rewrite the others as study objectives. These objectives should be specific statements that reflect the steps you will take to answer your research question. For research question 2 in Activity 2.4, the following objectives might be useful:

- Explore the nature of their working and 'on the street' life.
- Identify factors that leave working street children in Karachi vulnerable and at risk.

- Map out the strategies employed by working street children in Karachi to cope with hardship.
- Identify differences between boys and girls as well as possible explanations for these differences.

By addressing these four study objectives, you will automatically begin to 'paint a picture' that answers your overarching research question: 'What factors affect the struggles and coping strategies of working street children in Karachi?'

In practice, try to include a subheading in your study protocol entitled 'Research question and study objectives'. Draw on your personal motivations and the literature review to write a brief and summarized problem statement, which clarifies what evidence gaps exist. Then present your research question(s) and study objectives, explaining that your attempt to answer the research question(s) will help fill the knowledge gap.

Qualitative study design

Once you are happy with your research question and study objectives, you can begin to determine which study design is most appropriate to answer your research question. The first thing to be clear about is the approach you will be taking.

Selecting a study approach

There are many different study approaches in qualitative research. You can choose to follow one approach, from start to finish, or you can let yourself be inspired by the different approaches and choose elements from a selection. Either way, it is important that the study protocol clearly outlines your approach. Your study might follow one of the following four study approaches that are relevant to development research.

Community-based participatory research.   CBPR is a 'a partnership approach to research that equitably involves community members, organizational representatives and researchers in all aspects of the research process' (Israel et al., 2005). Related to participatory action research, CBPR is a study approach that involves giving voice to local people so that they can identify and collectively communicate and address local needs. It recognizes that communities have a wealth of knowledge and particular skills that can contribute to the research process. If you decide to follow a CBPR approach, you should establish a partnership between a local community, group, or organization, and, through dialogue with them, identify and agree on the research question. It would also involve building their research capacity so that they are in a position to take an active role in conducting the research, from data collection to the analysis and dissemination of findings. This could be through the use of Photovoice (see Chapter 6).

Implementation research.   Implementation research is a pragmatic approach to research in the field of development and service delivery. It lends itself well to monitoring, evaluation, accountability, and learning (MEAL), as it considers 'any aspect of implementation, including the factors affecting implementation, the processes of implementation, and the results of implementation' (Peters et al., 2013). Implementation research is an inquiry that draws on an analytical interest to make better programmatic decisions. It typically involves an interrogation of factors that influence programme implementation, with a particular emphasis on informing future implementation strategies. This includes formative evaluations.

Case study research.   Case study research is a qualitative research approach where you study an issue through one or more cases (Creswell, 2012). A case could be an individual, a community, a school, a hospital, or a development programme. Case study research often involves multiple methods (such as those presented in this book) and a detailed examination of the case from many different sources of information. Case study research therefore enables you to paint a very comprehensive picture of how the issue under study manifests itself within the case or cases. If you follow a case over time, you can observe changes as well as the factors that impact change.

Phenomenological research.   Phenomenological research seeks to investigate human experience of a particular issue, or phenomenon. In phenomenological research, you gather information from individuals who have had a particular experience, and describe both 'what' they experienced and 'how' they experienced it (Moustakas, 1994). Phenomenological research is an appropriate approach if you are looking to: 1) understand the context of the issue: 2) describe the experiences of study participants; 3) explore the meanings participants attach to these experiences.

These are four out of a countless number of qualitative study approaches. Study approaches in qualitative research overlap considerably. Common to them all is the fact that they are exploratory and observational, meaning they

---

Activity 2.5 Linking study interests and approaches

Draw a line between the study interest and approach you think would be most appropriate to investigate the topic.

Study interest or topic	**Study approaches**
Barriers and facilitators to programme implementation	Phenomenological research
Empowering working street children to communicate their experience	Case study research
Working street children's experiences of living on the street	Community-based participatory research
Health of children living and working on the street	Implementation research

Feedback is available at the end of the chapter.

try to explore and observe what is happening in a given context. However, being clear about your study approach helps you, as well as your audience, understand what you are trying to achieve through your study.

Whichever one or two study approaches you choose to take inspiration from, it is important for you to try to stick to them throughout the research. Your study approach will affect your design and how you go about developing the study protocol. In practice, this means that you are encouraged to include a subheading in your study protocol entitled 'Study approach'. Within this section you should explain that, to answer your research question, you will adopt a particular study approach. Briefly explain the characteristics of the study approach you adopt and justify why it is particularly relevant to your research question.

Setting up a study team

Who will be conducting the study? To conduct your planned study, how many people, or organizations, need to be involved? What will they each bring to the study? Being clear about these questions will help you involve the right people and organizations early on in the planning process. If you plan to interview 10 to 15 people in a single location, there may not be a need to involve many people. In fact, one or two people might be sufficient. If, however, you are looking to involve a large number of study participants, across different contexts, a much larger study team is required. You also need to consider whether community members should be part of the study team.

Depending on the scale of your proposed study, a research project often has one or two principle investigators (PIs). They lead and manage the research, often with the help of co-investigators (COs). A study team may also include research assistants who help with the data collection, interview transcription, and so on. Whether the investigators are in-house staff or have been commissioned to do the job depends on the availability and skills of in-house staff. It is advisable that qualitative studies with an evaluation focus are commissioned from consultants or academic researchers, primarily to uphold the objectivity and perceived integrity of the evaluation.

Some larger qualitative research projects may also establish reference committees, also known as advisory boards, which usually consist of experienced researchers and/or community members, including children. The core group of researchers can consult this committee and receive advice from it. If the study requires the buy-in and collaboration of a number of different organizations, representatives from these organizations can form part of the reference committee.

Practically speaking, try to include a subheading in your study protocol entitled 'Study group'. List who the PIs and COs are, including their names, titles, contact details, and research experience. Give details of any reference committee you may set up to support the project, including who the members are as well as their roles and potential contributions to the study. Explain the collaborative nature of the project, including the organizations involved in the research and their respective roles and responsibilities.

Identifying a location and selecting study participants

When you begin to plan for a qualitative study, you often have a setting and a group of study participants in mind. Your research motivation and literature review should ideally justify the broader study location. However, the specifics of the exact location, or who the study participants will be, often remain undecided. Any qualitative study depends on access to 'the field', meaning access to the setting in which you would like to conduct your study as well as to the individuals you would like to include. It is therefore important that, early on in the planning stage, you begin to negotiate access to 'the field' and obtain the necessary permissions to conduct the study.

For development practitioners, negotiating access is often not a major task, particularly if they have worked in the setting and know the 'gatekeepers' professionally. 'Gatekeeper' is a term used to describe the people who can authorize and facilitate access to a specific setting and people. A gatekeeper may be a local leader, the head of a local organization, or a government official.

While it is recommended that you make arrangements to access the field early on, the recruitment of study participants can wait until the study is underway. Having said that, it is important to plan how you will go about recruiting participants. There are a number of different strategies you can adopt. The first thing to be clear about is what qualifies someone to be part of your study and what disqualifies them. This can be clarified through the development of inclusion and exclusion criteria. The criteria depend on your study and the evidence you are seeking to obtain, but they could be related to age, gender, or ethnicity, or you might want to include the presence or absence of an illness or participation in a programme.

You also need to be clear about the stratifications, or layers of characteristics (gender, age, locations, socio-economic class, ethnicity, for instance), you want your participants to represent. If you are looking to compare responses between females and males, for example, it is advisable that you keep the layers of stratification to a minimum. The more stratified your sample is, the harder it will be to compare and attribute responses to a particular characteristic, such as gender.

Once you have clarified what should qualify, or disqualify, someone from participating in your study, you need to decide how participants should be

---

Activity 2.6 Consulting your gatekeepers

If you were to conduct a study on working street children in Karachi, which gatekeepers would it be advisable to consult? Write down one gatekeeper who can possibly grant you permission to conduct the study and one who can facilitate access to the working street children.

Feedback is available at the end of the chapter.

identified and selected. Here are seven commonly used strategies for purposefully selecting study participants (see Patton, 1990 for more selection strategies):

- *'Snowball' effect*: You can select participants based on recommendations from others who know of potential participants who fit your inclusion criteria and can contribute with rich information.
- *Extreme or deviant cases*: You can select participants who represent extreme or deviant cases, such as those who either excel or fail at something, or have an unusual experience.
- *Typical*: You can select participants who represent the typical case, the normal, and the average.
- *Intensity*: You can select participants who have a rich fund of information. They typically have significant experience of the issue under study and can communicate this well and with reflection.
- *Key informants*: You can select participants based on their role and knowledge of a community. Typically, they are leaders or professionals. You know they will have something useful to say about the issue under study.
- *Convenience*: You can select participants who meet your criteria based on convenience. To save money and time, you could select participants who are near to your office and speak your language. This is the least preferred option, but occasionally the way forward given resource constraints.
- *Random purposeful*: You can select participants randomly if your purposeful sample size is large. This is not to facilitate representativeness, but to reduce bias within a purposeful category.

You do not have to stick to one selection strategy. You can use as many of them as you like, as long as you justify your strategy.

How many research participants should you select? There is no fixed rule on how many participants qualitative research should have. The exact number would depend on: 1) how many different categories of participants you are including; 2) when saturation has been reached, which is when you stop hearing anything new and interesting; 3) what is realistically possible considering time and funding constraints.

Crudely put, it is our experience that some kind of saturation within a single category of participants is likely to be reached at around twelve participants, plus or minus five. So if you were to conduct research with a group of boys and girls working on the street in one neighbourhood of Karachi, you could identify twelve boys and twelve girls to participate, while being prepared for this number to increase or decrease slightly depending on when you feel that little new information is emerging from your participants.

In summary, try to include a subheading in your study protocol entitled 'Study location and participants'. Describe and justify the study location. Provide a detailed description of the location and explain why it is important for the study to take place in your chosen location. Explain how you plan to access the location, for example through community-based partners or government structures. Explain who your research participants will be, ideally making reference to your inclusion and exclusion criteria for each category of participant. Describe the process through which you will select and recruit the participants. This includes details of possible gatekeepers as well as the selection strategy (see above) that you adopt.

Choosing qualitative research methods

You can collect qualitative data in a number of different ways. Your choice of method is partly determined by your research question, your study approach, and the participants you have selected for the study. You should therefore not choose a research method until you are clear about the purpose of the study.

Some of the more prevalent methods used in qualitative research include the following:

- *Individual interviews*: A one-to-one conversational interview designed to obtain information from an individual (see Chapter 3).
- *Focus group discussions*: A facilitated and organized discussion around a topic (see Chapter 3).
- *Participant observation*: A data collection method where you experience and observe the social context of your research participants (see Chapter 4).
- *Participatory learning and action*: Tools that enable community members to collectively identify, plan for, and act against issues affecting their quality of life (see Chapter 5).
- *Photovoice*: A method where people, through photography, capture, represent, and communicate their perspectives about issues within their community (see Chapter 6).

When choosing qualitative research methods, you might consider the following:

- *Level of participation of your research participants*: Will you follow the community-based participatory research approach and empower your study participants to take an active role in the data collection? If so, you are likely to draw on more participatory methods, such as Photovoice or participatory learning and action tools. Note: this does not exclude you from using more traditional data collection methods, such as interviews and focus group discussions.
- *Thick description*. Are you trying to understand how context mediates behaviour? Thick description involves obtaining detailed information about the factors in a given social context that influence and mediate behaviour, or an issue being studied. You would benefit from adapting a case study approach and using a mix of methods, including participant observation.
- *Social competencies of research participants*. Different qualitative research methods require different capabilities and levels of literacy. You should

therefore use methods that match the social competencies of the study participants. For example, methods used for adults and young children are sometimes different, or applied differently.

- *Individual or collective methods.* Some methods are designed to obtain collective experiences, while others focus on the individual. For example, focus group discussions or participatory learning and action tools focus on the experiences of groups of people. Individual interviews, on the other hand, focus on the experiences of the individual. Methods focused on the individual ensure that individual voices are heard. This is important in contexts where children or certain ethnic groups do not feel comfortable about speaking out in public forums. Methods focused on the collective provide an insight into socially accepted norms, opinions, and experiences as well as frictions.

Reflecting on the above, ask yourself which methods would be best suited to obtain the kind of information you are looking for from the categories of people you will include in your study. Other considerations you may factor into your decision include previous experience of using a particular tool, as well as time and resources.

It is always a good idea to include more than one data collection method, or one category of study participant, in your study. Generating information from a variety of sources can, through the process of triangulation, shed light on the issue being studied from different angles, supporting and strengthening your findings.

As part of your planning, it is also useful to think about the procedures you will follow when collecting the data. Procedural considerations include the following.

Who will gather the data? To answer that question you need to consider the skills required for each of the chosen methods. This includes previous experience of data collection, interpersonal and language skills.

What guidance is required to facilitate data collection? For the purpose of consistency and procedural transparency, all data collection methods need to be steered by guidance notes. Individual interviews, for example, could be guided by a topic guide, which is a list of topics that need to be discussed in the interview (see Chapter 3 for more detail). Photovoice participants could

---

Activity 2.7 Choosing qualitative research methods

What qualitative research methods could you use to answer the research question: 'What factors affect the struggles and coping strategies of working street children in Karachi?'
    Write down two or three methods that you think could be used and your justification for why these methods would be particularly useful.

Feedback is available at the end of the chapter.

also be directed by guidance on what to take pictures of, for example anything or anyone who helps them cope with hardship (see Chapter 6 for more detail).

What is the timing of data collection?   Timing can mean many things in the data collection stage. You need to consider how long the data collection should go on for, and whether you will be collecting data from the same group of people at different points in time: for example, before a programme begins and after it has ended. You also need to consider the estimated length of time for each data collection method. You could plan an interview with an adult to last 80 minutes while limiting interviews with children to 40 minutes, for instance. You might also consider the season when you will conduct your study. A study taking place during a cold winter is likely to reveal slightly different results from a study undertaken during a hot summer. Finally, you need to consider the sequence of your data collection methods. For example, you might use Photovoice with a large group of working street children, and from that experience select a handful of children for follow-up individual interviews.

How do you capture and store data?   As with any type of research, it is important that data is captured, stored, and accessible for the analysis. To capture spoken words of an interview or focus group discussion, you might want to record and transcribe the interviews. Similarly, thoughts from observations should be written down in a diary, and photographs or drawings could be accompanied with a written reflection by the study participant. All items of data should be given identifiers and archived so that they can be retrieved by the study team.

In practice, try to include a subheading in your study protocol entitled 'Data collection'. Describe the qualitative methods you plan to use in your study. Explain why you think these are the best methods to use in your planned study, and relate this discussion to your research question and your study approach as well as your categories of participants. Describe who will be gathering the data. Clarify what instruments and guidance will help facilitate the generation of data. Develop the instruments and guidance and include them in the study protocol as appendices. Describe and justify the timing of your planned data collection activities. Explain your plans for capturing and processing the data. It is recommended that you include a table illustrating how many research participants you will include in your study together with the data collection methods to be used for each category of study participants.

Overcoming socio-ethical dilemmas

Anyone involved in conducting research has a responsibility to 'do good' and 'avoid doing harm' in the process. This may sound obvious, but in practice it is often hard to predict how your engagement with research participants and a local community can have a positive or negative effect. To ensure that your research activities do no harm to your participants, you need to aim for the following.

Transparency. It is important that study participants know what they are getting themselves into when they agree to participate in a study. As a researcher you therefore need to introduce yourself to the research participants and explain the aim and objectives of the study as well as the potential risks and benefits from participating. The research participants also need to know how to get in contact with you or one of your colleagues in case they have any questions or concerns. If you are conducting research with children, this needs to be communicated in a way that is appropriate to them.

Voluntary participation. The process of identifying and selecting study participants is not always straightforward and you need to ask yourself how voluntary their participation is. Power asymmetries exist everywhere, and you need to consider how your position, or that of a gatekeeper (the person who directs you to your study participants), may have influenced the decision of research participants to participate. If a girl living and working on the street of Karachi is invited to participate in a study by a male adult development worker, power asymmetries relating to gender, age, and social position may all influence the girl's decision to say yes. As a development practitioner, you need to be acutely aware of how your position may raise expectations of support that are unrealistic. Lastly, in some contexts it can be difficult to explain what 'research' is, making it hard for participants to understand what their participation means in practice. You therefore need to consider very carefully how you can best proposition someone so that their participation is genuinely voluntary.

Make it worth their time. Time spent participating in the study is time taken away from the respondent's daily tasks and living. It is therefore important that your study is not an inconvenience, or is at least worth any inconvenience it may cause. You may consider finding a way to compensate for the time people spend on the study, or you could think about using a methodology and design that involve the research participants in a way that facilitates learning and action – and therefore benefits them. If there are no immediate benefits to their participation, at least make it clear how their voices and participation can potentially benefit others in the future.

The cost, and in some cases risk, of participation differs between research participants. If you are working with a particularly vulnerable group of research participants, such as child soldiers or men who have sex with men, there may be certain risks involved in their participation (such as involuntary exposure), and so you need to consider whether their participation is worth that risk.

Feedback. Researchers have a reputation for parachuting into a community and disappearing without sharing the study results with the research participants or the broader community in which the study took place. Research participants not only have a right to know what you are saying about them, they also have the right to either verify or correct interpretations that have been made, as well as to use the results to instigate changes locally.

To operationalize these aims and considerations, a number of measures, or ground rules, have been formally established and are considered integral to good research practice. These ground rules include those listed below.

Informed consent. All respondents need to provide informed consent. Informed consent encourages transparency about the study and implies that a respondent needs to be fully informed about the study before he or she can consent. Consent can be given orally, but should ideally be in writing or through a thumb print. The process of obtaining informed consent involves an information sheet that provides details about:

- who is conducting the study;
- the purpose of the research project;
- the voluntary nature of participation;
- details about what will happen if the respondent decides to participate, including the length of time their participation will require;
- the right to withdraw without consequences;
- confidentially and secure data storage;
- risks and benefits of participation; and
- how the information gathered will be used.

The information sheet can either be read out or a physical copy given to the respondent. After they have been informed about the study, and what their participation entails, they can sign a consent form that contains a statement such as: 'The study has been explained to me/I have read the information sheet and I agree to take part.' Informed consent should be obtained from all respondents. If the research participants are below the age of 18, or mentally impaired, consent from parents or custodians also needs to be obtained. Some data collection methods, such as those gathering visuals of third-party individuals, require an additional set of consent forms. We discuss third-party consent with reference to Photovoice in Chapter 6.

Safeguarding of participants and researchers. Anyone coordinating a study is responsible for the safeguarding of research participants and researchers. You therefore need to consider very carefully any potential risks of conducting the study and put in place measures to safeguard and protect those involved. This includes the safety of researchers conducting research in contexts associated with certain risks, such as infectious diseases, poor road safety, crime, or conflict. Travel insurance, risk mitigation, and evacuation plans need to be in place.

Plans also need to be in place to protect participants from any harm associated with the study. For example, researchers conducting research with children ought to undergo checks to ensure that the risk of abuse is minimized, and work in pairs to reduce unsupervised one-to-one contact with children. If the topic being studied is sensitive and research participants may react negatively to the experience of sharing information, support services also need to be available for participants to be referred to.

Ethical review of the study protocol.   To obtain advice, and to help make sure that you have considered and taken steps to overcome the potential socio-ethical dilemmas that may arise from your study, you are strongly encouraged to send your study protocol for ethical review. Most universities and research institutes have a research ethics committee. Increasingly, larger NGOs are setting up their own research ethics committees too.

While these 'good practice' measures are important to follow, it should not be assumed that a study is ethical and avoids doing harm just because it adheres to these practices. Ultimately, the best way to conduct a socio-ethical study is to engage in dialogue with research participants and people from their local community, and to come to a common understanding of what the potential socio-ethical dilemmas may be and how best to overcome them (Skovdal and Abebe, 2012). This will also help you understand how you can implement the ground rules in a way that is culturally appropriate.

In summary, include a subheading in your study protocol entitled 'Socio-ethical considerations'. List some of the potential socio-ethical dilemmas that may arise from your study as well as actions you will take to mitigate and overcome these dilemmas. Explain who will review your study protocol with the aim of offering advice on how your proposed study can 'do good' and 'avoid doing harm'.

Data analysis

Qualitative data analysis pays attention to the 'spoken word', context, consistency and contradictions of views, frequency and intensity of comments, and their specificity, as well as emerging themes and trends. It is a process that seeks to reduce and make sense of vast amounts of information, often from different sources, so that impressions that shed light on a research question can emerge. It is a process in which you take descriptive information and offer an explanation or interpretation. You may have identified the methods you will use to gather information. But what will you do with this information? Do you handpick citations that support what you are interested in? Or is there a systematic way of interrogating and analysing your data?

We do not recommend that you choose citations to support your argument or story. Such practice does little to honour the spectrum of views and perspectives that you have gathered. However, precisely because qualitative data analysis relies on the impressions and interpretations of key researchers, it is vital that qualitative analysis is systematic and that researchers report on their impressions in a structured and transparent form.

To plan for qualitative data analysis that is systematic and transparent, there are four things you need to consider and plan for.

- *Units of analysis*: To recruit research participants who can provide you with information, that, when analysed, can answer your research question, you need to be clear about your units of analysis. These are the entities that are at the centre of your analysis and they might include individuals, groups, communities, geographic areas, sources of information, or an issue. In other words, it is the 'what' or 'who' that is being studied. Units of analysis are used to create summary descriptions of these elements and to explore differences between them. The 'individual' unit is most common and refers to the analysis of individual behaviours: for example, women's participation in a women's group. A 'group' unit, on the other hand, could be used to explore the differences and similarities between women's groups in two distinct geographic contexts. Each unit of analysis can also be segregated into different levels. For example, the 'individual' unit of analysis can be segregated into gender, age, and ethnic group. Qualitative studies often use a mix of these units of analyses and levels. However, the more units and levels you include, the more complicated the analysis gets. Try to limit it to a maximum of three.

- *Data capture, preparation, and management*: Once you enter the field of study, data is all around you. However, it does not qualify as data until you have captured it in a systematic way. 'Spoken words' therefore need to be recorded and transcribed. Observations need to be noted, either through written notes, drawings, pictures, video, or audio recordings. Capturing views and perspectives, as well as behaviours and impressions, and transforming them into physical data that can be stored and managed require careful planning. You need to consider how best to capture, prepare, and manage the information you gather as well as the resources needed to do so. In the following chapters we provide more detail on how best to capture and prepare the data you have gathered.

- *Deductive or inductive approach to analysis*: There are broadly two approaches to qualitative data analysis. The 'quick' approach is simply to index your data according to a predefined framework that reflects your aims, objectives, and interests. This deductive, or top-down, approach is relatively easy and is closely aligned with policy and programmatic research that has predetermined interests. This approach allows you to focus on particular answers and abandon the rest. The second approach takes a more exploratory perspective, encouraging you to consider all your data, allowing for new impressions to shape your interpretation in different and unexpected ways. This inductive, or bottom-up, approach is a little more challenging and time consuming, but can consider a broader spectrum of views and give rise to more nuanced learning. More often than not, qualitative analysis draws on a mix of both approaches. In Chapter 7, we describe analytical strategies that draw on these two approaches.

- *Computer-assisted qualitative data analysis software*: Qualitative research often generates huge amount of data and information, including interview and focus group discussion transcripts, field notes, literature, videos, photographs, and blog and social media updates. It can be challenging to keep an overview of what is being said by whom, where, and when. Computer software has been developed to assist with the interrogation of qualitative data in a way that is formal, time-saving, transparent, and manageable. It is not a must to use qualitative data analysis software, but if you conduct qualitative research regularly, it is worth investing time familiarizing yourself with it. NVivo and ATLAS. ti are two of the most commonly used subscription-based software programs. There are also free and open-source alternatives, such as CATMA for Windows, Macintosh, and Linux, TAMS Analyzer for Macintosh, and Coding Analysis Toolkit (CAT), which is web-based.[1] For more information, see Chapter 7.

In summary, include a subheading in your study protocol entitled 'Data analysis'. Explain the 'what' or 'who' that is being studied and analysed. Describe your plans of how best to capture, prepare, and manage the information you will be gathering. Clarify whether you will be adopting an inductive or deductive approach, or a mix of the two, and state which analytical procedure, or strategy, you will use. If you plan to use computer-assisted qualitative data analysis software, explain the software of your choosing.

Cost and timescale

Conducting good qualitative research is neither cheap nor fast. It is not uncommon for development organizations to embark on qualitative research with an inadequate budget and timescale. While this may well generate some useful information, shortcuts made due to funding and time constraints are likely to undermine the quality and rigour of the research. As this book is about strengthening the quality of qualitative research, we want to stress the importance of estimating costs and timescales and allowing enough money and time to carry out the project. Good and systematic qualitative research needs to be sufficiently resourced. To plan for this, you can develop a timetable that outlines your planned activities (see Table 2.2 for an example), and a table that estimates the costs for carrying out these activities (see Table 2.3 for an example).

Having a budget and a timescale that are realistic is crucial to maintain rigour. If you do not have sufficient resources to carry out your planned study, we recommend that you revise the design of your study, for example by changing its scope, so that you are able to conduct a rigorous qualitative research within the budget available to you.

In summary, include a subheading in your study protocol entitled 'Costs and timescale'. Explain who will fund the study and how much money will be available. Describe the human resources required to carry out the study. Include a budget, specifying key items and activities. Include a timeline and a plan of when different activities will be carried out.

Table 2.2 Example of what a qualitative research timetable might look like

Research activity	Jan	Feb	Mar	Apr	May	Jun	Jul	Aug	Sep	Oct	Nov	Dec
Discussions with partners	■	■										
Literature review		■	■									
Designing the study			■	■								
Draft research tools				■								
Recruit respondents				■	■							
Pilot tools and revise					■							
Fieldwork						■	■					
Transcribing data							■	■				
Analysing data								■	■			
Writing report									■	■		
Disseminating report										■	■	■

Table 2.3 Example of what a qualitative research budget might look like

Research activities	Costs
Labour	
Research assistants	
Days spent by the lead researcher	
Travel	
Flights	
Local public transport	
Driver allowance	
Car rental	
Lodging	
Research equipment	
Mobile phones	
Laptop	
Hard drive and USB sticks	
Digital voice recorders	
Research material and services	
Transcription	
Stationery	
Phone and internet credit	
Software (Windows and NVivo)	
Dissemination	
Workshops	
Printing and binding of report	
Total	

Conflicts of interest

In research, conflict of interest refers to situations where financial or other personal considerations may cloud and compromise – or appear to compromise – a researcher's professional judgement in conducting or reporting research. For example, if a researcher gains financially from producing certain results, this may cause him or her to bias the results in favour of financial gain. Conflicts of interest can undermine even the most systematic qualitative studies. Being clear about potential conflicts of interest in your study can either help you make arrangements that can remove them, or ensure you disclosure the potential conflicts of interest.

In practice, include a subheading in your study protocol entitled 'Conflicts of interest'. Declare the affiliation or involvement of study team members with the development activities being studied. Specify the relationship between each study member and involved organizations and entities (the programme, for example), such as their employment or role in implementing a programme. Explain the potential and perceived conflicts of interests that may exist in the project.

Activity 2.8 Potential conflicts of interest

Development practitioners often conduct research in programmes developed and funded by the same organization that pays their salary. What potential conflicts of interest may arise from this? Write down your thoughts.

Feedback is available at the end of the chapter.

Quality criteria of qualitative research

When planning and carrying out qualitative research, this should be done with an awareness of criteria to assess the quality of that research. As with quantitative research, 'good practice' exists for qualitative research. In this chapter we have offered some guidance on how you can plan for a qualitative study that follows 'good practice'. We will now draw on the quality criteria put forward by Gaskell and Bauer (2000) to illustrate the importance of planning a qualitative study and offer final advice on how you can conduct good-quality qualitative research.

- *Be systematic*: Approach the study methodologically and thoroughly. Do not take shortcuts or make decisions because 'it is the easy choice'. By being systematic you can demonstrate procedural clarity in: 1) how you arrive at the research question; 2) why your data collection methods are appropriate; 3) how you go about recruiting research participants; 4) the process of capturing and managing data, for example by recording and transcribing the data; 5) how you analyse the data, and reduce large amounts of information to a story that answers your research question.
- *Demonstrate reflexivity*: Demonstrate awareness of how you, the researcher, may shape the study. This includes your personal motivation

to conduct the study, as well as how your background and interests may influence the data collection process and the writing up of results.

- *Be transparent*: Provide detailed descriptions of how you carried out the study and how you came to your results and conclusions. Readers of qualitative work need to have enough information to be able to assess your interpretations. This requires you to document the (systematic) research process with a lot of detail, as well as including plenty of citations and data to back up your arguments.
- *Be honest*: Demonstrate that you are aware of shortcomings and limitations of the study. Declare what they are. Also demonstrate caution in making unsubstantiated claims. Be humble about your results and refrain from making huge generalizations.
- *Be open to surprises*: Be open to new and different perspectives, even if they do not match your expectations.
- *Triangulate findings*: Investigate your research question from different angles, both by including the perspectives of different actors and by using a different set of data collection methods.
- *Demonstrate relevance*: Revisit the literature and show how your study relates to the existing literature. You can do so by demonstrating how your study supports, contradicts, or builds on the findings of other researchers.

Summary

There are many things to consider before carrying out a qualitative study. This chapter has outlined and discussed some of the more important considerations that can help you plan for effective qualitative research. To approach the planning of a qualitative study systematically, we have suggested that you use the process of developing a qualitative study protocol as a platform to define your research purpose, identify a research question, and develop a feasible and ethical study design that can be used to answer your research question. We have covered many things, and it may seem overwhelming, particularly if this is your first time conducting a qualitative study, but it may well be worth learning as this will help you plan for more effective and convincing qualitative studies. We hope that by breaking down the planning into bite-sized chunks, and into a process for developing a study protocol, we have helped you to see it as a doable and rewarding approach.

The following chapters offer more detailed procedural clarity and guidelines on the process of generating data as well as on how to identify and report on findings.

Endnote

1. The software is available from the following websites: NVivo, <www. qsrinternational.com>; ATLAS.ti, <http://atlasti.com>; CATMA, <www.

catma.de>; TAMS, <http://tamsys.sourceforge.net>; CAT, <http://cat.ucsur.pitt.edu/> [all accessed 24 July 2015].

References

Creswell, J. W. (2012) *Qualitative Inquiry and Research Design: Choosing Among Five Approaches*, London: SAGE Publications.

Gaskell, G. and Bauer, M. W. (2000) 'Towards public accountability: beyond sampling, reliability and validity', in M. W. Bauer and G. Gaskell (eds), *Qualitative Researching with Text, Image and Sound*, London: SAGE Publications.

Israel, B. A., Eng, E., Schulz, A. J. and Parker, E. A. (2005) *Methods in Community-based Participatory Research for Health*, San Francisco CA: Jossey-Bass.

Moustakas, C. (1994) *Phenomenological Research Methods*, Thousand Oaks CA: SAGE Publications.

O'Leary, Z. (2004) *The Essential Guide to Doing Research*, London: SAGE Publications.

Patton, M. Q. (1990) *Qualitative Evaluation and Research Methods*, 2nd edn, Thousand Oaks CA: SAGE Publications.

Peters, D. H., Adam, T., Alonge, O., Agyepong, I. A. and Tran, N. (2013) 'Implementation research: what it is and how to do it', *BMJ* 347, doi: 10.1136/bmj.f6753.

Skovdal, M. and Abebe, T. (2012) 'Reflexivity and dialogue: methodological and socio-ethical dilemmas in research with HIV-affected children in East Africa', *Ethics, policy & environment* 15 (1): 77–96.

Wisker, G. (2007) *The Postgraduate Research Handbook: Succeed with Your MA, MPhil, EdD and PhD*, Basingstoke: Palgrave Macmillan.

Feedback on activities

Feedback on Activity 2.2 Motivational factors behind the study

A local development practitioner could be motivated by the following factors:

- Appalled by seeing the struggles of working street children first-hand, simply through living in Karachi. This could affect the study positively by providing the practitioner with stimuli to see the study through.
- Aware of the demand for a programme targeting working street children. This could affect the study positively, both from being implemented by a practitioner with an overview of existing services, and also from the recognition that working street children have unique needs that need to be flagged and addressed.
- Recognition from leaders in Karachi if the study emphasizes the positive role of the city council in supporting working street children. This could affect the study negatively by biasing the results.

An international development practitioner could be motivated by the following factors:

- Appalled by the statistics and news reports that highlight the vulnerability of working street children in Karachi. This could affect the study positively by providing the practitioner with stimuli to see the study through.

- Developing a programme that responds to a lucrative funding call. This could affect the study either positively or negatively. The study could form part of a needs assessment, resulting in programme development. However, the study could also be used to unfairly represent working street children as victims in need of aid.

Feedback on Activity 2.4 Deciding on a research question

The second question is probably the most appropriate research question. It is clear, focused, and gives an indication of what the study sets out to do. The first question is too simple and can incorporate anything. The third question is unclear. It does not give any indication of what you will be studying and assumes that children need support. You can still develop recommendations for policy and practice from an investigation of the second research question.

Feedback on Activity 2.5 Linking study interests and approaches

If you want to study the barriers and facilitators to programme implementation, you are engaging in a monitoring activity that reflects implementation research. If you want to empower working street children to communicate their experience, for example through a situational analysis in the planning of a programme, you could adopt a community-based participatory research approach. If you are looking to understand street children's experiences of living on the street, also as part of the planning of a programme, you could adopt either a CBPR, phenomenological, or case study research approach. If you want to explore the health of children living and working on the street, a case study research approach would be appropriate. If you follow the cases over time, the case studies can be used both to inform the planning of a programme and for monitoring and evaluation.

Feedback on Activity 2.6 Consulting your gatekeepers

A member of the city council may grant you permission to conduct the study, while a leader of a community-based organization supporting working street children in Karachi may facilitate access to the children.

Feedback on Activity 2.7 Choosing qualitative research methods

Photovoice could be used to enable working street children to identify, represent, and communicate their struggles and coping strategies.

Individual interviews with a selected group of working street children could be used to gain insight into their values, understandings, feelings, experiences, and perspectives. Interviews could also be used with service providers to obtain their perspectives on the struggles and coping strategies of working street children.

Participant observation could be used by the research team to better understand – through seeing, feeling, and intimate familiarity – what life is like for working street children.

Feedback on Activity 2.8 Potential conflicts of interest

Development practitioners actively involved in the programme being studied may have a personal interest to show that they have done a good job and could potentially be inclined to bias the results to primarily show the successes.

Even if you, as a development practitioner, may not get a bonus or salary increase from producing certain results, your salary comes from the same organization that may have an interest in you producing certain results.

Even if you and your organization have no interest in biasing the results, the perception that you may have an interest is enough to require you to disclosure your affiliations.

CHAPTER 3

Interviews and focus group discussions

Abstract

This chapter aims to equip the reader with a full understanding of the role of interviews and focus groups, and knowledge of each step to be taken in designing and carrying out an interview or focus group study. It begins by setting out the purposes of interviews and focus groups. Individual interviews are useful for understanding local points of view, or for gleaning key facts from key informants. Focus groups are useful for understanding collective responses or norms regarding an issue. These data collection methods can be used to improve practice at each stage of the programme cycle. Clear guidance is given regarding how to design an interview or focus group study, from writing research questions, through sampling and recruitment of participants, to creating a topic guide and conducting the interview.

Keywords: Qualitative research; interviews; focus group discussions; topic guide; sampling

Learning objectives

After reading this chapter, you will be able to:

- identify the purposes of interviews and focus group discussions in monitoring, evaluation, accountability, and learning (MEAL) work;
- explain the strengths and weaknesses of interview methods; and
- plan, design, and conduct an interview or focus group discussion study.

Key terms (definitions)

- *In-depth interview*: A one-to-one conversation between researcher and participant, providing information on the participant's point of view.
- *Focus group discussion*: A discussion among four to eight participants, facilitated by a researcher, generating data on the research topic through peer discussions.
- *Topic guide*: The researcher's list of issues and questions guiding the conduct of the interview or focus group.

Introduction

In-depth interviews are the most commonly used qualitative data collection method. Focus group discussions are very popular too. These methods provide

http://dx.doi.org/10.3362/9781780448534.003

an efficient and rapid way of gathering information from individuals or groups of people. Most commonly, interviews and focus groups are used for studies that investigate people's views, experiences, understandings, beliefs, or norms. They can tell us about the norms in a beneficiary community, prior to initiating an intervention, for example. Or they might be used to assess a community's experience of an intervention as a part of an evaluation study. In general, they offer us a window onto the views of other people.

Key informant interviews are used in a different way: to provide us with quick access to important facts, from carefully selected individuals who have access to those facts. Such interviews might be used to inform a rapid situation appraisal. We will discuss both of these types of interviews during the chapter.

Interviews and focus group discussions have contributions to make to each stage of the programme cycle. We will give examples in the course of the chapter to make their various possible contributions clear.

What are interviews and focus group discussions?

What is an interview?

An interview is a conversation between an interviewer (the researcher) and an interviewee. It is a conversation that is less open and undirected than everyday chit-chat, but at the same time less structured than a questionnaire, which asks a series of questions one after the other. In an interview conversation, the interviewer takes a leading role, guiding the conversation to cover the topics of the research, but allowing the interviewee to explain his or her point of view at some length, and to give examples and reasons for their views. As interviewers, we want the interviewee to do more of the talking than we do – because our goal is to learn their perspective.

Practically speaking, an interview usually lasts between 40 minutes and one hour. In less than 30 minutes, we often do not have time to get into the depth we need. Participants often start to get tired and lose their attention after an hour – though this depends on how exciting the topic is!

The researcher uses a 'topic guide' to guide his or her questioning during the interview. This might be about one page in length, and it asks a series of open-ended questions. The interviewer is likely to follow up answers with probing questions, or requests for examples.

The interview usually takes place in a private setting, to allow the interviewee to speak freely.

An in-depth interview is usually a one-to-one situation, although sometimes an interviewer might interview a pair of people if they prefer. Alternatively, an interviewer might sometimes be accompanied by a co-researcher, or an interpreter.

What is a focus group discussion?

In a focus group discussion (henceforth a 'focus group'), we bring together a group of people to discuss an issue. Similar to an individual interview, the discussion takes the form of a conversation, although this time the participants talk to each other and not only to the interviewer (often called a moderator or facilitator, in the context of a focus group). Like an interview, a focus group will have a topic guide, although this will often be a shorter and simpler one, because, ideally, the focus group moderator will speak even less than they do in the individual interview context.

Practically, a focus group is made up of about four to eight participants. The participants should all have enough of a common interest in the topic under discussion to be able to have a common discussion together. At the same time, they are likely to have somewhat different perspectives. Ideally, a focus group discussion gains a momentum of its own, as participants bounce ideas off each other, and respond to what others have said.

Why conduct interviews and focus groups?

What are interviews and focus groups for?

We will discuss and distinguish two main uses of interviews. The first is to understand local people's experiences and points of view. The second is to glean important facts from key informants.

Understanding local points of view.   A prime reason for the failure of numerous development and humanitarian projects is that they have failed to engage with beneficiaries' points of view. Programmes and projects need to respond to local people's concerns. They need to make sense to local people, and to win their support and commitment. Yet they are often not initiated by local people. Interviews and focus groups offer development workers opportunities to understand how local people think about the problem at hand. They enable us to explore local communities' norms, beliefs, concerns, expectations of a project, or wishes for the future. Interviews and focus groups allow people to talk in their own terms, giving us opportunities to learn the words they use, their priorities and concerns.

Individual one-to-one interviews allow the researcher to probe a person's thinking in depth. Focus groups give us a more collective point of view on how the group as a whole discusses a topic. So interviews are good at exploring individual thinking, emotions, and personal issues. Focus groups are good at exploring shared norms, common knowledge, shared beliefs, and common debates.

Thinking about interviews and focus groups as telling us about 'local points of view' means that we are not looking for objective facts, but for subjective experience. Thinking about interviews and focus groups in this way, if people say they are angry about increasing police corruption, we can be confident in concluding that they perceive that the police have become more corrupt, and that they are angry about this. But we cannot conclude with any certainty whether, objectively, corruption has become worse.

Gaining key facts from key informants.   When we consider interviewees as key informants, we are taking a different approach. If we want to scope out basic information, or to do a rapid appraisal of the situation in a particular setting, we might seek out key informants to bring us up to speed. We would select key informants who have rich and concrete knowledge of our area of interest. For instance, a leader of a women's group should be well placed to tell us about the existing support systems and resources available to women in her community. A senior police officer should be able to give a valid account of the situation regarding crime and security in a particular area. A senior social welfare official should be able to outline formal sources of support for vulnerable citizens.

With this sort of interview, we are more interested in objective facts about the situation. By asking very concrete questions, which have concrete answers, we increase the chances of truthful, verifiable answers. Of course, we must always remember that interviewees may have limited knowledge, or a particular interest to protect, and that their interviews are not fully objective or complete. But by interviewing a variety of people, cross-checking where possible, and remaining aware of the possibility of bias, we can justifiably use key informant interviews for a rapid situation appraisal.

Roles of interview research at each stage of the programme cycle

Given that humanitarian and development projects exist to serve, support, mobilize, and empower beneficiary communities, understanding communities' points of view plays a crucial role throughout the programme cycle (as depicted in Chapter 1).

Needs assessment and situational analysis.   Prior to even designing or planning an intervention, interview and focus group research can be used to build an understanding of local priorities, concerns, and wishes for the future – so that the intervention is something that the community can buy in to, and commit to.

For example, to inform a policy paper for a campaign on security in Africa, Oxfam commissioned a study of the security situation in South Sudan (Kircher, 2013). Some 22 focus groups with communities and 70 key informant interviews were carried out. These interviews and focus groups portrayed a situation of increasing violence, identifying inter- and intra-communal conflict, cattle raids, and violence against women as particularly worrying. With this research as a foundation, the author was able to produce a set of recommendations for Oxfam's programme and advocacy work, which were based in solid evidence of the situation on the ground.

In a different context, Hossain and Green (2011) used focus groups to study poor people's experience of food price hikes. They used participatory methods – including asking people about what is in their weekly 'food basket' and what it costs – to explore whether they had experienced a price hike, and how they had adjusted.

Local context analysis.   Moving closer to an intervention, and becoming more concrete, interview and focus group research can usefully investigate local norms, beliefs, and language to understand where challenges lie, and what kinds of changes are realistic and acceptable for local people.

For example, Wajid and colleagues (2010) conducted a focus group study of the acceptability of community midwives in Pakistan while community midwives were in training, and before they were posted in communities. The study aimed to explore communities' perceptions and expectations of community midwives, and any potential barriers to their effective work. By understanding local points of view, the study was able to make evidence-based recommendations for how to set up the community midwives programme to make it most likely to succeed.

Jejeebhoy and her colleagues (2013) conducted formative research, using focus groups on gender-based violence, to understand the context of violence and thereby inform programming. Their rich report gives a profound insight into the norms held by young men and women in villages in Bihar, India. Through individual interviews with husbands who were described by their wives as being either violent or nonviolent, they further explored the characteristics of perpetrators and non-perpetrators, to try to understand the possibilities for more positive, less violent masculinities.

Formative evaluation – barriers and facilitators.   Once a project has commenced, interviews and focus groups can be used for formative evaluation, to explore participants' experiences and perceptions of strengths and weaknesses of an intervention. Again, the assumption is that local knowledge is crucial to understanding what is working and what is not working.

In the world of design and technology development, 'user experience' research is highly valued. This is research that gives users a piece of technology to use and then explores with them how they use it, what works for them and what does not work, and barriers and facilitators to their use.

The USAID WASHplus project (2013), which examined the user experience of five different types of cookstoves in Bangladesh, provides a good example. For this study, researchers gave householders one out of the five different types of stoves to trial. They then interviewed them, using a semi-structured interview designed to identify barriers and motivators to change. The study found that two stoves were preferred to traditional cookstoves by many, but also identified the perceived flaws in their design, and challenges to their effective use.

An analogy to 'user experience research' can be made to any project that is in its early stages. A development project might not actually be distributing a concrete form of technology but might be trying to initiate a new process, with new behaviours, services, resources, or messages. Users, or beneficiaries, have crucial experience of the early days of those new behaviours, services, resources, or messages, and can feed back to practitioners about what, so far, is working and not working. They can identify barriers and facilitators, obstacles and ways of overcoming those obstacles. Adapting to such feedback can be vital to the success of a project.

Evaluation and impact studies.   In the evaluation phase, we often want to understand how people experienced an intervention: what they found useful or unhelpful about the project, and in what ways they consider it to have been successful or unsuccessful. Interviews or focus groups can be held to assess local perceptions of a project. Key informant interviews can be used to ask those people who have been closely involved in implementing a project to reflect on what seemed to work or not to work, and on lessons that could be learned from the experience.

The coalition Action for Large-scale Land Acquisition Transparency (ALLAT) commissioned Joan Baxter (2013) to investigate the social, economic, nutritional, health, and environmental impacts of large-scale land acquisition by agribusiness companies in Sierra Leone. She used focus groups and interviews to examine the effects on rural Sierra Leoneans of leasing land that had previously been used for subsistence and small-scale income generation. Participants talked about how their lives had changed over the past few years, and whether the large foreign investors had lived up to what communities expected of them. Her research revealed the enormous costs to local people of the land acquisitions and the failures of regulations to protect them.

Clearly, interviews and focus groups are being used for a great variety of purposes. With the various examples presented here, we hope we have illustrated some of the ways in which interviews and focus groups can be put to use to ensure that programmes and campaigns are based on evidence of local people's concerns, priorities, and everyday lives.

Interviews or focus groups? How to choose

What is the difference between an interview and a focus group? How should we choose whether to use one or the other?

Table 3.1 Should I use interviews or focus groups?

Use interviews if...	Use focus groups if...
You want to probe individual experiences in detail	You are interested in broader social norms among the community as a whole
You want to talk to people who all have very different views on the topic	Your target group has enough commonality to get a common discussion going
You have specific questions where key informants have access to the particular information you need	You have general questions and want to hear people discuss and debate at length
Your informants are in physically far-apart places, or are unable or unwilling to travel to a central location	It will be straightforward to gather between five and eight people in one place for the focus group discussion
You prioritize in-depth information from a smaller number of people over more general information from a larger number	You wish to rapidly involve as many people as possible

Both interviews and focus groups can tell us about local people's points of view. Interviews generally allow for more in-depth probing of individual experiences. Focus groups are a good way of getting a more collective view of what people assume to be the norm.

Designing an interview or focus group study

Step 1: Write research questions suited to interviews and focus groups

Map out the logic of your research problem.   The first issue of research design is to make sure that your selected method is the best one to be able to answer your research questions. First of all, you need to know that, by conducting interviews or focus groups, you will gather the information you need in order to solve your research problem. Ask yourself the questions: Why am I going to interview these people? What do I hope to get out of the interviews? What conclusions can I draw, based on that information?

Table 3.2 Steps in interview and focus group research design

Step 1	**Write research questions**	Map out the logic of how your interview or focus group is going to provide the information you need
		Write research questions suited to uncovering people's perspectives, e.g. experiences, beliefs, norms
Step 2	**Plan your sample**	Identify your target group
		Think about diversity: which sub-groups should be included?
		Set a goal for your sample size
		Plan your sampling strategy
		Plan your recruitment strategy
Step 3	**Write your topic guides**	Write your topic guide(s)
		Pilot your topic guide – do the questions work?
Step 4	**Conduct the interview or focus group**	Plan logistics (where, when, who)
		Record the interview
		Transcribe or make notes
Step 5	**Analyse the data (see Chapter 7)**	Prepare for analysis by rehearsing your research questions, and what you want to get out of the data
		Code the material
		Organize your codes to provide answers and a story
Step 6	**Write up (see Chapter 8)**	Write up your findings, using quotations from the data to illustrate your points

For example, focus groups with communities about child protection issues can give you information on local norms and resources. But they offer only indirect and uncertain access to information about formal policies, or about the impact of advocacy campaigns on government policies.

In evaluation research, interviews and focus groups are likely to give you information about *perceived impact*, but less likely to give you information about *actual impact*.

Write questions about people's perspectives. If your research questions are about people's perspectives – for example, their experiences, beliefs, attitudes, norms, priorities, perceptions, and so on – then an interview or focus group is likely to be a good fit.

Box 3.1 Examples of research questions for interview or focus group studies

Interview studies

How does HIV stigma affect the lives of individual people living with HIV/AIDS in Khartoum?

What are the factors impacting on the healthcare-seeking behaviours of new parents in rural Nepal?

What reasons do people give for their use or non-use of a new IT system to aid farming?

What beliefs and values are expressed by men who do not perpetrate domestic violence in a context in which many people believe it to be normal?

What is the current situation regarding formal services supporting child protection in the Somali region of Ethiopia? (Key informant interviews.)

Focus group studies

What are the current attitudes, behaviours, and practices regarding child protection issues among communities in the Somali region of Ethiopia?

What community support and resources exist to deal with child protection issues in the Somali region of Ethiopia?

What kind of sexual health education programmes would be deemed to be socially acceptable by young people in South Sudan? (And, separately by their parents? And by their teachers?)

What are the local norms regarding domestic violence in rural Bihar?

Activity 3.1 Write research questions

Think about a current issue you are facing in your work. Is there a question that is bothering you and your colleagues? Is there a gap in your knowledge about a particular group?

Imagine how an interview study or a focus group study might help you.

– Write one research question for an interview study
– Write one research question for a focus group study

Feedback is available at the end of the chapter.

Step 2: Your sample

In Chapter 2 (in the section titled 'Identifying a location and selecting study participants'), we outlined the main considerations in sampling and recruiting participants. You will find more detail in that section. Here we summarize the steps.

Identify your target group.   Your sample comprises all the people who actually take part in your interview or focus group study. You will start with a set of aims for your sample – how big it should be, who the target group is – but we are often surprised, in the course of data collection, and have to adapt to the real-world circumstances.

The first thing to do is to decide on your target group. If you are targeting young people, you will need to define what you mean by 'young people'. What age range are you referring to? Do you include those in school and out of school? Are there particular geographical areas of focus?

Think about diversity in your target group.   Once you are clear about your target group, it is worth thinking widely again about who else might be informative about your issue. If you are interviewing young people, might a perspective from their parents, teachers, or local community leaders offer a useful contrasting or contextualizing angle? Are there important differences between rural and urban young people that you want to tap into? Or between employed and unemployed young people? Do you want a gender balance in the sample?

Do not assume too quickly that age group or gender is the most important line of difference in your sample. Think about your topic. What is likely to be the most important line of difference (or, in research language, 'stratification') between people in relation to this topic? Is it whether they are men or women? Or whether they are self-employed, employed by somebody else, or unemployed? Work out how to build that important line of difference into your study. You are using a 'stratified sample' if you have consciously divided your sample into more than one clearly defined group: for example, men and women, or urban and rural participants.

For focus groups, the composition of the group is important. Participants need to feel sufficiently comfortable and at home together to be able to discuss important and sometimes sensitive issues. Some degree of shared culture and norms is important. So be aware of how you define the target group for each focus group. You need to aim to maximize the chances that participants will open up and speak freely in front of each other.

Sometimes participants in focus groups know each other already: they might be classmates in a school, or neighbours, or a group of friends. This has the advantage that participants already have a relationship, and are likely to start talking and discussing relatively easily. Conversely, the group history means that there may be established hierarchies, norms, and patterns of communication set up, so that some people dominate, or some topics are deemed 'off limits' or controversial. There are pros and cons to using both existing social groups and groups of people who do not know each other. As before, it is important to be aware of the dynamics and how they might influence the data. The example in Box 3.2 shows how this can work.

Box 3.2 The sample in a large-scale qualitative domestic violence study

The table below shows the sample used for a large-sale qualitative study about domestic violence. Jejeebhoy and colleagues (2013) assumed at the start that gender, marital status, and age group would be important lines of difference in their data. So they separated their participants according to those factors in their focus groups.

They conducted three focus groups with unmarried young women (aged 15–24) and two with unmarried young men (of the same age group). They also conducted four focus groups with married young women and four with married young men. Moving to the older age group (25–50), they conducted four focus groups with married adult men and four with married adult women.

They used a short survey questionnaire to establish factual demographic information and the extent of participants' experiences of domestic violence.

Then, in a second stage, they purposively recruited the husbands of women who had participated in the focus groups. At this stage, they stratified the husbands according to whether their wives had reported violence or non-violence, in order to try to understand the difference between men who were perpetrators of domestic violence and those who were not.

Table 3.3 Data collection methods for domestic violence study

	Group	Number of FGDs/Interviews
Focus group discussions (FGDs)	Unmarried youth	5 (3 with young women and 2 with young men)
Focus group discussions	Married youth	8 (4 with young women and 4 with young men)
Focus group discussions	Married adults	8 (4 with women and 4 with men)
Survey, using a structured questionnaire	Married female FGD participants aged 15-24 and 25-50	8 (4 with women and 4 with men)
Survey, using a structured questionnaire	Available husbands of married female FGD participants	36 (19 husbands of women aged 15-24 and 17 husbands of women aged 25-50)
In-depth interviews	Selected husbands of women who participated in FGDs, based on reports of violence in survey	21 (10 husbands of women reporting nonviolent husbands, 11 husbands of women reporting violent husbands)

Source: Adapted from Jejeebhoy et al. (2013: 2).

Set a goal for your sample size.   Whenever somebody asks us 'How many people should I interview?', we have to answer 'It depends.' The more diverse the sample, the more people you will need to interview in order to have a sense that your study has covered the main issues (or reached 'saturation', see Chapter 2).

It is difficult to be confident about claims made by a study with fewer than 10 interviews or about three focus groups (a total of about 18 people).

You should think about each sub-group in your sample (men/women; urban/rural) as a group in their own right. So, if you are separating your sample into men and women (because you expect there to be a difference between them in relation to the topic), you should interview about 12 men and 12 women. Alternatively, you might use two or three focus groups with each separate group.

Weighing up the resources available, the ease or difficulty of recruitment, and the diversity of the groups, decide on a target sample size.

Identify your sampling strategy. How are you going to identify people to take part in your study? How are you going to ensure that the sample is broadly representative of the population, and not overly biased? For more information on different approaches to sampling, see Chapter 2, especially the section on 'Identifying a location and selecting study participants'.

Qualitative research often uses **purposive sampling**. This means that the sample has been designed to cover important segments of the population, or important experiences defined by the research. It is not a random or perfectly representative sample; rather, it is consciously chosen to cover important groups or experiences. For instance, a purposive sample might aim to interview both men who perpetrate domestic violence and those who do not (even if these men are not equally represented in the population). Or it might be designed to sample equal numbers of people from different ethnic groups.

As always, the design of the sample involves weighing up what is ideal, from a research point of view, with what is achievable. The most important point is to be consciously aware of how you are sampling, and how that might affect the data. You should be able to justify the approach you have taken.

In practice, and especially in difficult settings, qualitative research often uses a **convenience sample**. This means that few restrictions are imposed by the researcher, who has to include in the sample whoever is available and willing to be interviewed, as long as they meet the basic criteria.

Plan your recruitment strategy. How will you access and recruit participants for your study? You need a process to identify places or gatekeepers through which to meet potential interviewees and invite them to take part.

It is often a good idea to start with multiple gatekeepers, not just one – so that you have a chance of getting a diverse sample, not just the friends or contacts of one particular person. So, for example, try to contact people in contrasting NGOs, or from different administrative districts, to help you with recruitment. Use people with different roles, and with contacts to different social groups.

Notoriously, for focus groups, one of the main challenges is actually getting six people together in the same room at the same time. Time and again, researchers report that they thought they had done a good job with recruitment, only to find that three participants turned up for their focus group, with the others dropping out at the last minute. Researchers usually advise over-recruiting for focus groups, assuming that some people will not make it to the venue. So plan ahead for such eventualities. Where you hold the focus group will be a key consideration – make sure it is as accessible as possible, and that you can cover transport, and possibly childcare, to make participation possible.

Recruiting and holding the focus group at a location where your target group spends time anyway – a school or workplace, for instance – can be a good idea.

You will need to prepare an information sheet and consent form (see the section on 'Overcoming socio-ethical dilemmas' in Chapter 2). Be prepared to explain the research informally and verbally, and do not expect everybody to be able to, or want to, read through a formal information sheet.

Make sure you know exactly what you are asking the person to do – answer the questions where, when, why, who, and what. Consider what the participant might get out of it. Are you offering any incentives? Travel costs? Refreshments? Explain the value of the research. And make sure not to give or even imply any false promises. People often hope that our research will lead to direct and concrete benefits for them. Researchers must be honest and careful about the expectations raised.

Step 3: Write your topic guide

The topic guide is a one- or two-page document that the researcher brings into the interview or focus group to remind himself or herself of the issues they are aiming to cover. It is designed to structure a conversation that takes place over the course of about an hour. It breaks down the research question into more concrete questions that the participants are capable of responding to at some length.

Easy-to-answer, concrete questions. A good topic guide asks intuitive questions to participants, questions that they understand, and questions on which they can elaborate at length. Asking participants for concrete stories is a good idea. Asking them the research questions directly is usually a bad idea! For example, would you prefer to answer the question 'What does "health" mean to you?', or 'Tell me about what you do to keep healthy', or 'Tell me about the last time you visited the doctor'? Most people find it much easier to tell concrete stories (the last time I visited a doctor, for example), than to answer abstract questions (such as 'What does "health" mean to you?'). If our research question is to understand indigenous concepts of 'health', we are likely to need to find indirect ways of getting at this abstract concept. Researchers, professionals, and programme managers use abstract concepts such as 'health', 'child development', 'child protection', 'sustainability', and so on. Ordinary people often do not use these concepts and so we need to translate between our research interests and the language of participants in order to have a good interview.

Checklist: A good topic guide

- Asks 'user-friendly', easy-to-answer questions in words familiar to the participants.
- Asks participants to talk about issues they are familiar with.
- Does not ask participants the research question directly.
- Has a logical flow and structure.
- Is no longer than one page for a focus group or two pages for an interview.
- Covers three to seven main topics.

Keep the list of questions short and simple.   We want to make sure that we are allowing participants time to elaborate their responses in their own words, and reporting their own concerns. A relatively short topic guide can help here – rather than a rapid-fire set of questions requiring short answers. A topic guide often has somewhere between three and seven main topics for discussion, with perhaps a few more specific questions or probes for each topic. Limiting the number of topics allows us time to address each topic in some depth with participants. Short and simple topic guides also help the sense of coherence and flow of the interview, and helps the researcher to feel in control. When interviews flow well, the researcher often finds that he or she is able to remember the topics and to guide the conversation skilfully, without being strictly tied to the wording or order in the topic guide.

The topic guide should contain the most important questions, whose wording has been carefully thought through. But, in the natural flow of conversation, the researcher should use probes and prompts fluidly, in response to what participants say.

Organization and flow.   We want the interview to flow naturally and comfortably. Changes of topic should ideally be quite natural, as one topic comes to an end and leads into the next. We want to avoid the dynamic of a question–answer survey interview, in which the interviewer clearly takes the lead and asks for short answers. There should be some sense of a logical order and flow to the interview.

A topic guide opens with an introductory section, in which the aim is to build rapport, get to know the participant(s) a little, and set the context for the interview. It usually starts with very easy-to-answer and concrete questions.

Introductory questions could be, for example: 'To set the scene, could you tell me a little about your role to date in this intervention project?', 'As you know, we are interested in girls' education. Please can you tell me about your own education to date?', or 'Thank you for volunteering to take part in this study. May I ask what interested you about the project? What connection do you have with the topic of study?'

Then the topic guide moves on to the body of the interview. Here, the researcher will address around three to six topics, one after the other, to cover the research questions and interests. There should be some sense of logic to the flow of the questions. That logic might, for example, mean moving from personal experience, to speaking about others' experiences, and then speaking about services, as in the domestic violence example in Box 3.3.

A different logic would be to follow a timeline. You might begin by talking about childhood, then adolescence and adulthood, for example. Or you could begin by speaking about the time before a particular intervention took place, then move on to describing the participants' experience of the intervention, and then their perceptions of its impact, and their hopes for the future.

Finally, there is a closing phase after the researcher has asked the main questions. The final tasks are to allow the participant to have a final word, and then to close the interview, with gratitude and respect.

Box 3.3 A brief topic guide for a focus group exploring the situation regarding domestic violence in a community

Section 1: Introduction

Thank you for taking part in this study. As you know, we want to understand the situation regarding violence against women. We know this is a difficult and sensitive topic. Please do not feel you have to speak about your own experience unless you wish to. At any time, you can call a stop to the interview, or say that you do not wish to answer a particular question. Do you have any questions before we start?

Section 2: Understandings of domestic violence

- What are the ways in which violence is committed against wives?
- Probe for physical violence including slapping, emotional violence, and sexual violence.
- Probe for examples.
- Is violence ever acceptable? Under what conditions?
- Probe for examples.

Section 3: Personal and community experiences of domestic violence

- How common are the forms of violence you have mentioned?
- Discuss each different type of violence in turn (physical, emotional, sexual).
- Probe for examples.
- Probe for what is considered 'normal' and 'to be expected'.

Section 4: Appropriate responses

- What should a woman do when she experiences any of these forms of violence?
- Probe about support from family and friends; traditional leaders; the police; NGOs; state services. Ask about leaving a violent marriage, and so on.
- What should a family member or friend do if they know a woman is suffering domestic violence?

Section 5: Closing

- Thank you for sharing your knowledge with me. The impression I have gained is that... and...Does that sound accurate? Is there anything you would like to add or change?
- Explain the next steps.

Source: Adapted from Jejeebhoy et al. (2013).

There are two typical final questions in an interview or focus group. The first just asks whether the participant has anything to add. The second is a little more demanding on the researcher. The researcher, who has been digesting the material during the interview, can ask a question to check that they have interpreted the material correctly. It can be useful to finish with this sort of 'interpreting' question, which sums up what the researcher has understood to be the main issue arising in the interview, and gives the participant a chance to correct that interpretation, or change or add to it.

The interview or focus group should then close with an expression of gratitude to the interviewee, a mention of any follow-up steps to be expected, and the completion of any remaining practicalities, such as reimbursement of travel fares or giving directions to the participant's next destination.

The closing section could follow one of the patterns shown below:

- Well, this brings me to the end of my questions. Thank you for speaking with me so honestly. Is there anything else you would like to add before we close? Is there something I should have asked about, to understand this issue, but that I didn't?
- So, summing up, what I understand from your interview is that your experience is…and your first priority is to sort out…Have I got that right?

Activity 3.2 Improve these topic guide questions

Your colleague is conducting their first qualitative research study about child protection in Somalia. Hers is a good-quality study and she does not make the mistakes below, which are made up for the example! Your colleague shows you her topic guide below, and asks for feedback. Are these good questions for a focus group with parents? If not, can you improve them?

1. What do you think are the main child protection issues in your community?
2. How do you discipline your children?
3. Are there differences in school attendance between girls and boys?
4. I have noticed children selling things on the street. Why are they not in school?

Feedback is available at the end of the chapter.

Source: Adapted from Lelieveld (2011).

Step 4: Conduct the interview

Interview facilitation style.   Good interviewing skills build on your normal, everyday communication skills. One of the most important determinants of the quality of your interview or focus group data is how comfortable your participants feel. Participants often feel surprised, uncomfortable, or even somewhat threatened by the odd situation of an interview. You want to establish rapport and a relationship with them, one in which they feel valued and respected, that their voice counts, and that you are interested in their point of view.

Each interview and focus group will ideally be led by the topic guide, but will take its own direction. It should feel like a conversation, in which the researcher is responsive to the issues being raised by the participant. The participant should be the person doing most of the talking, in their own words, telling stories and speaking from their own point of view. The researcher strikes a balance between being responsive to the participant, but gently guiding him or her to speak about the topics of interest to the research.

Activity 3.3 Creating a good interview dynamic

In their study of food price hikes, Hossain and Green (2011) encountered the following response from one of their participants. These feelings are often encountered.

'Do not ask me all these things, I know nothing. If you [the research team] and I discuss these things, what will be the impact? Will the price of food items come down? I don't think so!' (Transport worker in Notun Bazaar, Dhaka, quoted in Hossain and Green 2011: 6.)

How would you respond to this person to engage him or her in a productive interview?

Feedback is available at the end of the chapter.

Table 3.4 Types of interview question

Introductory	Can you tell me about...(be concrete)...
Follow-up	Mmm...; nod; repeat key words Pick up on specific research interest
Probing	Can you say a little more? Why do you think...?
Specifying	Can you give me an example?
Direct (later phase)	When you mention 'competition' are you thinking sportsmanlike or destructive competition?
Indirect	How do you think other people view...?
Structuring	Thank you for that. I'd like to move to another topic...
Silence	[Leave time for participants to fill silences or elaborate]
Interpreting	So what I have gathered is that...

Source: Kvale and Brinkmann (2008: 135–6).

And so each interview will take a slightly different course, and might address the issues in the topic guide to varying degrees or in a different order.

Types of interview question. As well as the carefully-worded questions of the topic guide, we use a range of other expressions and types of questions to explore participants' thinking around a topic. The table below sets out some examples of these.

Focus group moderation. A challenge particular to focus groups is managing the group dynamics. The main aim is for participants to take over the discussion and talk to each other, not only to the focus group moderator. Moderators want to avoid a dynamic in which participants each take short turns, waiting for the moderator to signal that it is their turn to speak. A good topic guide, which introduces topics that are familiar, and perhaps somewhat controversial, should help prevent the 'short turn-taking' dynamic. A good sample is important: conversation is likely to get going among people who are comfortable in the group, and who have sufficiently similar experiences to serve as a common starting point.

We also aim to create an environment in which each person contributes, and in which people listen to each other. Sometimes one or two people start to dominate, or one or two people remain silent. The moderator then needs to actively manage the conversation to try to rebalance it. They might use body language, turning away from the dominant person and towards one of the quieter ones. They might explicitly say something like 'Let's hear from this side of the room' or 'Let's hear from somebody who has not had the opportunity to speak yet'.

Recording and transcribing.   Typically, interviews and focus groups are audio-recorded and then transcribed. Sometimes they are recorded with detailed notes rather than a verbatim recording.

Following the transcription, the final steps are analysis and writing up. These phases are addressed in Chapters 8 and 9.

Typical challenges and possible responses

Social desirability

Interviews – and focus groups even more so – are social situations. Participants speak about their lives in front of possibly unfamiliar, high-status researchers in an interview – or in front of both an unfamiliar researcher and their peers in an interview. They may be showing their best side as well as answering questions. They may try to give the 'right' answers, or the answers they believe researchers want to hear, in an effort to be polite and helpful.

This is why interviews and focus groups are not very good methods for conducting outcome evaluations. Interviews and focus groups can teach us about how local people perceive the impact, successes, and failures of interventions. But they are weak tools for assessing actual impact.

All studies need to consider the context of the interview: who conducts the interview; their status and relationship to participants; what participants believe the interview to be about; and the moral codes regarding the topic of the study. All of these issues, and more, will influence how participants decide to talk about the topic, and they need to be taken into account

Interviews study what people say, not what they do

Building on the above point, interviews and focus groups get at what people say, but not necessarily at what they actually do. People do not always have insight into what they do, or they may not want to tell us what they actually do. Chapter 4, 'Participant observation', will explore ways of getting beyond people's verbal reports to understand what they do in practice.

Generalizability

In our discussion of sampling, it has become clear that a small-scale interview study cannot and should not strive for 'representativeness', nor should it claim to generalize for the whole population. However, with careful sampling, we can claim that the study includes a diverse population and has aimed for 'coverage' of the main social groups.

Connecting the study to other literature and experiences can validate an interview study's findings. If others have found related or similar things in similar contexts, that lends plausibility to the study.

Summary

Interviews and focus groups are ways of learning about *local people's points of view* on an issue. Interviews and focus groups can be informative throughout the programme cycle. Interview and focus group topic guides should be 'participant-friendly' and easy to follow. A diverse sample is often a benefit to interview and focus group studies. Interviews and focus groups are based on open-ended questions that allow participants to convey and elaborate on their experiences.

References

Baxter, J. (2013) *Who is Benefiting? The Social and Economic Impact of Three Large-scale Land Investments in Sierra Leone: A Cost–Benefit Analysis*, London: Christian Aid, <www.christianaid.org.uk/images/who-is-benefitting-Sierra-Leone-report.pdf> [accessed 23 July 2015].

Hossain, N. and Green, D. (2011) *Living on a Spike: How is the 2011 Food Price Crisis Affecting Poor People?*, Oxford: Institute of Development Studies and Oxfam GB, <www.oxfam.org/sites/www.oxfam.org/files/file_attachments/rr-living-on-a-spike-food-210611-en_4.pdf> [accessed 23 July 2015].

Jejeebhoy, S. J., Santhya, K. G. and Sabarwal, S. (2013) *Gender-based Violence: A Qualitative Exploration of Norms, Experiences and Positive Deviance*, New Delhi: Population Council, <http://r4d.dfid.gov.uk/pdf/outputs/ORIE/Qualitative_report_Formative_Study_VAWG_Bihar_DFID_India.pdf> [accessed 23 July 2015].

Kircher, I. (2013) 'Challenges to security, livelihoods and gender justice in South Sudan', Oxfam Research Report, Oxford: Oxfam, <www.oxfam.org/sites/www.oxfam.org/files/file_attachments/rr-challenges-security-livelihoods-gender-south-sudan-130313-en_0.pdf> [accessed 23 July 2015].

Kvale, S. and Brinkmann, S. (2008) *InterViews: Learning the Craft of Qualitative Research Interviewing*, Thousand Oaks CA: SAGE Publications.

Lelieveld, M. (2011) *Child Protection in the Somali Region of Ethiopia*, London: Save the Children UK, <www.savethechildren.org.uk/sites/default/files/docs/FINALChild_Protection_in_the_Somali_Region_30511.pdf> [accessed 23 July 2015].

USAID WASHplus Project (2013) *Understanding Consumer Preference and Willingness to Pay for. Improved Cookstoves in Bangladesh*, Washington DC: USAID, <www.cleancookstoves.org/resources_files/consumer-preference-bangladesh.pdf> [accessed 23 July 2015].

Wajid, A., Mir, A. M. and Rashid, Z. (2010) *Assessing the Potential Acceptability of a New Cadre of Community Midwives for Pregnancy and Delivery Related Care in Rural Pakistan: Findings from a Qualitative Study*, Islamabad: Population Council, <http://paiman.jsi.com/Resources/Docs/paiman-cmw-report.pdf> [accessed 23 July 2015].

Further reading

Morgan, D. L. (1997) *Focus Groups As Qualitative Research*, 2nd edn, Thousand Oaks CA: SAGE Publications.
Oxfam (2013) *Shifting Sands: Changing Gender Roles Among Refugees in Lebanon*, Oxford: Oxfam, <www.oxfam.org/sites/www.oxfam.org/files/rr-shifting-sands-lebanon-syria-refugees-gender-030913-en.pdf> [accessed 23 July 2015].

Feedback on activities

Feedback on Activity 3.1 Write research questions

The interview study question should address questions about individual experience, beliefs, or perspectives, to be probed and elaborated in depth. The focus group question should address local norms or collective views, on a topic that is of interest so that participants will be able to generate a long conversation about it.

Feedback on Activity 3.2 Improve these topic guide questions

1. Question 1 makes the classic error of asking participants the research question, rather than an easy-to-answer question using local words. Ordinary people do not speak the language of 'child protection'. This question should be turned into something more everyday.
   - Alternative: Do you have any worries about the safety of children in your community?
2. Question 2 is challenging to answer in a focus group. If it is something that is morally loaded, people may feel that they are put 'on the spot', and that their disciplining practices might be disapproved of. Focus groups often address community practices in general, rather than asking the participants to reveal intimate details of their own lives. And, finally, it is quite an abstract question. The participant might ask themselves: What is meant by discipline? What is the context of the question?
   - Alternative: Let's imagine a child does something seriously wrong, like stealing. Typically, how might their parents discipline them? What about a shopkeeper? A police officer?
3. Question 3 is probably being asked to the wrong participants. We might expect head teachers or school administrators to be able to give a clear and factual answer. To parents, we would ask more general questions of attitudes and opinions.
   - Alternative: How important is education to most people in this community? Do parents make sure their children are in full-time education? Until what age, usually? Probe: For boys? For girls?
4. Question 4 is again targeted at the wrong people. Would we expect our focus group participants to be able to provide a meaningful answer? The question suggests that the researcher does not really understand the context.
   - Alternative: Some people have raised concerns about children who work during the day rather than going to school. Do you have any concerns about the safety of children who are vendors? What about children who work in agriculture? Or in other places?

Feedback on Activity 3.3 Creating a good interview dynamic

- This transport worker voices two common concerns:

1. The participant is not an expert, and has no particular authority or special knowledge to share. At the recruitment stage and again at the start of an interview, we often work to reassure people that we are interested in learning from their own experience, or that there are no right or wrong answers.
2. Research is unnecessary. It is part of the ethical responsibility of researchers to ensure that their work justifies the enormous goodwill and contributions offered by participants. In the case above, the researchers might have argued that, if we do not document people's experience of price hikes, those in positions of power may continue to ignore the problem. Powerful testimonies can influence the public, and the powerful. The researchers might be able to reassure participants of the efforts they will make to publicize their findings, in the interest of having an effect on policies.

CHAPTER 4

Participant observation

Abstract

This chapter aims to equip the reader with a full understanding of the role of participant observation in development research, knowledge of key terms and design considerations, and skills for undertaking participant observation research. It begins by defining participant observation, and then setting out the rationales for using participant observation at different stages of the programme cycle, illustrated with key examples. The main sections of the chapter go through each of the practical decisions to be taken and documented when designing a participant observation study, from justifying the selection of participant observation as a method, through describing its purpose and implementation, to case selection, sampling, and writing field notes. A template for writing field notes is presented and explained.

Keywords: Qualitative research; participant observation; field notes; ethnography

Learning objectives

After reading this chapter, you will be able to:

- explain when and why to use participant observation;
- plan a participant observation study;
- write up field notes; and
- use participant observation to contribute to monitoring, evaluation, accountability, and learning (MEAL).

Key terms (definitions)

- *Participant observation*: A data collection method in which the researcher learns about the daily lives and broader context of a community by spending time observing and participating in community life.
- *Ethnography*: A type of study that presents an overall picture of a community, its culture, context, and practices. Multiple methods may be used, usually including participant observation.
- *Reality check*: A specific development of participant observation methodology for the purposes of evaluation, in which researchers live with families to understand the impact of a programme in their everyday lives.

http://dx.doi.org/10.3362/9781780448534.004

- *Field notes*: Also called a 'field diary', field notes are the record of participant observation data, written up by the researcher, usually daily.
- *Reflexivity*: A critical awareness of how the particular position, expectations, and role taken up by the participant observer may have affected the field, research participants, and data.

Introduction

The method of participant observation is absolutely foundational to the disciplines of sociology and anthropology. In their efforts to understand how social groups function, sociologists and anthropologists, since the early twentieth century, have gone to live in the communities that they study, in order to gain a deep understanding of how those communities work. They have spent their time participating in everyday life, observing people's practices and interactions, chatting with local people, figuring out the local hierarchies and power dynamics, and writing all of this up in daily fieldwork diaries. They then typically move back from the 'field' to their desks, to reflect on and analyse their field note data, ultimately producing an account of life in that community which is richly grounded in concrete practical experience.

More recently, participant observation as a method and ethnography (including 'rapid ethnography') as a more general research approach have gained increasing attention in a wide range of applied fields. Given connections between anthropology and development, it is no surprise that participant observation has found an important role in applied development research. The areas of health services research, management, and education have also all been making increasing use of participant observation. Along with interviews, participant observation is one of the core methods for qualitative development research.

Participant observation research allows the researcher to investigate people's practices – or, in other words, what they *do*. As we have seen in Chapter 3, interviews and focus groups are powerful means of investigating people's understandings and beliefs about particular topics – what they *say*. But interviews and focus groups are less good at investigating actual practices. What people say is not always the same as what they actually do. Participant observation researchers observe behaviour in its natural context. They also participate in that behaviour, as far as possible, so as to gain an insider's point of view. Participant observation methods can be used to understand how a particular development issue (such as child protection, water usage, or educational styles, for example) plays out in its real-life context. Such methods can also be used to understand the workings of a development intervention (for example, how beneficiaries relate to services, or the organizational culture of an NGO).

Most development workers are familiar with the idea of field visits. For workers who spend most of their time in the office, a visit to the place where a development programme is being carried out is often hugely informative. Field visits give the researcher a vivid picture of a community or a development programme. There are often surprises during such a visit; for example, we may find out that actual practice is not quite the same as was expected or intended. Participant observation as a research method is based on the same rationale. It is simply a more systematic way of observing, documenting, and analysing the experience of being in the field.

In this chapter, we will first set the scene for the use of participant observation methods, and then provide guidance on the practicalities of carrying out a participant observation study.

Box 4.1 Example of participant observation data

This is an excerpt from a report by Kostelny et al. (2013: 41). It comes from a section where they report their participant observation data on the theme of socio-economic status (SES) in urban slums in Mombasa.

Participant observations in regard to SES

Example of a high SES household in Giriama:
The mother owns a chapatti business by the roadside, and she really sells. From several observations, I noticed that she has many customers during the morning, lunchtime and evening. When visiting her house, she possesses a TV set, a stereo radio, and a sofa set. Things around the house look in order. Her husband works full time.

Example of a high SES household in Msikitini:
The man is the owner of his two-roomed house, and has built two others which he rents out. He works full time as a technician for the electric company, and has even put a solar panel in his house. This is the first house that I see that has a television set and a light bulb.

Example of a low SES household in Giriama:
The woman's house was a rental one with basically only a mattress on the floor which she used for sleeping. Set aside was the cooking area within the same room – a kerosene stove with two saucepans, looking dirty from the accumulation of soot. The children there were half naked – only wearing the top, dirty T-shirts with no bottoms...There was also a dirty basin with dirty clothes in it, and the mother at one point during the interview stopped to wash the child who had gone for a long call (defecate). She put the dirty clothes aside on the earthen floor and poured a little water and washed the child without soap. When lunchtime approached, the children asked for some food, and the mother replied to them that the food available was only for supper so they had better persevere till evening so that they eat and then sleep.

Example of low SES household in Msikitini:
The man lives near the place that has the public toilet. There is [a] permanent stench that comes in because of the breeze from the ocean which keeps blowing on that side. There are two girls – one seems 7 and the other 11 – who are not in school.

What is participant observation?

Participant observation is a method for learning about how people behave and interact, in their everyday, natural context. The method involves both participating in everyday life and observing the actions of others going about their everyday lives. The researcher takes on the role of participant observer. That means that he or she is present in the setting, or field, being studied. This includes anything from being an observing visitor to being embedded in the community or organization; taking part, for example, in the chores of everyday life or attending community events; participating in NGO meetings, or taking on a role in an NGO. Presence and participation in these activities are not goals in themselves, but are undertaken with a research mindset, in order to provide data in relation to one's research questions. Participant observation can be used to inform an understanding of what is important in this community; its norms and habits; the social relationships and hierarchies; the support available; the power dynamics and relations with institutions; and the context. Overall, the purpose of participant observation is to provide data on what occurs, as it happens, in its natural setting – rather than producing data that relies on research participants' verbal reports of what has occurred.

Observation is used in different ways in qualitative and quantitative research. Quantitative observation research uses a structured grid for making observations. In quantitative observation research, what is to be observed and how it is to be coded are clearly defined at the outset. The observer takes an objective stance and records observations as ticks in boxes, or numbers in a table. Structured observations of this sort are not dealt with in this book. Qualitative observational research is quite different. Research questions are more open-ended. The observer does not take an objective stance, but strives to participate in the setting and to get to know community members' norms, priorities, concerns, beliefs, and feelings. He or she uses his or her own experience to understand community life. Data is recorded in field diaries, using writing and perhaps drawings or photographs, in an open-ended form.

Why use participant observation?

This section begins by introducing the two most common rationales for using participant observation: accessing what people do (not only what they say), and discovering the unspoken and unofficial angles. It then moves on to identify the contributions that participant observation can make in providing important data at different stages of the programme cycle.

Access to what people do (not only what they say)

Direct access to behaviour in its natural context is the most highly prized strength of participant observation research. There are many reasons why people may not be in a position to report accurately on their behaviour or their context in an interview. They may not be aware of some aspects of their environment, for example if technical expertise is needed to appreciate the merits of certain building materials, or the ideal usage scenario for a primary healthcare centre. If the topic is highly charged, morally or politically, people may not be willing to report unfashionable, stigmatized, or challenging views to an unknown interviewer. Or people may simply take some things for granted, such as the 'proper' way to discipline children, or to store water, or to communicate with outsider interviewers – so that they just do not deem some things worth reporting. For all of these reasons, interviews can be limited means of understanding what people do, in contrast to what they say.

Participant observation, ideally, allows the researcher to spend time with community members participating in daily life, and thus accessing what people do, in the ordinary course of their activities. The object of interest, then, such as the use of primary healthcare, nutritional practices, or disciplining children, arise in the course of those everyday activities, and the researcher has the opportunity to understand them in context.

When we contrast what people do with what they say, we do not mean to suggest that what they 'do' is more true than what they 'say'. Participant observation data benefits from talking to people, as well as observing them. To understand the meaning of what they do, and why they do it, we need to engage in discussion with people. Indeed, it is often profitable to combine participant observation with interviews, in a mixed method study.

Discovering the unspoken and unofficial angles

Participant observation is often used as a way of tapping into the informal and unofficial ways that things work in a particular community. By participating with people in their everyday lives, and talking to them outside formal settings, or indeed outside the relatively formal environment of an interview, researchers come to learn how people may have criticisms about the way that things are done officially, or they might just observe how things depart from the ways they are 'supposed' to be. For example, in Sida's (2012) *Reality Check* report (which is covered in more detail below), it is notable that the bulk of the report's findings detail ways in which formal health services are not meeting the needs of local communities, or ways in which education policy is having unintended consequences. The researchers clearly gained sufficient trust of community members to allow them to voice their dissatisfactions and their sense of disempowerment in relation to formal policy processes.

Contribution of participant observation at key stages of the programme cycle

Participant observation is typically used to understand existing practices. This makes participant observation useful while planning an intervention, to better understand the status quo in a community. If participant observation is used in a longitudinal way, it can help researchers understand changes to practices. When interventions seek to change everyday behaviour or practice, participant observation is useful to allow the researcher to observe those practices in their natural setting, to find out whether and to what extent they have changed.

Local context analysis. Participant observation is an ideal method for investigating the status quo in a community. It can make a useful contribution to a needs assessment or rural appraisal. Such research might be used to inform the development of a suitable intervention programme, or to inform relevant policy. Information about existing resources and challenges can be obtained, as well as information about the context and factors that might support or limit the successful implementation of a programme.

Kostelny and colleagues (2013) conducted a 'rapid ethnographic' study to investigate community-based child protection mechanisms in two urban slums in Mombasa, with the goal of strengthening the national child protection system in Kenya. Using a range of qualitative methods, they aimed to produce grounded knowledge about how people actually respond to child protection threats in the community. Researchers spent four weeks in each slum, devoting most of the first week to participant observation and focus group discussions.

The researchers made observations in schools, markets, homes, and on the streets, and wrote up their observations daily as field notes. Simply by spending time in the community, the researchers were able to directly observe that some children were out of school during school hours, and that children were frequently punished with harsh beatings, carried out by parents, elders, teachers, and the police. The observation of children being out of school was corroborated by group discussions, in which adults rated this issue as the most serious harm to children. However, group discussions gave a low priority to harsh beatings, which contrasted with the researchers' observations that such beatings were commonplace and indicated that beating children may have been widely accepted as a norm, rather than a child protection issue.

As a result of their data collection, the researchers made a series of recommendations for Kenyan government policy, for NGOs, and for practitioners. For example, in relation to the harsh corporal punishment observed, the report recommended that the reduction of the use of corporal punishment in both school and family settings should be a high priority for government and practitioners, that practitioners should train parents in positive discipline methods, and that efforts to engage adults and children in discussions of child rights and child responsibilities should be undertaken.

Evaluation of infrastructure and its uses. As any development worker who has undertaken a field visit knows, simply observing the very broad-brush practical implementation of a project is an essential component of an effort to understand the impacts of a development programme. Walking around a community and observing the tangible and visible features of development programmes provide an outsider's view on the practical results of the programme, and give the researcher a more concrete sense of the setting than can be gained through an interview. Topics such as the construction and uses of buildings, the location of latrines or water pumps and how and when they are used, children's journeys to school, the use of cooking stoves, these are all suited to investigation by brief observational visits to the field.

Morgan, Naz and Sanderson (2013) conducted an evaluation of Christian Aid's relief efforts in the wake of severe floods in Pakistan in 2010. Their research was primarily qualitative, using interviews, focus groups, and meetings with key informants, supplemented with direct observations in the field (see the discussion below about using participant observation as a supplementary method). The authors conducted field visits to at least one project run by each of the partners. During these field visits, they conducted 'walkabouts' during which they observed how houses and latrines had been constructed, and whether they were used appropriately and maintained.

The walkabouts allowed the researchers to observe concrete details about infrastructure, rather than relying solely on research participants' verbal reports. These details made significant contributions to the findings. For example, in one village, the researchers received very positive feedback from focus group discussions with beneficiaries on the funded NGO's activities regarding hand pumps and latrines, and this positive feedback was confirmed by their observations. However, during their walkabout, they also observed that drainage channels dug by another NGO had become blocked, fetid, and a breeding ground for mosquitos. They would not have learned about this problem if they had relied solely on beneficiaries' reports. Building on this observation, the researchers speculated that there may be an issue of ensuring community ownership of all infrastructure, not only that specific to particular popular projects. Thus, in this case, the observations were in themselves directly informative about the issue of water safety. But they were also indicative of possible broader, more complex social challenges. Further research would be needed to investigate more deeply the sense of community ownership of infrastructure.

In other cases, the researchers observed the construction of houses, noting that they were well built and maintained, and that they allowed good ventilation. They also observed that the mesh covering the vents (to stop mosquitos entering) had become clogged, preventing smoke from escaping. Thus they recommended removing the vents and considering the removal of doors to the kitchens to allow better ventilation.

In this study, 'participant observation' was employed in a very minimalist way, involving much more 'observation' than 'participation' (so it is an example of 'non-participant observation', as discussed below). The researchers were interested in the material infrastructure, its condition and use, and their observational data on these topics added value to the study, particularly where the researchers identified issues that were not a concern for beneficiaries but were a problem from a technical point of view. This kind of 'minimalist' observational data can hint at, but cannot reveal in depth, the more complex human and social dynamics surrounding a project. Topics such as whether communities were adequately consulted, whether projects were well run, whether they addressed community priorities, and what the learning might be for future projects are likely to call for a more in-depth engagement. For all of these kinds of issues, it is necessary to talk to people, either through more engaged observations, where you incorporate your conversations with community members into your field notes, or by including interviews, focus groups, or participatory methods in your study.

Evaluation of the human and social impact of programmes. While infrastructure and its actual uses are relatively easily observable, the more complex human and social impact of development programmes calls for a more nuanced and participatory form of engagement. Topics such as changes to teaching styles, reasons for children dropping out of school, how families manage nutrition and diet, or choices of health services call for the researcher to spend time in the community. They need to spend time with families in their homes, to attend services rather than just observing their use, to talk to providers and community members, and to build up an understanding of how and why local people make use of development resources in the way they do. As the programme being evaluated becomes more complex, so too should the engagement of the researcher with the community and the programme, in order to fully understand them.

The 'reality check approach' is a participant observation methodology developed for the purposes of programme evaluation. It was initiated by the Swedish International Development Cooperation Agency (Sida) in Bangladesh in 2007, with the intention of foregrounding the realities of poor people's experience of development programmes – rather than evaluating programmes solely with reference to externally generated monitoring and evaluation indicators (Sida, 2012). It is an approach that aims to listen to poor people's voices and to put them on the agenda of policy makers.

The fundamental activity of the reality check methodology is that members of the research team stay with families, taking part in their everyday activities and in conversations with them. By placing researchers in the homes of families, the aim is that the researchers will gain a close-to-the-ground experience of everyday life for those families, and of their experience of development interventions. The researchers get a concrete understanding of what it is like to live in those circumstances, which helps put the interventions in context.

The flagship reality check study was a five-year longitudinal study of people's experiences of primary healthcare and primary education in Bangladesh (Sida, 2012). For this study, every year for five years, researchers visited the same families for a minimum of four nights and five days. Each researcher stayed with three families in a single community. In all, 27 families across nine different communities took part. In contrast to an impact evaluation study, which might look at changes in specific health and education outcomes, the study reported on how community members engaged with health and education policy changes, revealing significant unintended consequences in the ways in which policies were being put into practice. The study thus gave voice to communities' concerns about policies, in a context where community members also reported being fearful of making complaints, worrying that doing so would risk them being singled out, blamed, or excluded. Because the study was written up carefully to ensure anonymity, and because the researchers gained the trust of the communities, the research was able to reveal complaints about policies that were not being revealed through other routes.

Designing a participant observation study

This section outlines the main issues to consider when designing a participant observation study. These are also the issues that should be written up as part of the methods section of a report. Box 4.2 describes the important topics to be covered when writing up your methods. The following sections then elaborate on each of these topics in turn.

Box 4.2 Topics to cover in a methods section

1. *Rationale*: Justify the choice of participant observation as a method.
2. *Study design*: Explain the study design, and how participant observation contributes to it.
3. *Role of the participant observer*: Detail the role and level of engagement of the researcher.
4. *Case selection*: Justify your choice of cases to study.
5. *Sampling within the case*: Explain how you sampled times, places, and/or people to observe within your case.
6. *Data collection*: Explain the process of entering the field, what kinds of activities you took part in, and your relationships with community members, and describe how you wrote your field notes.
7. *Reflexivity*: Give a critical account of how your position may have influenced the data and interpretation.

Justify the choice of participant observation

The first task of design is to choose the most appropriate method for the research questions, given the opportunities, skills, and resources available. If you are choosing to use participant observation, explain the rationale for your choice. For this, you might refer to any of the rationales in the section on 'Why use participant observation?' above. What purpose does participant observation serve in your study? What kind of data do you hope to obtain by using participant observation that you would not get through other methods?

The role and varying uses of participant observation in the study design

Traditionally, in anthropology, researchers spend one to two years in the field, so that they come to deeply understand local customs, norms, cultures, and forms of social organization. Development researchers have much less time at their disposal, and, if they are to make productive use of participant observation methods, they have to adapt those methods to their needs. We maintain that there is still enormous value to be gained by using participant observation as a method, even if you have only a few days or weeks to spend on it. With limited time available, it is likely that the participant observation will be part of a mixed method study.

Interviews are designed as focused engagements with research participants, which compress their experiences into the space of about an hour. With a well-designed topic guide, a skilled interviewer, and a responsive research participant, most of that hour will produce data that is directly relevant to the topic of study. However, participant observation involves engaging with communities in real time, as they go about their everyday lives. Much of this time may be spent on activities that do not seem very relevant to the research questions. The data collection is less intensive during participant observation compared with interviews. This is one reason why interviews are more widely used than participant observation: they are efficient means of gathering information-rich data.

In our experience, if a researcher has less than a couple of months to spend in the field, then it is risky to use participant observation as the only or primary research method for a study. It is often difficult to achieve sufficient richness and depth in a short time to allow you to reach substantiated and solid conclusions.

Alternatively, participant observation may fruitfully be used as part of a mixed method study, often accompanying interviews, and sometimes in conjunction with action research or survey data. Rapid ethnographic studies often combine methods in such a way. We can distinguish two different uses of participant observation in such mixed method studies: as one method among equals, or playing a minor role, as an additional, supportive method. As one approach in a mixed method study, participant observation offers a rich source of data, which is combined with other sources to build up a complete picture. In the case of the Australia–Indonesia Basic Education Program (2010) reality check study, for instance, participant observation was used in conjunction with quantitative monitoring and evaluation studies – this is an example of using participant observation data in a mixed method study. In the evaluation of the impact of Christian Aid funding after the Pakistan floods, participant observation played a minor role, adding context and practical observations to already rich interview and focus group data.

Box 4.3 Three different uses of participant observation data in a study

As a primary method: Participant observation is the main source of data, and thus standards for the depth of data and duration of observation are high.

As one method in a mixed method study: Participant observation is one source of data, of equal standing with others (often interviews). The data needs to be substantial, but gaps can be filled through the other methods.

As a minor contextualizing method: Participant observation is not a substantial data source for your study, but is a brief, backup, or supportive method used to contextualize interviews or survey research, or to give the researcher a concrete sense of practice on the ground.

Each of these uses of participant observation data is valid and valuable. Even if there is little time to spend in the field, adding some observation of a development programme in action, to complement what people say about that programme, can provide vital context, or indeed contradiction.

Participant observer roles and degrees of involvement

It is not always possible to be a full participant in a community or NGO, especially if there is only limited time for a study. With a long timeframe, and the opportunity to become accepted as a member of a community, the researcher can participate fully and come to understand what it is like to be (almost) an insider in the community. However, the practicality of participant observation research is often somewhat different. Researchers distinguish between different types of participant observer role, and so an important part of the design of participant observation research is to clarify which kind of role is being adopted. Box 4.4 identifies three different roles for the participant observer that are suitable for applied development research.

Participant observation. In studies shorter than a few months, or studies with social groups different to one's own, it is often not possible to be accepted as a full participant. For instance, a development professional, with a successful career in an office job, access to good quality healthcare, and a comfortable home in the city can be accepted as a friend and supporter in a deprived rural environment, for a study of maternal health. But that professional is unlikely to be a full participant in maternal health practices in the community, unlikely to stay in the community for the duration of her own pregnancy, and unlikely to use the same maternal health services or traditional birth attendants as the women from the community. Nonetheless, a participant observation study is possible. The researcher could spend time with pregnant women and mothers in their homes, listen to the advice given to them by friends, family, and healthcare providers, and observe how they look after themselves and their children. She could also accompany women on their visits to maternal health services. She could base herself at the health post or clinic for some time, to observe the workings of maternal health services. These are all legitimate opportunities for participant observation research, although the researcher is not a full

---

Box 4.4 Three different roles for the participant observer

Participant observation: The observer is initially an outsider in the field, but takes on an active, participating role. They gain some acceptance by the community, and play a role in community life – thereby gaining the participant perspective. They use their outsider point of view together with their insider point of view to make interesting observations.

Non-participant observation: The researcher attends and observes actions and interactions in the field, but has a very limited role. The researcher observes and, in doing so, tries to understand action in its natural context. The researcher is never a complete 'non-participant' as his or her presence is likely to have some impact in the field.

Observant participation: The researcher is already a participant in the field (for example, a person researching their own community or an NGO employee researching their own NGO). Participation comes naturally but taking an observational stance is a challenge.

participant. As long as the researcher has a role to play in the setting, and interacts with people in the course of their usual daily action, then their work can be called 'participant observation'.

Non-participant observation. This term is sometimes used to signal that the researcher gathered qualitative observational data but had very limited participation in the field. It is often used for the observation of healthcare practices, when a researcher is based in a hospital or clinic, where it would be inappropriate for the researcher to play an active role without clinical training. In such cases, the researcher might sit in the corner of a consultation room or ward, be introduced to clients as a researcher, but do very little talking or interacting. However, even when we use the term 'non-participant observer', it is important to remember that an outsider who observes is not simply an objective observer. Just by being present, we are, even in a limited sense, a participant in the field. If we observe a healthcare worker's consultations, without intervening directly or contributing to the conversation, our very presence still changes that consultation. The healthcare worker is likely to feel self-conscious and to strive to implement 'best practice'. The client may form theories about our role – for instance, that we are there because the healthcare worker is particularly good or bad – and this may influence the consultation. Even when we appear to have a 'non-participant' position, it is important to recognize and reflect upon our impact in the field.

Observant participation. From the opposite starting point, some researchers study their own natural setting rather than other people's lives. This is the case when researchers have worked for several years within a particular organization and then start to carry out research on the activities of that organization, for example as part of a monitoring and evaluation activity or through a dissertation study in a higher education programme. This role is sometimes termed 'observant participation', to show that the researcher is first of all a participant but has to take up an observational stance on his or her own participation. In this setting, in contrast to the example above, the challenge is not participation but observation. A 'research approach' (see Chapter 1) means that the researcher steps back from their daily work, concerns, and strategies, with a research question in mind, to observe that daily work in order to understand the organization in a new way. You might, for example, conduct observant participation on your own organization, to learn about the organization's culture, or about how it uses rewards and reprimands of different kinds to shape staff behaviour, or to try to understand why some groups of staff are promoted more quickly than others, and so on. It can be very difficult to step out of the everyday concerns and take up this observational stance – and it is for this reason that we often employ external consultants to offer us a reflection on our own everyday work.

Reflexivity about our roles. Each of these options (participant observation, non-participant observation, and observant participation) is a respectable means of gathering useful data. The reason to differentiate them is not to say that one is better than another, but to be transparent and reflexive about our role in the field. The methods section of a participant observation study should report on the role of the researcher in the field, their relationship to community members, and how they were seen by community members.

Identifying your role is one part of the work of 'reflexivity'. Reflexivity is especially important in participant observation research. It refers to critical awareness about how your own positioning may impact upon the research. Our starting assumptions and expectations may lead us to some interpretations rather than others. Our position and social role in the field – as a woman, guest, stranger, or NGO worker, for instance – affects how community members perceive us, trust us, and interact with us. As part of your research approach, you need to document these important influencing factors as far as possible – rather than denying them.

Case selection and sampling within the case

Case selection.   Participant observation is an intensive method. That means it is used to gain an in-depth understanding of a small number of cases – as opposed to a general population-wide view. The 'case' is the broad location or community in which you carry out the research. A 'case' might be a project conducted by one NGO, or a village, or a school. A research project using participant observation will have time to investigate only a small number of cases, perhaps just one, or often two, three, or four. For this reason, the selection of the case or cases is very important.

If there is time to conduct participant observation in contrasting cases, this is often a good idea, as the contrast can be informative. So, depending on the topic of study, we might opt to do participant observation in one urban and one rural location, or in a more successful and a less successful project. Or, if our cases are schools, we might choose one co-educational school, one boys' school, and one girls' school.

As well as contrasts, there may be specific reasons for choosing particular cases. Perhaps there is little knowledge about a particular social or indigenous group, for instance, or perhaps one community has had particularly devastating experiences of flooding. In the study of child protection in Kenyan slums (Kostelny et al., 2013), two slums were chosen for substantive reasons, to fill specific gaps in current understandings. One site, Kilifi, was chosen because it was close to Mombasa, which was known to have a range of child protection challenges, and it was thought to possibly be a 'feeder' site, channelling children into sex tourism in the city. The other slum, located in Nyanza, was chosen because it has a very high rate of HIV/AIDS, and because little was known about child protection issues in that province.

Practical issues are also reasonable and relevant considerations for case selection. Is the site accessible? Are researchers available who speak the local language? Is the local community open to the research and likely to support it?

There is no single or right way to select your cases. The main point is that it is always important to have some rationale for the selection of cases, and to be aware of the context of those cases, including why they might be particular and unique.

For example, in the reality check study by Sida (2012), described above, the design of the case selection was intentional. The study was carried out in three districts in Bangladesh: one in the north, one central, and one in the south. In each district, three locations were chosen: one urban, one peri-urban, and one rural, making nine communities in total. And in each location, three families participated. This is a very extensive selection of cases for a participant observation study, and illustrates the careful design of the case selection. Often, however, researchers will not have resources to work in so many sites. As we have seen above, the study of child protection in Kenyan slums was conducted in just two slums. And many participant observation studies are conducted in a single community.

Sampling within the case.   Within the chosen case, there are further decisions to make. The researcher cannot attend every setting at every time of day, but must narrow down the places for observation. This is what we term 'sampling within the case'. We need to generate a sample of the activities that are going on. For instance, we may choose to focus our observation in particular places (a communal water pump, a school, an irrigation system, a clinic, or a street, for example), or with a particular group of people (such as an individual family, NGO employees, or farmers). The choice of person and place to observe depends, of course, on the research question.

Timing might be important. Are observations likely to be different at night or during the day? Is there a seasonal aspect? Is it relevant whether it is a holiday or a regular school or work day?

The degree of formality of the setting is often important. Can we have access to an informal setting as well as a formal one? Can we chat to people in the waiting room, as well as observing their clinical consultations, for example? Can we join people for tea after an NGO event, as well as attending the event? Can we spend time with schoolchildren during their breaks, as well as in the classroom? How have we negotiated access with 'gatekeepers' and community members?

Just as with the selection of cases, the selection of our sample within the case should be carefully thought through and justified. In particular, researchers need to be aware of how their sampling process, and the process of negotiating access, might influence their data, and they should be appropriately cautious in generalizing from their study.

Data collection

What do we observe?   Participant observation data is recorded in field notes, but what is 'data' in participant observation?

PARTICIPANT OBSERVATION 89

Activity 4.1 Design a participant observation study

You have been given the following brief, and are tasked with designing a study that includes participant observation.

A major USA-based philanthropist has funded a school-based sexual health promotion programme for young people in Nigeria, which aimed to advance a non-judgemental, empowering approach to enable young people to take informed decisions about their sex lives. An impact evaluation revealed little behaviour change among young people, teacher dissatisfaction with the programme, and lack of interest among young people. The programme will continue to run for three months, and the donor wishes to learn lessons for future programming.

Your job is to design a study to understand the reasons underlying the poor results and lack of engagement, and to make recommendations for future similar programmes.

Your budget allows for a research team of two junior researchers, with qualitative methods training and capable in local languages, who can spend four weeks each on data collection, and a further four weeks contributing to analysis and write-up. You will supervise the researchers, conduct some primary data collection, and lead the analysis and write-up.

To design the study, answer the following questions, adding one sentence to justify your answer, and one or two sentences to elaborate the details.

1. What role does participant observation play in your study (a primary method, one method in a mixed method study, or a minor, contextualizing role)?
2. What type of role will the researcher take on (participant observer, non-participant observer, or observant participation)?
3. *Case selection*: What community or communities have you selected to observe?
4. *Sampling*: Within that community, are there particular locations (primary health centre, school, family home, streets, and so on), times of day, or individuals that you will focus on?
5. *Procedure*: How long will you spend in each setting? What role will you play? What do your research questions direct you to observe?
6. *Reflexivity*: What are your expectations at the outset? How do local people perceive you? How might these expectations and perceptions influence your data collection?

Feedback is available at the end of the chapter.

We cannot expect to observe everything that happens in the field – nor do we wish to. We need to be selective and aware of our 'analytical gaze' (see Chapter 7). Our observations are guided primarily by our research interests and research questions. If we are interested in child protection, we should first reflect on what we mean by child protection and the range of observable behaviours that might be relevant to child protection, so that we are ready to observe them in the field. If we are interested in the uses that communities make of communal water resources, we should define which water resources we are including in our study, and then be prepared to observe all the behaviours leading up to the use of the resource, following the water to its ultimate destination, and probably engaging in conversations at the same time, or afterwards.

Participant observation data should ideally include two main types of data: 1) observations of what people do, or do not do; 2) reports of conversations with people to understand how they think about what they do, and why they do what they do. This also includes silences and the unspoken, meanings, notes on your observations of implicit knowledge, unspoken rules, and codes of conduct that exist within the setting being studied.

In observing what people do, we might have research questions that lead us to observe, among other possibilities:

- the ordinary knowledge, attitude, and behaviour of community members (e.g. their child-rearing practices, cooking practices, or water usage);
- power hierarchies and the positioning of people within a community or organization (e.g. relations and interactions between men and women, adults and children, and community leaders and community members);
- people's uses of infrastructure or technology (e.g. how people use the space in new housing or how people use smartphones for business);
- the implementation of development programmes (e.g. the behaviour of NGO staff and the interactions between staff and community members);
- organizational culture (e.g. interactions among staff in the NGO office, formal meetings in the NGO office, and visits to accompany frontline staff during their daily schedule).

Writing field notes. Participant observation data is recorded in field notes. Field notes are usually a descriptive record of the researcher's observations and experiences during the field work. Box 4.5 presents a template to use for recording field notes, drawing on a useful blog by Lorena Gibson (2013). It implements two important principles. First, we should make sure that we record as many practical details as we can. Second, we need to keep

---

Box 4.5 Field notes template

Location:
Date, time:
Observations:
Try to stick to observable facts, reporting:
    Who
    What
    When
    Where
    What people do
    And what people say
Interpretations:
    What do my observations tell me in relation to the research question?
    What is the significance of what I have observed?
    Why did people act like this?
    How did the situation come to be like this?
Reflexivity:
    How was I perceived?
    How might I have influenced the data?
    How do I feel about what I have observed?
Next steps:
    Is there anything I would do differently next time?
    What leads might I follow up on?
    Have gaps been revealed?

observations separate from interpretations, so that we maintain an awareness of the difference between them. You can use the text in bold as headings for your field notes. The plain text under the bold headings tells you what belongs in that section.

The template begins with practical details of location, date, and time. This is important contextual data that helps with the organization of field notes, and that can be important to the analysis.

The next category is 'observations'. In this section, write your descriptions of what happened. These descriptions should be rich in detail, so that the concrete observations are recorded faithfully (rather than quickly summarizing and assuming that our summaries are correct). So, for instance, rather than writing 'there seemed to be a good relationship between the farmer and the official', we should write something more like 'when the farmer entered the office, the official stood up to greet him, and asked about his uncle. He then offered the farmer tea, which was declined politely.' The mainstay of field notes is this kind of concrete detail, which hints at issues of interest but remains detailed and evidence-based. When making observations, we strive to suspend our judgement for the time being, so that we come to understand the behaviour in its context, and appreciate why it makes sense to people to act in the way they do.

At the 'interpretations' stage, we bring our judgement back in. Interpretations go beyond what is directly observable, to move towards providing an answer to our research questions. In offering interpretations, we might contrast different ways of doing things, or highlight how practice differs from what is said in interviews, or what policies expect. We might make a judgement about whether the behaviour is close to what is recommended or not. Or we may interpret the behaviour in the light of theory or other expectations we had. In the example of participant observation data in Box 4.1, the descriptions of the people's possessions and actions are the observations, and the labelling of these people as belonging to a particular SES group comprises the interpretation.

Under 'reflexivity', we record our critical reflections and impressions about our own involvement in the data collection. We reflect on how people in the field may have perceived us, or why they responded in the way they did. And we examine our own responses and feelings in the situation, documenting them as part of the context in which the data is being recorded.

Finally, we shift to a practical, future-oriented focus, noting what we have learned and possible next steps. Are new lines of inquiry suggested by what has been observed today? Is there something that I wish I had asked about?

Practically, writing field notes is a time-consuming process requiring significant effort and work. During the day, researchers typically write brief notes, or 'jottings', in the field, noting down just the keywords or main ideas that will jog their memories when it is time to write out the full field notes. Usually, field notes are written up daily, so that the researcher's memory is still fresh, and the details are easily brought to mind. It is important to leave sufficient time for writing up notes. It may take at least two hours to write up one day's field notes. In a study of child protection in Sierra Leone, the research

---

Activity 4.2 Practise writing field notes

Spend a day visiting a field site, with a research question in mind. Use the template to record your notes. Debrief with a colleague afterwards, checking if you have recorded sufficient detail and whether your interpretations are justified and backed up with data. Discuss the different kinds of things you have observed, whether your notes are comprehensive, and what you could include next time to add value to your notes.

Activity 4.3 Distinguish between observation, interpretation, and reflexivity

Read the hypothetical field notes below, and note whether each sentence is an example of observation, interpretation, or reflexivity (or something else). If you have three different coloured pens, you can underline or highlight the sentences accordingly.

15 June 2015, 8.45 a.m., entrance to the health post

I walked to the health post to arrive before the scheduled opening hour (9 a.m.). The building is a one-storey, brick construction, with a faded wooden sign above the door. It is set back from the dusty road, fenced off with concrete fencing topped with wire. Compared with the residences huddled together in the village, the location and the separation of the health post looked odd – like something that did not belong there.

The family I was staying with had grumbled that healthcare workers do not turn up on time or often do not arrive at all. The mother complained bitterly that she had made the effort to take her baby for vaccination on 12 April, just as the midwife had asked her to, only to be turned away. I tried to ask her why, but couldn't understand whether there were no vaccines, or no appointments, or nobody to administer the vaccine. I don't think she had a sense of the whys and wherefores of the health post, or even that she ought to expect a reasonable explanation.

So on my walk to the health post, I vaguely wondered whether I might have the interesting opportunity to observe wrongdoing, of people not turning up to work, or turning up late. As it happened, when I arrived, the door was being swept, some people entered, were greeted by the cleaner who evidently was used to them arriving. (I guess they were staff, but I will try to find out more.) Within 10 minutes (at 8.55), the physician arrived, neatly dressed, carrying a formal briefcase, greeted by her colleagues: 'Good morning, doctor.'

Feedback is available at the end of the chapter.

---

design had planned for the researchers to type up their field notes on laptops, to allow for easy sharing of the data within the research team. However, slow typing speeds and large quantities of data meant that professional typists had to be hired to type up the researchers' handwritten notes – which introduced significant further logistical hurdles, as team leaders had to manage the typists and check the quality of their work (Columbia Group for Children in Adversity, 2011). We give this example to emphasize how demanding it is to write up good field notes, and that sufficient time needs to be allocated for the write-up.

Challenges and responses

In this section, we discuss three of the main challenges to participant observation research, and possible responses to those challenges.

Access and acceptability

Participant observation is an intensive and possibly an intrusive method. People often feel self-conscious about being observed, and worry about being judged or evaluated. Trust needs to be developed between participants and researchers, so that the participants can grant researchers access willingly, and without suspicion or a sense of threat. A donor or NGO may negotiate (or demand) access for you, from community leaders or key informants. A community leader may give you access to a community event. But this does not mean that community members necessarily accept you or give you access to their lives. This access has to be negotiated continually, and founded on respect and trust.

Fluency in the local language is a key issue for access. Ideally, participant observation researchers are fluent in the local language, so that everyday life is accessible to them. When research is to be carried out in communities with different languages, or if the lead researcher does not speak the local language, a research team of participant observers is often formed. When working with a team of participant observers, regular meetings are important, to ensure that comparable and appropriate data is being collected. Training and regular (perhaps weekly) debriefings are key.

Alternatively, it is possible to conduct participant observation with the support of an interpreter. The interpreter can accompany the lead researcher in the field, facilitating conversations, and giving a running commentary to the researcher regarding what is happening. In such cases, it is typically better to train and treat the interpreter as a co-researcher, because his or her ability to notice events of interest to the research is central to what gets recorded as data. Similarly, if the interpreter can write field notes, this reduces the number of translations that the data goes through before being recorded (compared with the interpreter reporting to the researcher, who then records his or her version of events). When very practical matters such as the use of water drainage channels are of primary interest, language skills are somewhat less important, but when the research aim is to understand human and social processes, language is key. In such cases, it is probably ideal to employ researchers fluent in the local language.

Researcher bias

Participant observation research demands a deep engagement on the part of the researcher. Observations are made by the researcher, and written up by the researcher. Alongside the observations, the researcher also records their own experiences as a participant, their reflections on their role in the field, and their interpretations or theories about why things are the way they are. At each step of participant observation, the researcher himself or herself plays a significant role in noticing what is worth observing, then recording and interpreting the data. The researcher plays a significant role in shaping the data. A woman might have access to different spaces than a man. An older person might be treated differently from a younger person. A chatty and outgoing person might find it easy to start up conversations with strangers. A person with years of development management experience might find it difficult to escape the language of objectives and indicators and value for money, to try to understand programmes in the local language and from local points of view. Inevitably, the data we collect through participant observation is not simply objective data, but is shaped by our own perspectives and positions. Bringing our own perspectives to bear on the data is an essential part of the process – it is what makes the method instructive and insightful – but it is important to be aware of how our own position might have shaped the data.

As a response to this issue, reflexivity is particularly important. It is not possible, or desirable, to iron out the influence of the researcher on the data, but it is possible to document it, to reflect upon it, and then to make efforts to diversify the data if necessary. If gender seemed a crucial dimension, it might be possible to employ an additional researcher of the opposite gender to the original researcher. A programme manager could consciously make efforts to listen to community voices rather than impose management language. A researcher who sees himself as shy could work on ways of starting up conversations. Reflexivity, then, serves two purposes: 1) it alerts the researcher to potential biases or risks in his or her own approach, allowing adjustments to the data collection strategy; 2) it demonstrates a critical awareness of the engagement of the researcher and the possible limitations of that engagement.

Ethical issues

Participant observation raises particular challenges for the main ethical concerns of avoidance of harm, informed consent, and anonymity.

Avoidance of harm. We stated above that participant observation research often strives to access the 'unofficial' or 'informal'. It is possible that by revealing ways in which people's practices or opinions diverge from 'the way it is supposed to be', there are risks of harm for those participants. In the reality check study described above, participants were fearful of publicly complaining about services, concerned that they would be stigmatized or denied services as a result. Yet they revealed their complaints to the research team. Ensuring genuine anonymity is important here – as is the principle of informed consent.

Informed consent. Usually, it is a requirement of research projects that participants voluntarily give their informed consent. This means that the participants understand the nature of the research and its possible impacts, and that there is no pressure or coercion for them to take part. For any people who may figure prominently in your field notes, this principle remains key. However, when observing in a public place, it is not always appropriate or possible to actively seek informed consent from each person passing through. In such cases, it is important to discuss ethical issues with local advisers, not to hide the fact that you are doing research, and to be open about your research with anybody who shows an interest or who figures in the research in anything more than a passing observation.

Anonymity.   Research participants should always be able to expect anonymity: that is, they should not be identifiable in a research report. The main challenge in participant observation research comes at the case selection stage. If the case selected is highly particular, or is likely to be obvious to people who know the context, then the researcher must take into account the fact that the community, and prominent members of that community, may be identifiable from the write-up. Extra caution will then need to be exercised regarding what is revealed about the community or individuals, in the interest of avoiding harm. On the other hand, if the community is similar to many others, these issues are less troublesome.

Summary

Participant observation is a method for learning about *what people do*. It is useful for understanding the existing practices in a community, or for examining how a development programme is responded to and engaged with in a community. Participant observation is an intensive and time-consuming method to implement fully, but many projects can benefit from even a small-scale participant observation exercise. Participant observation data is recorded in field notes, in which it is important to distinguish between observation and interpretation. Participant observation can raise significant ethical challenges, which require careful attention and oversight.

References

Australia–Indonesia Basic Education Program (2010) *Indonesia Reality Check Main Study Findings: Listening to poor people's realities about basic education,* Australia Indonesia Partnership, <www.oecd.org/derec/australia/48473826.pdf> [accessed 31 July 2015].

Columbia Group for Children in Adversity (2011) *An Ethnographic Study of Community-based Child Protection Mechanisms and Their Linkage with the National Child Protection System of Sierra Leone,* London: Interagency Learning Initiative on Community-Based Child Protection Mechanisms and Child Protection Systems, <http://childprotectionforum.org/wp/wp-content/uploads/downloads/2011/11/Ethnographic-Phase-Report-Final-7-25-11.pdf> [accessed 27 July 2015].

Gibson, L. (2013) 'A template for writing fieldnotes', in Anthropod [blog] <http://anthropod.net/2013/08/14/a-template-for-writing-fieldnotes> (posted 14 August 2013) [accessed 27 July 2015].

Kostelny, K., Wessells, M., Chabeda-Barthe, J. and Ondoro, K. (2013) *Learning about Children in Urban Slums: A Rapid Ethnographic Study in Two Urban Slums in Mombasa of Community-based Child Protection Mechanisms and their Linkage with the Kenyan National Child Protection System*, London: Interagency Learning Initiative on Community-Based Child Protection Mechanisms and Child Protection Systems, <http://childprotectionforum. org/wp/wp-content/uploads/downloads/2013/05/Mombasa-Ethnographic-Report1.pdf> [accessed 27 July 2015].

Morgan, N., Naz, S. and Sanderson, D. (2013) *Pakistan floods response 2010–12*, London: Christian Aid, <www.christianaid.org.uk/Images/Pakistan-floods-evaluation-August-2013.pdf> [accessed 27 July 2015].

Sida (2012) *Reality Check Bangladesh 2011: Listening to Poor People's Realities about Primary Healthcare and Primary Education – Year 5*, Dhaka: Embassy of Sweden and Swedish International Development Cooperation Agency (Sida), <http://reality-check-approach.com/wp-content/uploads/2013/10/Sida-BD-Reality-Check-2011.pdf> [accessed 27 July 2015].

Further reading

Emerson, R. M., Fretz, R. I. and Shaw, L. L. (1995) *Writing Ethnographic Fieldnotes*, Chicago IL: University of Chicago Press.

Feedback on activities

Feedback on Activity 4.1 Design a participant observation study

A range of different options are plausible. Here we present just one example, but, of course, other designs are also appropriate, as long as they are well thought out and explained.

1. We would design a mixed method study, using participant observation in classrooms, and interviews with teachers and students. Participant observation would allow us to observe the dynamics of the sexual health promotion classes, whether teachers are implementing the curriculum as expected, and how learners respond. Interviews would address teachers' and learners' views on the sexual health promotion classes.
2. The researchers would be participant observers. We would recruit young researchers who share some characteristics with the learners, so that they could, at least to some extent, participate in classes with the learners, and spend break times chatting with them.
3. We would select four schools, giving each researcher responsibility for two schools in the same community. We would select communities based on an important and relevant dimension of comparison, such as urban/rural, or northern/southern district. Within the communities, we would select schools based on an important comparison, such as schools where the programme was more successful and less successful. If a mix of co-educational and single-sex schools received the programme, we would aim to reflect that diversity.
4. Within the schools, we would select one classroom to observe, including the teacher, other adults in the classroom (if appropriate), and the learners in our observations.
5. Researchers would spend two weeks in each school. They would spend five days conducting participant observation and would use the rest of the time for interviews. The researchers would attend school assemblies and sex education classes, and would spend time with learners before and after school and during breaks, to understand their local culture. They would request permission to spend time in the staffroom, or to have lunch or spend other free time with teachers. Researchers would note all references by teachers to sex or sexuality in the course of the day, to understand how teachers understand these issues. They would also note all references by learners to these issues. In addition, they would note the conduct of sex education classes and learners' engagement and responses.

Feedback on Activity 4.3

6. We begin the study knowing that the impact evaluation was negative. This awareness might lead us to emphasize negative points, so we remind ourselves to allow for positive points about the programme to emerge. Our own experience as adolescents makes us expect that teachers and learners will feel uncomfortable talking about sex, but we remind ourselves that we are researching in a very different place and time. The researchers' training includes attention to the importance of being non-judgemental, comfortable, and open. Finally, we must note the responses of research participants to the researchers. We have aimed to recruit young researchers, with whom the participants can identify easily, but we acknowledge that differences remain and are obvious. It may be difficult for the researcher to gain both the trust of learners and the trust of teachers.

Feedback on Activity 4.3 Distinguish between observation, interpretation, and reflexivity

Sentence	Observation, interpretation, or reflexivity
I walked to the health post to arrive before the scheduled opening hour (9 a.m.).	Context-setting remark
The building is a one-storey, brick construction, with a faded wooden sign above the door. It is set back from the dusty road, fenced off with concrete fencing topped with wire.	Observation
Compared with the residences huddled together in the village, the location and the separation of the health post looked odd – like something that did not belong there.	Interpretation
The family I was staying with had grumbled that healthcare workers do not turn up on time or often do not arrive at all. The mother complained bitterly that she had made the effort to take her baby for vaccination on 12 April, just as the midwife had asked her to, only to be turned away. I tried to ask her why, but couldn't understand whether there were no vaccines, or no appointments, or nobody to administer the vaccine.	Observation (of what people say)
I don't think she had a sense of the whys and wherefores of the health post, or even that she ought to expect a reasonable explanation.	Interpretation
So on my walk to the health post, I vaguely wondered whether I might have the interesting opportunity to observe wrongdoing, of people not turning up to work, or turning up late.	Reflexivity
As it happened, when I arrived, the door was open, the entrance was being swept, some people entered, were greeted by the cleaner who evidently was used to them arriving.	Observation
(I guess they were staff, but I will try to find out more.)	Interpretation (and next steps)
Within 10 minutes (at 8.55), the physician arrived, neatly dressed, carrying a formal briefcase, greeted by her colleagues: 'Good morning, doctor.'	Observation

CHAPTER 5
Participatory data collection methods

Abstract

A key tenet of development and humanitarian work is to ensure that the intended beneficiaries and target groups are involved in decisions that may affect their lives. Participatory learning and action tools are therefore routinely used by development practitioners to enable adults and children to analyse their life situations, identify solutions to local problems, influence duty bearers, and assess the impact of development programmes. This chapter introduces you to participatory research, which is a research approach that endorses the use of participatory learning and action tools. It introduces you to some of the many tools and methods that can aid participatory data collection at different stages of a programme cycle, and discusses some of the challenges and obstacles to using these methods.

Keywords: Qualitative research; action research; participatory methods; participation; reflection; accountability

Learning objectives

After reading this chapter, you will be able to:

- explain the benefits and limitations of using participatory data collection methods in qualitative research;
- recognize the considerations needed to facilitate an enabling and empowering environment for the use of participatory data collection methods in qualitative research;
- describe a variety of participatory data collection methods that can be used at various stages of a programme cycle in order to facilitate programme planning and monitoring and evaluation; and
- identify the practical steps needed to plan and facilitate data collection using participatory methods.

Key terms (definitions)

- *Community*: A group of people who have something in common. This may include living in the same geographical area or sharing common attitudes, interests, or lifestyles.

http://dx.doi.org/10.3362/9781780448534.005

- *Community participation*: A process (and approach) whereby community members assume a level of responsibility and become agents for their own health and development.
- *Participatory learning and action*: A collection of methods and approaches used in action research that enable diverse groups and individuals to learn, work, and act together in a cooperative manner, to focus on issues of joint concern, identify challenges, and generate positive responses in a collaborative and democratic manner.

Introduction to participatory research

Participatory research gives community members (adults and children) an opportunity to play an active role in directing research. It recognizes that community members have a wealth of knowledge and particular skills that can contribute to the research process. In the spirit of mutual respect for diverse skills and knowledge, participatory research encourages researchers and community members to work together and to learn from each other, to combine knowledge and create a context for analysis (Wallerstein and Duran, 2003).

Participatory research comes under many different names. You may have heard about 'community-based participatory research'(Minkler and Wallerstein, 2003), 'participatory action research' (Lewin, 1946), 'participatory rural appraisal' (Chambers, 1994), or 'participatory learning and action' (Rifkin and Pridmore, 2001). While there are small differences between these concepts, they all share a commitment to conducting research that provides a context for community members to generate knowledge about their community, develop a deeper understanding of local problems, and use this knowledge to instigate change (Minkler and Wallerstein, 2003). Participatory research is therefore not just about participating; it is also about influencing and contributing to development.

Participatory research as empowering

Paulo Freire (1973), a Brazilian educator, has explained how learning through participatory research can prompt reflection on – and possibly a more critical awareness of – the factors that keep people poor and disempowered. And this, Freire argues, is necessary for social change to happen. From this perspective, participatory research has the potential to empower people to become aware of the factors that affect them, and to give them the confidence to either demand change or, through their own initiative, take action. Community members participating in research about kinship care, for example, may realize that kinship care does not always lead to positive outcomes for children. This new understanding could result in the community coming together and taking a more active role in supporting children in kinship care (Chukwudozie et al., 2015). It could also result in community members organizing a petition to demand political support for changes in kinship care legislation.

Participatory research to enhance impact

Local people have a great deal of experience of what works, what does not, and why (Moser, 1998). Participatory research therefore lends itself particularly well to development work. In fact, the concepts of 'participatory rural appraisal' and 'participatory learning and action' were specifically developed to gather local input and to contextualize development programmes (Chambers, 1994; 1997). Participatory research thus has a long tradition in the field of development, enabling development organizations to involve the most marginalized members of a community in the planning and monitoring and evaluation of programmes. Development practitioners can facilitate participatory processes with both individuals and groups of people (for example, a community), enabling them to gather either a collective voice or the voices of individuals. Regardless of your approach, this not only increases local ownership, commitment, and buy-in of the development activities, but it ensures that they resonate with local needs and resources.

Participatory research can feed into wider advocacy policy work

Participatory research can influence duty bearers, including development organizations themselves. Participatory data collection methods often make use of visuals – bridging cultural and language barriers – and can provide duty bearers with an insight into issues, and a group of people, unfamiliar to them. Visual representations can therefore present a compelling argument to duty bearers, which in turn may prompt change. Development practitioners are duty bearers and have a responsibility to learn from and make use of the information they gather through participatory data collection methods (Newman and Beardon, 2011). For example, they might work with study participants to disseminate findings to other duty bearers. This could be through distributing reports or exhibiting posters with visualizations and summaries of study findings. In this way, participatory data collection methods can provide community members with a platform to advocate for change at different levels.

Why are we referring to participatory tools as research methods?

As we discussed in Chapter 1, local voices are important and powerful in shaping development policy and programing. However, with increased pressure for development practitioners to use robust forms of evidence to inform programming and strategy, there is a danger that local facilitation of participatory processes, however important they are, will not be taken seriously, or will amount to little more than colourful testimonies to illustrate 'hard' evidence. We therefore need to treat local voices as data, and approach participatory processes as evidence gathering. In doing so we will be able to package local voices as qualitative evidence, and increase the likelihood that local perspectives will trickle up the system and inform policy and practice.

However, it is not just a matter of 'repackaging' participatory processes, but also about how you, as a researcher, systematically capture, analyse, and report on the findings that emerge. This, we argue, can help bridge the gap between local efforts to facilitate participatory processes and learning at every level of a development organization. In this chapter we introduce you to a number of participatory data collection methods and guide you through the process of using these methods to systematically collect qualitative data.

Participatory data collection methods

Participatory data collection methods are a combination of approaches, tools, attitudes, and behaviours that enable programme stakeholders – children as well as adults – to take an active role in the production of knowledge.

Numerous resources have been written that describe participatory data collection methods (see Box 5.1). Often they are referred to as 'participatory tools' and have been written for particular audiences, such as development practitioners working within disaster risk reduction (e.g. *VCA Toolbox*), hunger and livelihood (e.g. *80 Tools for Participatory Development*), health and HIV (e.g. *Tools Together Now*), or those involved in monitoring and evaluation (e.g. *Tools for Monitoring and Evaluating Children's Participation*). There is likely to be a resource available in your field.

Hundreds of methods are available, and it can be a challenge to decide on which methods to use in a project. *Tools Together Now: 100 Participatory Tools to Mobilise Communities for HIV/AIDS*, from the International HIV/ AIDS Alliance (2006), usefully identifies seven categories of participatory methods:

1. *Mapping tools* seek to develop maps that contain information about local realities and practices.
2. *Time analysis tools* focus on temporal aspects of community life, looking, for example, at changes over time or between seasons.
3. *Linkages and relationships tools* seek to visualize the connections between different factors promoting or undermining well-being or health.
4. *Experiential tools* seek to bring forward community members' experiences.
5. *Prioritization and quantification tools* help community members seek consensus through ranking and scoring.
6. *Action planning techniques* systematize the planning and evaluation process.
7. *Training tools* prepare facilitators to use the tools in a flexible, engaged, inclusive, and participatory way.

These categories highlight the fact that participatory data collection methods can be used for different purposes, uncovering different kinds of information. The methods not only differ in terms of the kind of information they generate. Some require specific skills, both to facilitate (interpersonal skills, for instance) and to engage with (such as basic literacy); some require more time and materials than others; and some are better suited to people who share similar characteristics (gender, age, ethnicity, or health status, for example).

Box 5.1 Selected resources freely available online

International HIV/AIDS Alliance (2006) *Tools Together Now: 100 Participatory Tools to Mobilise Communities for HIV/AIDS*, <www.aidsalliance.org/assets/000/000/370/229-Tools-together-now_original.pdf>.

Pretty, J. et al. (1995) *Participatory Learning and Action: A Trainer's Guide*, <http://pubs.iied.org/pdfs/6021IIED.pdf>.

Save the Children (2008) *A Kit of Tools for Participatory Research and Evaluation with Children, Young People and Adults*, <http://resourcecentre.savethechildren.se/library/kit-tools-participatory-research-and-evaluation-children-young-people-and-adults-compilation>.

Lansdown, G. and O'Kane, C. (2014) *Tools for Monitoring and Evaluating Children's Participation*, <http://resourcecentre.savethechildren.se/library/toolkit-monitoring-and-evaluating-childrens-participation-tools-monitoring-and-evaluating>.

IFRC (2007) *VCA Toolbox*, <www.ifrc.org/Global/Publications/disasters/vca/vca-toolbox-en.pdf>.

Geilfus, F. (2008) *80 Tools for Participatory Development*, <http://betterevaluation.org/resources/guide/80_tools_for_participatory_development>.

It can therefore be a challenge to identify the appropriate mix of methods for a study. To help you decide, you may consider the following:

- *Study aim and research question*: Which methods can help generate information relevant to your study?
- *Skills of the facilitator*: Who will be facilitating the workshops?
- *Location*: What environment is needed to create an enabling context for the methods to be used successfully?
- *Timing*: Is there a time of the year, or during the day, when the methods are likely to work better? How much time do you have to facilitate workshops using participation data collection methods?
- *Materials*: What materials are required to facilitate the methods? And do you have a budget for this?
- *Participants*: What methods might be most appropriate for the composition of your participants? What are the risks of bias with these particular participants? Will it be possible to triangulate the data with another source or sources?
- *Ethics*: What issues and challenges might you encounter? How can you best mitigate these? Will it be possible to gain consent from your research participants?

Although you can identify methods that are more appropriate than others, given your topic and participants, it is important that you use the methods flexibly and adapt them to your specific context (Rifkin and Pridmore, 2001). The methods presented in this chapter or in other resources are by no means fixed; they can be modified to suit different participants and socio-economic and cultural contexts. Some methods may work well instantly, while others require more facilitation, or may need to be abandoned altogether. As a facilitator you need to be prepared to make changes 'on the spot'; you should not expect to comply with the guidance found in the literature, but to make the tools work within your context.

Table 5.1 Methods matrix

Method	Page	Context suitability				Informants suitability			Suitability within the programme cycle			Qualitative data output		
		Humanitarian	Development	Individuals	Groups	Adults	Children	Varied literacies	Planning	Monitoring	Evaluation	Visual	Oral	Written
Problem tree	7	•	•••	•	•••	•••	••	•	•••	•	••	••	•••	•
Body mapping	8	•••	•••	••	•	•	•••	••	•••	•••	•••	•••	•••	•
'H' assessment	10	•••	•••	•	•	•••	•	••		•••	•••	•••	•••	•
Stories of change	12	•••	•••	•••	••	•••	••	•		••	•••			•••
Daily diagrams	13	•••	•••	•••	•	•••	•••	•	•••		•	•••	•••	•
History profiles	15	•••	•••	••	•••	•••	•••	•	•••			•••	•••	••
Preference ranking	17	•	•••		•••	•••	•••	•••	•••			•••	••	•
Community mapping	19	•••	•••	•••	•••	•••	•••	•••	•••	•	••	•••	••	•
Spidergram	21	•••	•••	•	•••	•••	•••	•••	•		•••	•••	••	•

The dots represent the level of suitability: the greater the number of dots, the more suitable the method.

The chapter now details a range of participatory data collection methods. In the process, it underlines which of the seven categories they belong to as well as their purpose in relation to the different points within a programme cycle where qualitative methods can be used (as described in the paragraphs next to the swirls). See also Table 5.1 for an overview of the different methods and their suitability for different aspects of research.

Problem tree

The problem tree enables participants to visually and collectively explore the underlying causes and effects of a problem or an issue. It involves using the trunk, roots, and branches of a tree as metaphors and a platform to brainstorm, identify, and discuss the links between the causes and effects of a problem or an issue.

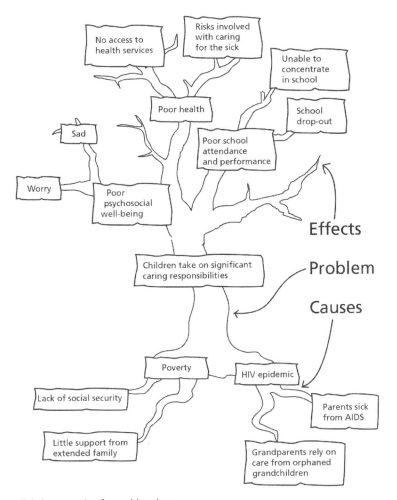

Figure 5.1 An example of a problem tree

As problem trees help you analyse the causes and effects of a problem or an issue, they are particularly useful to use at the planning stage of a programme. They can also be used to evaluate a particular component of a programme, looking at pathways to change as well as outcomes of the intervention.

45–60 minutes.

Flipchart paper, pens, Post-it notes, and possibly a digital voice recorder to capture discussions.

The problem tree method works best in a group setting, from as few as six to eight people in a focus group discussion through to a larger community meeting. However, it can also be used with individuals and serve as an activity to spark dialogue in an interview. It can be used with adults as well as children, irrespective of their literacy.

1. Explain the purpose of the exercise and make sure that the participants have all agreed to the problem or issue about to be discussed. It is important that everyone participating feels passionate about the issue.
2. Write or draw the problem or issue to be discussed in the middle of the flipchart and draw a trunk around it. The trunk effectively represents the problem or issue.
3. The participants should then be encouraged to identify all of the main root causes of the problem or issue. Each cause should be added below the trunk, representing a root.
4. For each root cause of the problem, ask the participants why they think this happens, and draw up smaller roots coming off the main roots, giving details of 'secondary' causes. Primary and secondary causes can be discussed as a collective, and you, as a facilitator, can write the themes on the problem tree. Alternatively, the participants can be encouraged to write or draw the causes on Post-it notes, and then place them on the drawn tree.
5. Next, encourage the group to identify the main effects of the problem or issue and draw branches that illustrate these effects.
6. Ask the participants to identify 'secondary' effects to each of the main effects and draw them on the tree as smaller branches coming off the larger branches. Figure 5.1 illustrates an example of a problem tree that looks at the causes and effects of young caregiving in western Kenya.
7. Discuss the problem tree with the group. What does it show? How does it relate to their lives? What are the links and relationships between the causes and effects? What are the most serious effects of the problem or issue? What causes and effects are changing? And for what reason?
8. Work with the participants to convert the 'problem tree' into a 'solution tree'. First discuss what possible solutions there might be for the causes and effects identified on the tree. Second, ask the

participants to write or draw their recommended solutions on Post-it notes and stick them on the appropriate roots and branches.

 While the completed tree is a valuable source of data, providing an in-depth understanding of the causes and effects of a problem or issue, the discussions that take place in the process of developing the tree provide equally valuable information. It is therefore recommended that you either audio or video record the discussions, or at a minimum have someone take very detailed notes of the discussions. The notes should also include information about the number and background of the participants involved in the exercise. These notes, or the transcripts of audio or video recordings, as well as the completed tree comprise data that can be used to answer your research question (see Chapter 7 on how to categorize, index, and analyse qualitative data).

Body mapping

As the name suggests, body mapping is a *mapping tool* that uses the drawing of a body to capture perceptions of a group of people and how they experience a particular a situation or programme. This can be done before and after an intervention, and thus highlight perceived changes. Even if the baseline was not captured, participants can be encouraged to reflect back and make notes on perceived changes arising from a programme. Body mapping can therefore be used to gain an understanding both of local perceptions of a group of people and of changes they may have experienced following a programme.

 Body maps can be used at any point within the programme cycle. For example, body maps can be used to analyse and understand an issue within a context, as part of the planning for a programme. They can also be used to examine beneficiaries' experiences of a programme while it is still being implemented and to explore people's perceptions of programme impact.

 60–90 minutes.

 Flipchart paper, pens, Post-it notes, tape, and possibly a digital voice recorder to capture discussions.

 The body mapping exercise works best in a small group setting with between four and 18 people. However, it can also be used with individuals and serve as an activity to spark dialogue in an interview. It works particularly well with children, but can also be used with adults. If you have a large group of participants, you can divide them into smaller groups of people with similar ages, the same gender, and so on. The method can be used with individuals of any level of literacy.

1. Explain the purpose of body mapping and agree with the participants what to show on the map. This depends on the focus of your study.

2. Either provide the group with a sheet of flipchart paper where the shape of a body has been drawn, or tape together four sheets of flipchart paper and invite a volunteer to lie down on the paper while another volunteer of the same gender draws the shape of a body. Make sure you use a non-permanent marker!

3. Explain that the body represents a typical boy or girl, or man or woman, from their community (for example, someone who lives with HIV, or has benefited from the programme) and encourage them to use the body parts as metaphors to explore and record their perceptions of the person (see Figure 5.2 below for examples).

4. To capture differences and changes, you can explain that the body now represents an individual who has benefited from a programme. Encourage the participants to use the body to discuss and draw up their perceptions of how the programme has contributed to change in the individual. You can adapt the tool and draw a vertical line down the middle of the body. One side can then represent perceptions of a 'bad' situation or before a programme, while the other side can represent perceptions of a 'good' situation or after a programme. For example, one side can represent a child living on the street before an intervention, while the other side represents a child living on the street after an intervention.

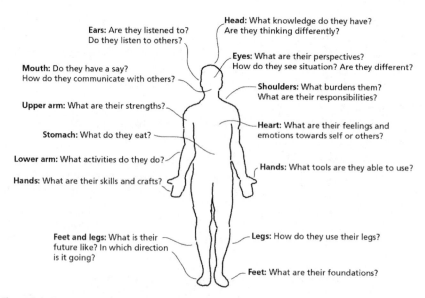

Figure 5.2 Example of how body parts can be used as metaphors to spark dialogue

5. Encourage the participants to either write down on Post-it notes possible action points that can help the person escape a 'bad' situation or explanations relating to the changes that have been observed in the 'before and after' scenario. Encourage the participants to place the Post-it notes on the body map.
6. Discuss the body map and the findings that emerge. How representative are the experiences captured in the body map? What differences might there exist between men and women, or boys and girls? What are the most significant changes that have been observed? Nudge the discussion in the direction of your research question.

The body map method can generate a lot of useful information about local perceptions of how a group of people experience a situation or a programme. The former allows you to use body maps for situational analyses, while the latter makes body maps useful for programme monitoring and evaluation, capturing the most significant change stories. Irrespective of its purpose, the discussions surrounding the process of developing body maps contain useful information and ought to be either audio or video recorded, or at a minimum have someone take detailed notes of the discussions.

'H' assessment

The 'H' assessment method is an *experiential tool* that can be used to identify local perceptions of strengths and weaknesses of a programme as well as to capture local recommendations on how to make improvements to the programme.

This method can be used to monitor progress and evaluate the impact of a programme.

45–60 minutes.

Flipchart paper and pens.

The 'H' assessment method works best in a group setting, including as few as six to eight people in a focus group discussion or a larger community forum. However, it can also be used with individuals and serve as an activity to spark dialogue in an interview. It can be used with adults as well as children. It can be used with a mix of people or in small groups of people of a similar age group, the same gender, and so on.

1. Explain the purpose of the exercise and make sure that the participants are aware of the programme about to be discussed.
2. In the middle of a large sheet of flipchart paper, write a large 'H' and include the following headings within it (see Figure 5.3):
   • name of the programme
   • strengths and successes ☺
   • weaknesses and challenges ☹
   • recommendations for improvements ☿

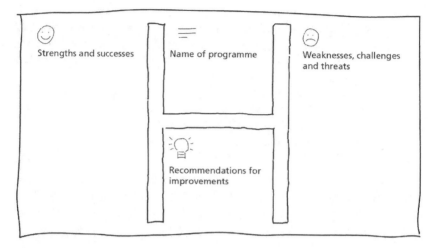

Figure 5.3 An 'H' assessment

3. Ask the participants to fill in the name of the programme they are benefiting from in the top middle panel. Here they can also make notes about who they are (for example, four boys and six girls, aged 12–17).
4. Starting from the left, ask the participants to first think about, and then list, some of the strengths and successes of the programme they have been part of. In the process, discuss the scope and reach of each of these successes (i.e. might some people have been left out?) as well as some of the factors that may have contributed to these strengths and successes.
5. Go to the right of the 'H' and ask the participants to brainstorm and list weaknesses, challenges, and threats to the programme. Discuss some of the underlying reasons behind these challenges.
6. Below the middle 'H' bar, ask the participants to list their ideas and recommendations for how the programme could be improved. In the process, discuss how each recommendation could be put into practice.

 The 'H' assessment on its own is a valuable source of data, providing an overview of what programme stakeholders perceive as key strengths and weaknesses as well as their recommendations for improvement. To aid your analysis of this information, you can encourage the participants to rank the lists within the chart, with number one indicating the greatest strength or weakness or the most promising action point. To capture the discussions, either audio or video record the session, or at a minimum have someone take detailed notes of the discussions, and use these, together with the completed 'H' assessment, to answer your research question.

Stories of change

The stories of change method in an *experiential tool* that builds on the 'most significant change' (cf. Dart and Davies, 2003) method. It involves collecting, discussing, and selecting stories about changes that have occurred in a given context as a result of a programme. These changes can be either positive or negative, and might include changes in knowledge, skills, attitudes, values, or behaviour, as well as access to and the quality of services. Stories of change can be captured in many different and creative ways, such as through Photovoice (see Chapter 6), diaries, drawings, and drama. In this guidance note we focus on written stories gathered in a workshop setting.

 Change stories can be gathered at the end of the programme to identify changes observed by participants since the start of that programme (evaluation). They can also be gathered every three or six months to identify changes over the past couple of months (monitoring).

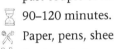 90–120 minutes.

Paper, pens, sheets of flipchart paper, and markers.

 Stories of change are first and foremost produced by individuals, but can be discussed at a community and peer group level. If the stories are discussed in a collective, participants can be encouraged to work together and cluster the change stories into themes and rank them according to their significance. The method as described here works best with individuals who can write, but it can easily be adapted to anyone who is illiterate by encouraging them to draw and narrate changes to a note taker.

1. Explain the purpose of the exercise and make sure that the participants understand it.
2. Use the flipchart paper to brainstorm with the participants and make notes of all the changes they have observed.
3. Hand out sheets of paper and pens and invite the participants to write two small essays about a positive and negative change they have observed over a specified number of months or years. Each essay can be prompted by the following questions:
   - Why is this positive or negative change important to describe?
   - How does this change relate to your life and/or the lives of people in your community?
   - What do you think has contributed to this change?
4. Once the participants have finished writing the stories, encourage them to read and share them. In the process, facilitate a discussion that enables the participants to identify common patterns and come to an agreement about some of the most significant positive and negative changes.

 The change stories are important pieces of data. Also, the discussions, if captured, can form part of your data collection. The ranking of change stories is an important first step in the data analysis and provides you with key information about local perceptions of progress and impact.

Daily diagrams

The daily diagrams method is a *mapping tool* that allows participants to explore their daily routines. It involves participants visually mapping out the activities they do on a typical day. Daily diagrams allow you and the participants to identify differences in daily activities between them (Rifkin and Pridmore, 2001). For example, this could include identifying the caregiving burden of some children, or differences between men and women, or between those living in rural and urban areas.

 Daily diagrams are particularly good for needs assessments and situational analyses. You could repeat the exercise at the end of the programme to see whether the people use their time differently now.

 90 minutes.

 A4 paper, sheets of flipchart paper, pens, and pencils.

Daily diagrams can be used both with individuals and with peer groups. This guidance note will first introduce daily diagrams to individuals and then have them come together in peer groups to discuss differences and similarities as well as to agree on an average and representative daily diagram. It can be used with both children and adults. The method as described here works best with individuals who can read and write, but it can easily be adapted to those with varied literacies by encouraging them to draw and narrate changes to a note taker.

1. Explain the purpose of the exercise and make sure that the participants understand what they are invited to do. Show them an example of what a daily diagram might look like (see Figure 5.4 for an example).
2. Brainstorm a list of factors the participants may want to include, such as hours sleeping, time for recreation, time spent with different people, participation in a programme, hours spent cooking, cleaning, generating income, studying, and so on.
3. Give the participants a sheet of paper and pencils and invite them to draw their own daily diagram, capturing the hours spent on different activities on a typical weekday. Reiterate that they need to account for all 24 hours in a day.
4. Give the participants another sheet of paper and invite them to draw a daily diagram capturing the hours spent on different activities on a typical weekend day.
5. Once the daily diagrams have been drawn up, ask them to get together in groups of similar characteristics (gender, age group, ethnicity, etc.) or experience (married, living with HIV, caregiving responsibilities). Within these groups, the participants can identify common patterns and develop a daily diagram that is representative of the group.
6. If you have more than one group, ask them to come together to discuss similarities and differences. If, for example, you had two groups – a group of men and a group of women – these two groups can come together and discuss differences between their daily routines.

Both the individual and the peer group daily diagrams make up valuable data about the activities that occupy people's daily lives. But also the discussions offer important insights and discussions that are worth capturing. It is therefore a good idea to either audio or video record the discussions or have someone take detailed notes.

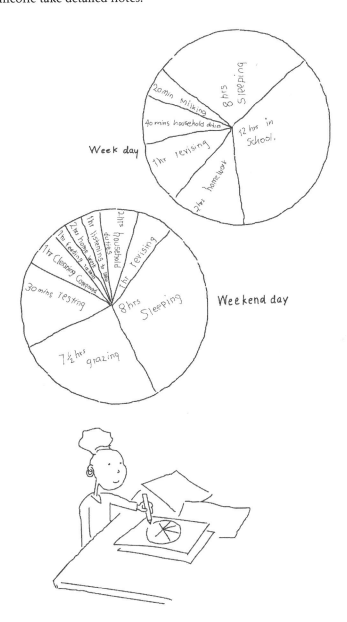

Figure 5.4 Daily diagrams drawn by a 14-year-old girl in Kenya

History profiles

The history profiles method is an *experiential tool* that involves charting historically significant events on a timeline. History profiles help you identify past experiences, which can help you and the participants contextualize and understand the present situation of an individual or the community (Rifkin and Pridmore, 2001). As it is possible to chart many different historical events, it is important that the exercise is guided by your research question. For example, individuals can identify events that have been significant in their life (such as migration, deaths within the family, or engagement with development programmes). On the other hand, community members, as a collective, can identify events relating to food production, disease patterns, political events, cultural traditions, infrastructure development, and service provisions, among other things.

History profiles are particularly good for needs assessments and situational analyses as information about the past and historical events can help you understand the present situation of individuals or communities.

45–60 minutes.

Pens and paper (for individuals), or a sheet of flipchart paper and a marker pen (for groups of people).

If your aim is to identify key life events of individuals, in order to understand their current situation, the history profiles should be identified by individuals. If, on the other hand, you are trying to understand key community events (such as droughts or disease outbreaks) and how these have influenced the present situation, the history profiles should be developed by a group of community members. This method can be used with both children and adults. As described here, it works best with individuals who can read and write, but it can easily be adapted to those with varied literacies by encouraging them to draw and narrate changes to a note taker.

1. Explain what the history profile method is about and ensure that the participants know how it is used. Agree on the focus of the history profiles (droughts or rainfall patterns, or individual migration and movement, for example).
2. Show an example of a history profile, either from an individual (see Figure 5.5 for an example) or from a group, depending on your aim.
3. Ask the individuals, or groups of individuals, to draw a horizontal or vertical line that represents a period of time they can remember. Timelines with children are likely to be in years, as Figure 5.5 illustrates. Timelines developed by elderly community members, on the other hand, could be in decades.
4. Ask the person, or the group of people, to mark significant events along the line.
5. You can then discuss the history profile, unpacking the significance of the marked events and their relevance to today.

1994	I was born at Simga village.
1996	I start in Nursery school.
1997	I went to stay with my sister where I continued my education.
1998	I went to standard two.
1999	Our first born brother died and I came back home for burial.
2000	I was in standard three at a place called Opuk Village.
2001	That year my sister also died. She was weak and then she died.
2002	I came back to stay with my mother.
2003	My real mother died, then my father married a step-mother.
2004	I went on with my education and I was in standard five.
2005	My father was also getting weak and then died. In the end I remained with my step-mother.
2006	I was in standard seven.
2007	Now I am in standard eight. I am still staying with my step-mother. I stay with her well.

Figure 5.5 Example of a history profile by a 13-year-old HIV-affected girl from Kenya

 The history profiles and subsequent discussions make up important data for any study where a historical insight can help you understand the present situation better.

 Preference ranking

The preference ranking method is a *prioritization and quantification tool* that enables community members to come to a consensus about what issues or actions to prioritize. It involves comparing and contrasting different options and voting on them (International HIV/AIDS Alliance, 2006; Rifkin and Pridmore, 2001).

 Preference ranking is particularly good for needs assessments as it involves community members ranking and prioritizing their needs. Preference ranking can also be used as part of an after-action review, if the programme is to continue and new needs have arisen.

 45–60 minutes.

Sheets of flipchart paper and pens.

Preference ranking requires a group or community setting. You can either facilitate preference ranking with the whole community, or split participants into peer groups that each produce their own preference ranking. It can be used with adults as well as children, irrespective of their level of literacy. Please note that the process of voting might not be implemented easily in all settings, and may on rare occasions be considered inappropriate.

1. Start off the exercise with an identified list of issues and problems, or actions and solutions, to prioritize. This list could be generated from other participatory data collection methods, such as the problem tree method. Or perhaps your qualitative interviews and focus group discussions uncovered a number of problems and solutions that you would like the community to rank according to their priority and preference. A list of between five and eight options to compare works best for this method.

2. Explain the purpose of the exercise and make sure that the participants understand what they are invited to do. Show them an example of a preference ranking (see Tables 5.2 and 5.3).

3. If you are working in a community setting, you can either proceed with the larger group or divide people up into peer groups (for example, according to gender, employment status, age, or ethnicity).

Table 5.2 Example of pairwise voting on community problems

Health problems	Soil-transmit-ted helminths	Malaria	Dengue fever	Sleeping sickness	Dysentery
Soil-transmitted helminths	–	Malaria	Soil-transmitted helminths	Soil-transmitted helminths	Dysentery
Malaria	–	–	Malaria	Malaria	Malaria
Dengue fever	–	–	–	Dengue fever	Dysentery
Sleeping sickness	–	–	–	–	Dysentery
Dysentery	–	–	–	–	–

Table 5.3 Example of preference ranking through pairwise voting

	No. of times preferred	Rank
Malaria	4	1
Dysentery	3	2
Soil-transmitted helminths	2	3
Dengue fever	1	4
Sleeping sickness	0	5

4. For each group, draw up a matrix where each option is written across the top row and down the left-hand column (see Table 5.2 for an example).
5. Cross out all the squares that have the same pair of options as well as all the squares below the line of double pairs. They merely repeat the pairwise options.
6. Starting with the top right-hand square, invite the participants to compare the two options. From the example in Table 5.2, you could ask the participants about which one of the two health problems they perceive to be greatest in their community: dysentery or soil-transmitted helminths? Allow the group to discuss the options before asking them to decide. You may need to take it to a vote by asking for a show of hands. Write their collective preference in the square.
7. Repeat Step 6 for each of the remaining squares, recording their preferences within the matrix.
8. On another sheet of flipchart paper, draw up a matrix that lists each of the options that have been compared (see Table 5.3 for an example).
9. Begin to count the number of times each option has been recorded as the preferred choice.
10. Rank the options according to the number of times they were preferred. The group has now ranked their options.
11. If you divided the community into peer groups, you may have more than one preference ranking matrix, and there may not necessarily be agreement between them. Women and men, or adults and children, for example, may have different preferences. Use this opportunity to discuss differences with the community. You can then either repeat the exercise with the entire community, or simply add up the preference scores from each group to get a community total.

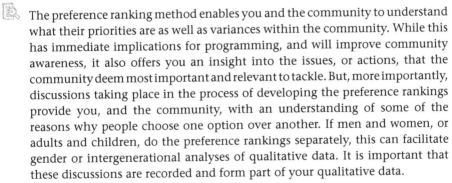 The preference ranking method enables you and the community to understand what their priorities are as well as variances within the community. While this has immediate implications for programming, and will improve community awareness, it also offers you an insight into the issues, or actions, that the community deem most important and relevant to tackle. But, more importantly, discussions taking place in the process of developing the preference rankings provide you, and the community, with an understanding of some of the reasons why people choose one option over another. If men and women, or adults and children, do the preference rankings separately, this can facilitate gender or intergenerational analyses of qualitative data. It is important that these discussions are recorded and form part of your qualitative data.

Community mapping

The community mapping method is a *mapping tool* that enables community members to draw their community and highlight places, boundaries, people, infrastructure, or resources of importance (Rifkin and Pridmore, 2001).

Depending on the aim of your study, you can give the community map a focus. If you are interested in knowing how people cope with poverty, you can ask the community to develop a resource map. As a development practitioner you may be interested in what other interventions are available in a given context, and you could invite the community to chart the services, facilities, and activities relevant to a particular issue.

Community maps can help you engage community members at the start of a project to get them involved, as it allows them to visually present their knowledge. This knowledge can be used to foster awareness about local strengths and weaknesses and serve as a platform to discuss the importance of the different elements drawn on the map, any concerns about the community, and what they would like to see changed.

120 minutes.

Sheets of flipchart paper and pens.

Community maps can be drawn by individuals or smaller peer groups. To make sure that everyone participates, it is advisable that the groups are no larger than eight people, or that they can all sit around the sheet of paper. It can be used with adults as well as children, irrespective of their level of literacy.

1. Explain the purpose of the exercise and make sure that the participants understand what they are invited to do. Show them examples of community maps. Figure 5.6 illustrates a community map created by children with caregiving responsibilities in rural western Kenya, prominently featuring a community centre (the building with the antenna, and a compound with a granary and cattle dip).
2. Divide the community into peer groups, and provide each group with flipchart paper and pens. This will allow you to compare the different groups and discuss variances. Ask each group to brainstorm the kinds of things they want to include in their map. This could be anything that is important to them, or, depending on the aim of the study, it could have a focus, such as health services or land distribution.
3. Invite the peer groups to draw their maps, starting with marking the boundaries of their community and charting major roads and paths.
4. Bring the groups together and facilitate a discussion around the maps. Encourage the participants to ask questions about the elements that appear on the different maps. In this process, identify similarities and differences between the peer groups.

The groups are likely to draw quite different maps of the same community. Their emphasis, or the centre of the community, may reflect their varying perceptions of what is important to them. The maps and discussions about group differences constitute important data. However, community maps also provide researchers with invaluable background information about the community. They can provide you with reference points that can facilitate

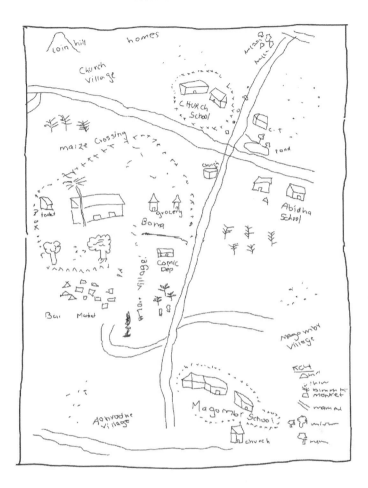

Figure 5.6 Community map created by caregiving children in western Kenya

understanding and discussions between you and community members, whether that takes place in interviews or in a needs assessment.

Spidergram

The spidergram method is *a mapping tool* that allows you and the community to assess local perceptions of change as a result of a programme, highlighting programme strengths and limitations. Spidergrams allow you to assess change using between five and eight indicators, by marking a score for each indicator on the spidergram. The marks can be joined up to illustrate a spider's web. If this is done before and after a programme, the spidergram can illustrate the perceived change.

Spidergrams can be used to assess people's perceptions of their knowledge, skills and behaviours in relation to an issue or their participation in a development programme. Rifkin and Pridmore (2001) use spidergrams to assess community participation and have identified five indicators: 1) needs assessment; 2) leadership (local leaders involve the broader community); 3) organization (programme links to other activities); 4) resource mobilization (local contributions to the project); 5) management (community members take a management role). Scores of 1 or 2 indicate narrow participation, while scores of 4 or 5 show wide participation (see Figure 5.7).[1]

Spidergrams can be used to evaluate and review particular aspects of a programme, such as participation or programme change.

120 minutes.

Sheets of flipchart paper and pens.

Spidergrams are best facilitated in group or community settings. You can either use the spidergram exercise with the whole community, or divide

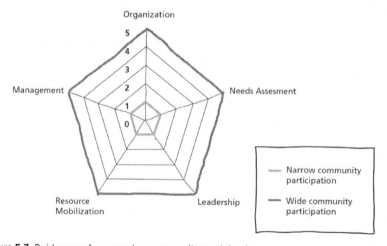

Figure 5.7 Spidergram for assessing community participation
Source: Baatiema et al. (2013).

the community into peer groups that each produce their own spidergram. You can then bring the peer groups together and encourage them to explore differences in perceptions between the groups. It can be used with adults as well as children, irrespective of their level of literacy.

1. Explain the purpose of the exercise and work with the community members to identify what they will be assessing as well as the indicators that should be used. They might assess community participation or community competence in any programme-relevant area. If you are working in a programme that seeks to build the capacity of communities to respond to the hardship faced by orphaned and vulnerable children (OVC), you might consider the following indicators: knowledge and skills in relation to OVC care and support; opportunities for community members to discuss and plan for the plight of OVC; recognition of local strengths and coping resources; confidence in their ability to support OVC; community solidarity; and links with outside sources of support (Skovdal and Campbell, 2010).

2. For each indicator, work with the community to identify a couple of questions they can discuss in order to give it a score.

3. Show them how to draw a spidergram that includes the agreed indicators. Explain to the participants that each arm of the spidergram represents a continuum, with scores going from 1 to 5. Mark the five points on each of the spidergram arms (see Figure 5.7 for an example).

4. Divide the community into peer groups and invite them to draw their own spidergrams, as well as discuss and score each of their indicators. Once each indicator has received a score, a line can be drawn between them, illustrating a spider's web.

5. Bring the groups together and give them an opportunity to present their spidergrams, explaining the reasons behind their scores.

6. Once all the spidergrams are displayed, it is possible to see differences and similarities between the peer groups, which can then discuss and explore these differences.

7. If this activity is done at the start of a programme, as part of a needs assessment or baseline, the spidergrams can be saved and the exercise repeated, for example at the end of the programme, to visually illustrate change (if the scores are different from the baseline!).

The spidergram method enables you to systematically gather information about key indicators relating to a topic, such as community participation within a programme or competence as a result of a programme. It can be used as a monitoring tool to identify the weaknesses and strengths of a programme. As with most participatory data collection methods, the outcome, a visual illustration of change, is not the only form of data. The discussions leading up to the scoring, as well as discussions exploring and explaining differences between peer groups, ought to be recorded and form part of the data collection.

What next?

We have now introduced nine different participatory data collection methods and offered some practical steps for how you can facilitate workshops using these methods. The next chapter introduces you to one additional participatory data collection method – a method called Photovoice.

Common to all participatory data collection methods is that they are flexible and can be used in countless different ways, serve different purposes, and be used at different stages of the project cycle (see Figure 1.3 in Chapter 1). It therefore important that you do not use our guidance as *the* way to do it, but merely take inspiration from our suggestions as you develop your own plans. You need to keep your research question in mind and adapt the methods – not only to fit your question, but also to match community interests and capacities.

You might have used participatory tools before, like the ones described above, in your capacity as a development practitioner. So how is it different using them as participatory data collection methods? The key difference is that you make every effort to capture the discussions that take place in the process as well as observe group and power dynamics, and their influence on the generation of data. These discussions, coupled with the visual representations that the community members produce, are important forms of data that can be systematically analysed, just like transcripts from individual interviews. Ideally, you should be able to audio or video record the discussions, if informed consent permits this, and have them transcribed. At a minimum you should have a dedicated note taker capturing the detail of the discussions as well as the dynamics of the participants.

Many of the methods introduced here also lend themselves well to 'before and after' assessments. While these can spark discussion about change in the community, and can provide the communities with a visual representation of this perceived change, you will have to be careful about attributing the change to a particular programme. Although this can also be usefully discussed by the community, attribution can be measured only by using a sophisticated quantitative research design.

Common pitfalls in using participatory data collection methods

Using participatory data collection methods does not come without challenges. To a large extent, the success of participatory methods depends on the facilitator recognizing how human relationships and dynamics shape local perceptions of events, and the production of information (data). To help you navigate complex social relations and gather the perspectives of *all* members of a community, we will now discuss some of the more common pitfalls in using participatory data collection methods.

Complexity of community

One should not underestimate the messy nature of 'community'. Many participatory data collection methods are facilitated in a community setting, making it important for you to define what you mean by 'community'. Communities tend to be tied together by having something in common (Howarth, 2001). This could include having a shared goal. A woman's group, for example, might have a shared goal of protecting a group of vulnerable children. A community could also be made up of people who share a belief system, such as a religion, or a hobby, such as football. A community could also consist of a group of people who share an identity, such as those living with HIV, or are part of a shared geographical space, such as a village. It is important to recognize that people can belong to more than one community and that people within a community may not always share the same values and agendas, even if they are part of the same community.

Activity 5.1 Reflecting on the diversity of communities

Communities are not homogeneous entities. This activity encourages you to reflect on the diversity of a community.

1. Make a list of communities you belong to.
2. Think about what qualifies you to be a member of these communities and how each of these communities plays a role in facilitating your well-being.

Feedback is available at the end of the chapter.

Power relations

Any community is riddled with power dynamics and politics, which can be very difficult for outside facilitators to pick up on. However, this does not mean that they do not exist. One should therefore be careful not to take certain community functions and structures for granted, but instead pay attention to how gender, ethnic, and intergenerational dynamics are played out, any possible feuds between families and neighbours, and the role of community leaders in shaping the process. Participatory data collection methods may bring to light issues within a community that instigate change and challenge power relations and the status quo. Such changes are not always welcomed by those with power and, in some hostile environments, they can leave the community more vulnerable and marginalized.

Participation

Participation means different things to different people (Fraser, 2005) and can be used to either facilitate transformative change or serve as a disguise to convince local people to accept the agendas of others (Cooke and Kothari, 2001). Often, participation is used to mean something in between. As a facilitator, you need to be aware of your role in facilitating the process, and how the interests of your organization may influence the data. You need to find a balance between facilitating processes that delegate power and control to the community, and that let community members have a say in setting the agenda, while still working within the framework of your organization.

Capacity building

Be careful not to underestimate the need for capacity building. Both you and the community need to be fully trained and equipped to facilitate workshops using participatory data collection methods. Inadequate support and training can lead to community apathy, frustration, and demotivation, making it difficult for you and the community to gather useful information for the study. Equally, capacity building activities should not assume that you, or community members, have no knowledge or experience to incorporate and build on.

Time commitments

Participatory data collection methods can be time-consuming. Even if a workshop takes no more than two hours, the preparations involved, and the transcription of workshop discussions, add significantly to the time spent on conducting research. For community members, volunteering time can be a challenge, and some members may feel overstretched and burdened by the process.

How to be a good facilitator

Facilitation is what distinguishes participatory data collection methods from more traditional research methods, for example where a researcher is asking questions that reflect his or her interests. By taking on the role of a facilitator, the researcher is handing over a level of power and control to the participants, enabling them to steer the process and become researchers of their own life situations. To achieve this, it is the role of the facilitator to do the following:

- *Introduce yourself and explain why you are there.*
- *Be transparent and open*: You need to gain the trust of the participants. One way to do this is to be open and transparent about your purpose and role in facilitating these activities.
- *Show interest*: Another way to gain their trust is to show a genuine interest in their life situations. Be prepared, committed, and interested.
- *Establish ground rules*: Work with the participants to establish ground rules, which include respecting diverse opinions, confidentiality, timekeeping, and active participation.
- *Be clear in your instructions*: Explain the methods very carefully and make sure that all participants know how to use them as well as their relevance.
- *Support the participatory process*: This involves not being too focused on the content and the specific output (such as a community map and transcripts of discussions), but being concerned with the process and how this contributes to learning. Let the participants take an active role and be careful not to impose your own ideas.
- *Understand your participants*: Constantly assess the dynamics of the group and the role of power in shaping these. Also be aware of group members' different abilities and use methods that fit all skill sets and comfort levels. For example, you may use the methods slightly differently depending

on whether you are working with children or adults. Most participatory methods can be made child friendly.

- *Be flexible*: Adapt the methods to match your understanding of the participants and the context. Use local materials where possible. Expect things to go differently from planned. Be prepared to interpret a situation and adapt tools on the spot to match the varied abilities of participants and directions of discussions.
- *Be inclusive*: Make sure that even the most marginalized community members are given the opportunity to participate in and contribute to the study – this includes children.
- *Be aware of the dynamics of the participants and the non-participants* and the impact these can have on the activity and its outcomes.
- *Build trust between participants*: If the participants come from all walks of life, you need to build trust between them. This can be done through icebreakers and trust-building activities.
- *Recognize local resources*: The participants are more likely to feel involved and motivated to participate if you build on existing knowledge, skills, and assets within the community.

Your aim is to facilitate participation data collection workshops in a way that transcends power hierarchies and conflicting values and knowledge systems, and to ensure that people successfully work together to generate new knowledge. This requires good interpersonal and cross-cultural communication skills.

- *Be an engaged and active listener*: Listening is not just about hearing what someone says, it is also about showing them that you hear and understand what is being said. You can do so using your body, for example by sitting in front of the person speaking and looking at them. Avoid sitting with crossed arms, but nod your head in response to what is being said. Facial expressions, such as smiling or showing surprise or sadness, can also help the speaker see that you are listening. Verbal prompts of encouragement ('Ah', 'Mmm', 'I see', and so on) can also be helpful. Remove all possible distractions such as screens, phones, and other activities that might distract from or disturb the discussion.
- *Be inquisitive and ask effective questions*: You can help facilitate learning and reflection within a community by continually asking questions that can explain the why, when, where, who, what, and how of an issue that manifests itself in a community. You can ask the participants for concrete examples to illustrate their arguments or to expand and explain their points further. By asking questions you also convey an interest in the person who is speaking. Refrain from doing much talking yourself – this includes expressing your own ideas, which might bias the discussion.
- *Allow for silence*: Sometimes with shy or nervous people or groups unfamiliar with group activities, it can take time to get the group talking. Sometimes an icebreaker can help, but silences can also push people to start discussions.

- *Be patient and relaxed*: Participants are more likely to take an active role in the research if they feel there is room for trial and error. This requires you to be relaxed and not too rigid about meeting deadlines or following protocols.
- *Be tolerant and open to new ideas*: Diverse views and opinions will be shared only if participants feel that everyone, including the facilitator, respects different viewpoints. Even if you disagree with what is being said, respect that other people have this view and treat it like any other viewpoint being expressed.
- *Be aware of your own bias and how your experiences and beliefs will influence your interpretation of certain situations*: This is also known as 'reflexivity', which is when the researcher has a self-awareness of the impact that their own beliefs and experiences have on their interpretations of the data. It is important to keep this in check, especially if the issues being discussed confront or are at odds with your own beliefs.

Being a facilitator of participatory data collection methods is arguably not for everyone. It requires you to observe, interpret, and facilitate human interactions on the spot, all in the spirit of facilitating learning, and generating information in a participatory manner. The more prepared you are, the more time and energy you will have to be a 'good' facilitator. So although you cannot plan for every eventuality, it is very important that you plan guidelines for each of the methods you anticipate using, as well as setting out details about their sequence. To aid your planning, you may consider these points:

- *Time and resources*: It is important for you to be realistic about what can be achieved with the time and budget available. Plan ahead with the assumption that the process will take longer and cost more than originally expected. Focus on 'need to know' versus 'nice to know' if you are short of time.
- *Skills of the facilitator*: When identifying a facilitator, whether it is yourself or a colleague, make sure that they have the attitudes and behaviours discussed above. You may need to arrange for the facilitator to be trained.
- *Trained and neutral translator*: If you are working in a multilingual setting and require translation, it is important that you identify a trained and neutral translator who directly translates, not interprets. A lot can be lost in translation, either during discussions or in the writing up and analysis stages.
- *Purpose of the study*: The research question should guide the planning process. Break up the research question into smaller objectives. When information gathered from each of the objectives is combined, you will be in a position to answer the research question. These smaller objectives can help you identify appropriate methods, as well as who to involve.

- *What participatory methods to use*: Familiarize yourself with a large number of participatory data collection methods (see Box 5.1 for resources). Identify methods that would be appropriate for exploring each of your objectives.
- *Develop guidance notes*: Once you have identified the methods you will use to generate information that can answer your research question, develop guidance notes for each of the methods. These notes should include a schedule of the session and should specify roles and responsibilities, materials needed, and time spent on each activity, as well as listing step-by-step instructions.
- *Data capture and storage*: Think about how each of the methods can be used to generate data. Make plans for this data to be captured and stored in a safe place. We discuss this in more detail below.
- *Research ethics and child safeguarding*: As with any type of research, lead facilitators need to be sensitive to risk and keep participants safe. You need to obtain informed consent and ensure confidentiality, as well as encourage all participants to keep the discussions confidential. If you are working with children, you also need to put in place child safeguarding mechanisms, such as never letting an adult facilitator be alone with the children (see Chapter 2 for more detail).

Data capture and management

Throughout this chapter we have stressed the importance of capturing the information that is generated as a result of the participatory data collection methods. The reason for this is that good qualitative research is able to account for the ways in which certain findings and arguments emerge. As a qualitative researcher, you need to demonstrate how you come to a particular conclusion. A first and important step in achieving this is to capture what is being said and what is being observed by the research team.

While it is easy to record and transcribe an interview between two people, it is much more challenging to capture the discussions between a group of people. Given the many roles and responsibilities of the facilitator, it is therefore recommended that each session also has a recorder. This is a person

---

Activity 5.2 What makes a good facilitator?

Through body mapping, this activity encourages you to think about what skills, knowledge, attitudes, and behaviours a good facilitator should have, or not have.

1. Draw a silhouette of a body.
2. Use the body illustration as a metaphor to map out the skills, knowledge, attitudes, and behaviours a participatory, learning, and action facilitator needs (taking inspiration from the body map illustrated in Figure 5.2). You could write down the knowledge, attitudes, and behaviours of a good facilitator on the left side of the body, and those of a poor facilitator on the right side of the body.

Feedback is available at the end of the chapter.

who observes, takes notes, and manages all the information gathered. More specifically, it is the role of the **recorder** to:

- capture everything that is being said – this is best achieved through audio or video recording of the sessions, but if this is not possible, the recorder has to write down in as much detail as possible what is being said;
- write down the details of the participants (age, gender, ethnicity, employment status, and so forth);
- obtain informed consent for the recorded data to be used in a study;
- take notes regarding the physical and social environment where the session takes place, human behaviour and interaction, use of language, and non-verbal communication, such as how adults and children or men and women interact;
- take pictures or video film of what is happening – for the purpose of backup, storage, and data analysis, it is important that the recorder takes a picture of each visual output (for example, a community map or a problem tree);
- write down reflections and interpretations of what is being observed (while maintaining a degree of reflexivity); and
- make sure that all the data produced from the process is kept somewhere safe – the participants may require a box with a lock to store all their visual outputs and notes, while the recorder may need a password-protected computer or USB device to safely store images, transcripts of recorded discussions or handwritten reflections, digital audio or video files, notes of observations, and scanned copies of the consent forms.

These efforts to capture local reflections and discussions, as well as the process where participants narrow down their thoughts and register the most important ones in a diagram, provide you with tangible data that can be looked at and analysed at a later stage. In fact, the visual outputs that participatory data collection methods produce make up an important first step in data analysis. They also offer you an important indication of what the participants perceive to be key findings and would like the focus of the study to be. As a researcher engaging with participatory methods, you have a responsibility to honour this focus in your continued analysis. However, this does not mean that you cannot identify new themes or report on other findings.

Summary

This chapter has introduced you to participatory research, covering the background and rationale for this approach to research, as well as some practical methods that you can use to both facilitate learning among your participants and obtain data for your study. The chapter has also explained what it takes to be a good participatory researcher, or facilitator of participatory data collection methods. This includes an awareness of the potential pitfalls in using participatory data collection methods, as well as skills and behaviours that can nurture the participatory process. Finally, the chapter has discussed some of the ways in which you can capture data generated from qualitative participatory methods.

Endnote

1. A score of 0 should not be given as this would imply no participation at all. There will always be some level of participation, however narrow it may be.

References

Baatiema, L., Skovdal, M., Rifkin, S. and Campbell, C. (2013) 'Assessing participation in a community-based health planning and services programme in Ghana', *BMC Health Services Research* 13 (1): 233.

Chambers, R. (1994) 'Participatory rural appraisal (PRA): analysis of experience', *World Development* 22 (9): 1253–68.

Chambers, R. (1997) *Whose Reality Counts?: Putting the First Last,* London: Intermediate Technology.

Chukwudozie, O., Feinstein, C., Jensen, C., O'Kane, C., Pina, S., Skovdal, M. and Smith, R. (2015) 'Applying community-based participatory research to better understand and improve kinship care practices: insights from the Democratic Republic of Congo, Nigeria, and Sierra Leone', *Family and Community Health* 38 (1): 108–19.

Cooke, B. and Kothari, U. (2001) *Participation, the New Tyranny?,* London: Zed Books.

Dart, J. and Davies, R. (2003) 'A dialogical, story-based evaluation tool: the most significant change technique', *American Journal of Evaluation* 24 (2): 137–55, doi: 10.1177/109821400302400202.

Fraser, H. (2005) 'Four different approaches to community participation', *Community Development Journal* 40 (3): 286–300.

Freire, P. (1973) *Education for Critical Consciousness,* New York NY: Seabury Press.

Howarth, C. (2001) 'Towards a social psychology of community: a social representations perspective', *Journal for the Theory of Social Behaviour 31* (2): 223–38.

International HIV/AIDS Alliance (2006) *Tools Together Now: 100 Participatory Tools to Mobilise Communities for HIV/AIDS,* Brighton: International HIV/ AIDS Alliance, <www.aidsalliance.org/assets/000/000/370/229-Tools-together-now_original.pdf> [accessed 30 July 2015].

Lewin, K. (1946) 'Action research and minority problems', *Journal of Social Issues* 2 (4): 34–46.

Minkler, M. and Wallerstein, N. (2003) 'Introduction to community based participatory research', in M. Minkler, N. Wallerstein and B. Hall (eds), *Community-based Participatory Research for Health,* pp. 3–26, San Francisco CA: Jossey-Bass Wiley.

Moser, C. (1998) 'The asset vulnerability framework: reassessing urban poverty reduction strategies', *World Development* 26 (1): 1–19.

Newman, K. and Beardon, H. (2011) 'How wide are the ripples?: From local participation to international organisational learning', *Participatory Learning and Action* 63: 11–18.

Rifkin, S. and Pridmore, P. (2001) *Partners in Planning: Information, Participation and Empowerment*, London: TALC and Macmillan Education.

Skovdal, M. and Campbell, C. (2010) 'Orphan competent communities: a framework for community analysis and action', *Vulnerable Children and Youth Studies* 5 (S1): 19–30.

Wallerstein, N. and Duran, B. (2003) 'The Conceptual, Historical, and Practice Roots of Community Based Participatory Research and Related Participatory Traditions', in M. Minkler, N. Wallerstein and B. Hall (eds), *Community-based Participatory Research for Health*, pp. 27–51, San Francisco CA: Jossey-Bass Wiley.

Feedback on activities

Feedback on Activity 5.1 Reflecting on the diversity of communities

Your examples will show how diverse communities are, how they overlap, and perhaps even how they influence behaviour.

Feedback on Activity 5.2 What makes a good facilitator?

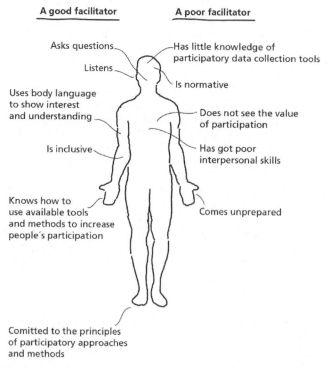

Figure 5.8 Body map illustrating the characteristics of a good or poor participatory research facilitator

CHAPTER 6
Photovoice: methodology and use

Abstract

This chapter describes how development practitioners can use Photovoice to improve development and humanitarian responses. It offers 10-step guidance in how to plan and design a Photovoice project. Photovoice is a participatory research method that enables community members to photographically capture and depict their perceptions of community life and the local conditions that affect their lives, or a programme. The method actively encourages participants to use the photographs to share their perspectives on community life, through either written or spoken narratives about the significance of their pictures. Photovoice is accessible to people of most ages and abilities and can be a fun and engaging activity, facilitating communication across cultural and linguistic barriers, as well as power hierarchies.

Keywords: Photography; Photovoice; advocacy; participatory research; qualitative research

Learning objectives

After reading this chapter, you will be able to:

- give a detailed explanation of what Photovoice is and its background;
- outline the advantages and disadvantages of using Photovoice;
- develop a plan for implementing Photovoice; and
- conduct qualitative research using Photovoice.

Key terms (definitions)

- *Photovoice*: A methodology that enables people to identify, represent, and enhance their community and life circumstances through photography.
- *Community-based participatory research*: An approach to research that enables participants to gather information, reflect upon it, and use this as an opportunity to instigate some level of action.

Introduction to Photovoice

Photovoice is a community-based participatory research method that was developed by Caroline Wang and colleagues in the 1990s (Wang and Burris,

http://dx.doi.org/10.3362/9781780448534.006

1997; Wang et al., 1998). Photovoice involves handing out cameras to a group of people and encouraging them to tell their stories through photography, capturing their impressions and perspectives on an issue. They can be encouraged to capture stories about a health issue, their life circumstances, or a programme. However, the images should not stand alone, but should either be complemented with a written or spoken story explaining the significance and meaning of the picture, or be used to spark discussions about the pictures within a group of people.

As the pictures are taken by community members themselves, Photovoice provides participants with a level of control over what they want to share, and the stories that are told. The participants set the agenda for the storytelling or discussion, enabling them to become researchers of their own lives and communities.

Pictures, combined with personal testimonies, can have a powerful effect on people who view them. They can bring to the fore hidden or silenced voices. They help to make issues real to others by illustrating concrete concerns and solutions. Pictures can effectively transcend cultural barriers and power hierarchies and instigate emotional reactions that may lead to change. Photovoice therefore provides an excellent opportunity for community members to reach out to more powerful stakeholders, such as development practitioners, policy makers, and government officials, and advocate for change (Pies and Parthasarathy, 2007). This is aided by the fact that Photovoice is often initiated by external actors who may have an interest in getting a glimpse into how community members view their community or the life circumstances that they find themselves in, and may effectively be more responsive to the stories that emerge from the Photovoice project.

Photovoice has become a very popular research method and is enthusiastically used by a countless number of development practitioners, health professionals, and researchers around the world. The value of Photovoice as a means of engaging marginalized groups has long been recognized. Not only are the photographs and stories important sources of information, the process of capturing, discussing, and sharing the images provides great benefits. Research suggests that the process of Photovoice can contribute to the self-development of the participants by fostering recognition of the need for change, improved self-awareness of local circumstances, and personal worthiness and confidence, as well as awareness of social resources and problem-solving abilities (Castleden et al., 2008; Skovdal, 2011; Teti et al., 2013). In other words, the Photovoice process has the potential to be empowering for participants. This, coupled with a focus on advocacy and change, is what sets Photovoice apart from other photography-driven research methods. Wang and Burris (1997: 370) summarize Photovoice as having three goals:

- to enable people to record and reflect their community strengths and concerns;

- to promote critical dialogue and knowledge about important issues through large and small group discussions of photographs; and
- to reach policy makers.

The use of photographs taken by the study participants to generate learning and instigate change is what makes Photovoice a valuable addition to more traditional qualitative data collection methods. The social justice intent of Photovoice makes it a particularly valuable research tool for development practitioners working with monitoring, evaluation, accountability, and learning (MEAL), policy, and advocacy.

Since Photovoice was first used among women in China's rural Yunnan province (Wang and Burris, 1997), the method has been used for a variety of different purposes, involving both adults and children. These include:

- to **engage youth** in community needs assessments (Stack et al., 2004);
- to **involve community members** in community health assessments (Wang and Pies, 2004);
- to **promote critical awareness** and active grassroots participation (Carlson et al., 2006);
- to **identify the coping strategies** of children living in difficult circumstances (Skovdal et al., 2009; Skovdal, 2011);
- to **explore women's experiences** of breast cancer (Poudrier and Mac-Lean, 2009);
- to **explore how minority groups view themselves** (Graziano, 2004);
- to **promote women's empowerment** (Duffy, 2011);
- to **learn from the experiences of children** who are orphaned and living with HIV in a Ugandan group home (Fournier et al., 2014);
- to **involve community residents in the evaluation** of a community health initiative in the US (Kramer et al., 2013);
- to identify and **understand environmental characteristics** associated with tobacco use among young people in the US (Tanjasiri et al., 2011);
- to **identify solutions** to local problems (Downey et al., 2009)
- as an **intervention to reduce self-stigma** and enhance proactive coping with prejudice and discrimination among people with mental illnesses (Russinova et al., 2014); and
- to **promote more health-enabling behaviour** among young people (Short, 2006).

In Chapter 5 we discussed the contributing role of Brazilian educator Paulo Freire (1973) in shaping and promoting the use of participatory data collection methods. Freire argues that it is through a process of learning and raising self-awareness that poor and marginalized people gain the confidence to challenge the structures and systems that contribute to their marginalization. Photovoice translates these principles into practice.

Take, for example, a class of schoolchildren who under normal circumstances may not get the opportunity to collectively and critically reflect on factors that influence their daily lives and advocate for change. If you invite them to participate in a Photovoice project, through images they can capture, highlight, and reflect on the dangers of walking or cycling to school. This may be due to heavy traffic on roads with no pedestrian walkways, or crossing roads without traffic lights. They can collectively identify key dangers and present their pictures and stories to local leaders, who may decide to invest in changes to the infrastructure, such as installing walkway bridges or traffic lights to minimize the danger of travelling to school.

Photovoice in the programme cycle

Photovoice projects can be delivered and facilitated at any stage of the programme cycle.

At the *planning stage*, Photovoice can be used by community members (adults as well as children) to capture the issues that affect them and to develop a more contextual understanding of the context in which a programme is embedded. In addition to understanding the issues that affect community members, this might include an analysis of their coping strategies, giving us an insight into the innate resources and support structures that you can build on and strengthen through a programme. Using Photovoice to gather community voices at the planning stage can help ensure that a programme targets people's articulated needs and resonates with their lived realities (Skovdal et al., 2014).

During the *implementation stage*, Photovoice can be used as a monitoring and formative evaluation tool to understand and map out the different contextual and operational factors that contribute to programme success or failure, highlighting important programmatic lessons that can inform changes to current or future programming. For example, Photovoice can provide community members with an opportunity to depict and communicate any potential unintended consequences of a programme. The implementing agency can use this information to make improvements to the programme. Photovoice can also be used to understand what facilitates programme success, encouraging the implementing agency to do more of 'what works'.

At the *evaluation stage*, cameras can be handed out to community members with an invitation to capture stories of change. These stories may carry more or less significance and can illustrate both positive and negative changes. The important thing is that the change stories reflect locally perceived changes as a result of a programme, which may, or may not, reflect expected outcomes. In addition to looking at perceived changes, Photovoice can also be used to gather community perspectives on programme strengths and limitations at the evaluation stage, contributing to an understanding of the factors that enabled or prohibited programme impact.

Planning and design

Photovoice is a demanding research process, requiring significant time and resource commitments. Facilitators also need to exhibit a variety of interpersonal skills and have in-depth knowledge of Photovoice. While this chapter cannot impart interpersonal skills, it can provide an in-depth understanding of Photovoice and an insight into the requirements of a facilitator.

To set up a Photovoice project that is feasible in a given context, there are a number of things to consider. In this expanded section we: 1) outline some of the questions you need to ask yourself early on in the inception phase; 2) discuss different aspects of the planning process. The section is followed by 10-step guidance on how to implement a Photovoice project. These two sections are inspired by Blackman and Fairey's (2007) excellent *The PhotoVoice Manual* and build on previous guidance notes described by Skovdal and colleagues (2014) for Save the Children.

Questions to consider

Before you start any planning, you ought to consider the following questions:

What is the purpose of the Photovoice project? What is the research question it seeks to shed some light on? As with any research method, Photovoice requires you to be clear about its purpose from the onset. At what stage in the programme cycle do you intend to use Photovoice and for what purpose? Is it to engage children and youth, and use their voices to inform the development of a programme? Or do you want to use Photovoice to generate insight and evidence about a programme? Clarity around the purpose of the Photovoice project will help you clarify how much of a social justice intent you need to work towards and will help you identify an appropriate team for facilitating the project.

Where will funding come from? Given the time and staff intensity of facilitating a Photovoice project, consideration of the cost may determine the scope of the project. It is therefore important that you are realistic about what resources, both staff time and money, you require to facilitate the project. It is recommended that you develop a budget at the inception phase. This should consider your equipment needs, travel, human resources, plans for dissemination, and a generous contingency. This will help you determine whether funding needs to come from internal or external funds, or a mix of the two.

How much time is required? There are no fixed rules regarding the ideal length of a Photovoice project. Photovoice projects can last from anywhere between a day and a year, or even more. It ultimately depends on how you design the project. To determine the length of your planned Photovoice project you need to consider how much time you, and the participants, are able to commit or think you will need to capture their stories.

Some stories may be easy to capture, whereas other stories require more reflection, or rely on particular or shifting seasons. In some circumstances, it may suffice to give the participants a week to capture their stories. In other circumstances, it may be beneficial to have the participants come together in a workshop to reflect on their photographs, and to use this as an opportunity for them to return to their communities and take more deliberative photographs (Castleden et al., 2008). Using Photovoice this way, and over a longer period of time, is supported by Vaughan (2014), who argues that reflection and critical thinking develop over time – and that it takes time to develop the group relationships that can support action and effective dissemination to address the issues identified through photography. *Who should you partner with?* The success of a Photovoice project relies partly on the involvement of key stakeholders and partners. These stakeholders may include:

- *Senior management*: Given the high resource intensity of Photovoice projects, it is important that senior management within your organization supports and recognizes the potential of Photovoice. So make sure they are on board from the outset.
- *Experienced facilitators*: A Photovoice project can succeed or fail depending on its facilitator(s). Please see Chapter 5 for a discussion on what it takes to be a good facilitator. While you may be able to facilitate the process yourself, or at least parts of it, you may also recognize when someone else may be better suited to the role. In that case, you can reach out to colleagues or external facilitators who have expertise and previous experience of facilitating participatory workshops – or, better yet, Photovoice.
- *Local organizations*: It is advisable that the project is implemented in partnership with a local organization. The organization can serve as a gatekeeper to the participants and can help you make sure that the project is implemented in a way that is sensitive to local ways of working. A local organization can also help sensitize the broader community to the project, as well as support the dissemination of findings.
- *Local government departments*: By partnering with local government departments you can attract their attention and help ensure that local voices are listened to. Conducting a Photovoice project with local government departments increases the likelihood that the research findings will result in change at a service delivery and policy level.

How will findings be disseminated? As giving voice to community members is at the core of Photovoice, it is important from the outset to think about who the target audience should be. You can do so from a research, advocacy, or community development perspective.

- *Research audience*: The findings of the Photovoice project have research merit and can offer insight and evidence on a number of issues of interest to academics and policy and decision makers.

- *Advocacy audience*: The images and their captions provide powerful stories that can help service providers better understand the life circumstances of community members at a local level and initiate changes accordingly. At a global advocacy level, the photographs can draw attention to social injustice and help advocate for structural change.
- *Community members themselves*: Photovoice helps community members identify and represent certain aspects of community life. It is a process that instigates learning about the socio-economic structures and socio-cultural factors that have an impact on their lives. Photographs and stories discussed at a community level can help community members see how they are part of both the problems identified and the solutions.

Once you have identified who your target audiences are, you can begin to develop a dissemination strategy that describes: 1) how you plan to engage with the different actors; 2) the media you will use to help facilitate the dissemination of findings; 3) the desired reach and social change you would like to see come out of this process.

Once you have considered the above questions, you are an important step closer to knowing whether you can, or should, proceed with the planning of your Photovoice project.

Specifying the aim of your project

An important first step in the planning of a Photovoice project is to translate the purpose that has been guiding your interest up to now into a set of concrete aims and objectives. Aims are meant to 'paint a picture' of what the Photovoice project is looking to achieve. They are often broad statements that describe either your intentions or the desired outcome. Examples of aims include the following:

- To give local community members a *voice* about a healthcare reform.
- To explore women's *perspectives* of local maternal and child health services.
- To explore the *role of Photovoice* in facilitating children's participation in needs assessments.

These three aims are merely illustrative of some of the different ways in which an aim can be phrased in order to stress a purpose. The first aim seeks to give community members a voice. This is highly relevant if you want to conduct Photovoice with a group of people who are ordinarily silenced and have little to say about decisions that affect them. This aim is particularly relevant if your target audience will be advocates and policy makers. The second aim stresses the importance of gathering the perspectives of a particular group of people on a particular subject. Such an aim may be relevant if your purpose is to engage with academics and policy makers. The third aim is relevant if you are looking to explore the role of Photovoice, as a method, in generating information used for a particular purpose, which in this case is needs assessments.

Objectives, on the other hand, are meant to reflect intentions that can help you meet the aim of the project. It is helpful if the objectives are specific, measurable, appropriate/achievable, relevant/realistic, and time bound (SMART). Objectives may include those listed below:

- To develop partnerships that link community members with more powerful actors.
- To develop the photography skills of participants.
- To establish an exhibition of photographs and stories.
- To develop training tools and guidance for future Photovoice projects.

With your aims and objectives set out, you are ready to establish a team of people who can help you implement the project.

Setting up a team

You cannot set up a Photovoice project on your own. You will need to bring together teams of people and harness their different skill sets. This requires you to have a good overview of what capacity and skills are required and to have access to networks of people whom you can invite and draw on. Depending on the scale of your project, and on whether it involves programme- or issue-focused research, you might consider setting up different teams with specific objectives.

An advisory team.   This team would consist of a collection of people who have particular sets of skills and know-how that you can draw on to inform the development and design of the project. They may include experts on the issue or programme under investigation, researchers with previous experience, or local decision makers. Advisory teams can be set up at local, regional, and national levels.

A project team.   The project team takes the overall responsibility for the design and implementation of the project. Tasks can be delegated to sub-teams who may be responsible for design, logistics, community engagement, ethics, and facilitation.

An advocacy and dissemination team.   This team would be charged with the responsibility of ensuring that the project communicates the voices and perspectives of participants to the intended audiences and meets its social justice intent. If you work for a larger organization, this team can bring together colleagues from advocacy, communications, monitoring and evaluation, and report writing departments.

Irrespective of what teams you set up, it is important that the teams include representation from the participant group, including children, if they are involved in the programme.

Selecting participants and a setting

There is no hard and fixed rule on how to select participants for a Photovoice project. In fact, you can select participants in many different ways. What is important is that the people who participate have expressed an interest to be involved and reflect criteria that define the target group set out in your aims and objectives.

If many people matching your criteria have expressed an interest in participating, you can use different strategies to narrow down the number of participants. These might include one or more of the following:

Random sampling.   If you have a list of 100 people who have expressed an interest in getting involved, you can roll a dice and select every second, third, or fourth name on the list, depending on the number of dots you get, until you have a number of participants you can feasibly work with.

Purposeful sampling.   You can also select participants purposefully, either out of convenience, such as selecting participants who live in close proximity to where the project will take place, or because you want to learn something that requires you to purposefully select participants based on their background. For example, you may want to include participants who represent either extreme or typical cases or meet a particular criterion you have set. If, on the other hand, you struggle to identify potential participants, you can ask local stakeholders or other participants if they can recommend others to participate. This is also referred to as snowball sampling.

Stratified sampling.   Again, if too many people have expressed an interest in taking part, you can select participants based, for example, on their demographic characteristics. This is relevant if you want to compare and contrast the responses and images of different target groups, such boys or girls, or community members from different communities.

Whichever sampling strategy you use, it is recommended that you work with local partner organizations in the recruitment of participants. Their knowledge of the local setting can ensure that you identify and engage with participants in a way that is culturally appropriate. You can also recruit through educational establishments, sports associations, or community-based and faith-based organizations, to mention just a few options.

You might wonder how many participants you should look to recruit. This very much depends on your project objectives, the budget, and the staff time available to you, but 10 to 20 people is typically an ideal size. Of course, more people can participate. As Photovoice can take up a lot of time, expect some participants to drop out during the process. Keep that in mind when you recruit participants.

Ethical considerations

Photovoice is an ethical minefield. The public nature of photography infringes the privacy and anonymity of people who may appear on the photograph, and it makes it difficult for the photographer to keep the location anonymous (Harley, 2012; Wang and Redwood-Jones, 2001). As such, a number of ethical considerations need to be made. These include, but are not limited to, those listed below:

- *Private space*: Take care not to enter into someone's private space without permission or consideration of what this may mean to them. This includes not taking a picture of a person, or entering someone's home to take a picture, without permission. It also includes being aware of how community members will react to having people walking around and documenting their community through photography.
- *Embarrassing facts*: Take care not to disclose embarrassing facts about anyone or any community location. This includes not taking photographs of someone doing something that may incriminate them (for example, someone smoking a cigarette in a no smoking area) or if they are in a compromised position (for example, sick and bedridden).
- *Misrepresentation*: Be mindful about not giving the 'models' – those who consent to appear in a photograph – a false or incomplete impression of how the image will be used.

So what can be done to overcome some of these ethical dilemmas?

- *Training on ethics*: Those facilitating Photovoice need to be attuned to the ethical dilemmas of using this method and be in a position to adequately guide the participants in ways of working that can minimize ethical risks. This can be done through workshops that help the participants reflect on the specific ethical dilemmas of using Photovoice in their setting and on the ways in which they can overcome these challenges.
- *Being flexible and responsive*: Photovoice is flexible and is open for creative and alternative solutions to ethical dilemmas. If, for example, the participants want to tell a story that involves a picture of someone doing something incriminating, or someone in a compromised position, they can be encouraged to draw a picture instead. This way, an important story can be told without capturing it in a photograph.
- *Accountability and transparency*: Given the public nature of photography, the public space becomes a subject of Photovoice research. It is therefore important that those moving around or living in that space are informed about the Photovoice project and invited into a dialogue about the project, its participants, and its activities. This is an opportunity not only for you to disclose the aims and objectives of the project to the wider community, but for everyone to discuss potential ethical dilemmas and how best to overcome them. These discussions are important for the safety of the Photovoice participants (see Box 6.1).
- *Safety*: To safeguard the welfare of the Photovoice participants, it is important to conduct a risk assessment that maps out all the potential

risks associated with participation. In the process of planning and implementing the project you can take steps to mitigate risks. It is also important that you fully disclose the risks you have identified to the participants before they agree to take part. This leads us to informed consent.

- *Informed consent*: Obtaining informed consent is a key measure to address some of the ethical dilemmas that arise from conducting research. Blackman and Fairey (2007) have recommend three different types of consent forms in a Photovoice project.

1. *Informed consent from Photovoice participants*: This form discloses the aim, objectives, and potential risks and benefits of participation, as well as stating that participants have the right to withdraw from the project at any point they wish. The form should also guarantee confidentiality and anonymity where possible. Once the project has been fully explained, as well as their rights and responsibilities, written or oral consent can be sought. If the participants are under the age of 18, additional consent should be sought from their guardians.

Box 6.1 Example of accountability and transparency in a Photovoice project

Save the Children in Bangladesh used Photovoice to involve children in a needs assessment for a hunger and livelihoods programme in rural Bangladesh. Through community meetings it was agreed that children were to be equipped with T-shirts with a camera printed on them, a cap, an ID card, and/or a research bag that carried the logo of Save the Children. It was also agreed that the participants should carry information sheets giving details about the Photovoice project and its aims and objectives, which they could then distribute to people as they walked around the community.

Figure 6.1 Bangladeshi children participating in a Photovoice project
Source: Tanvir Ahmed/Save the Children Bangladesh

2. *Informed consent from 'models'*: This form constitutes an agreement between the Photovoice participant (the photographer) and the person(s) who appear in the photograph (the 'models'). The agreement seeks permission from the 'model' to take their picture and use it for a particular and declared purpose. The form is required if one or two individuals can be clearly identified in the photograph; if a picture is taken inside someone's home; or if the pictures are documenting the life of an individual. For many Photovoice participants, 'model' consent is particularly difficult to negotiate. Different strategies to obtain or avoid 'model' consent may arise from consultation with the wider community. It could include refraining from taking pictures of people, obtaining collective community permission to take pictures, or Photovoice participants staging scenarios and taking pictures of each other.

3. *Photo release consent*: This third and final form is primarily used to give permission to the project to use the photographs for the purpose of research and advocacy. It is a form that clarifies copyrights and whether the participant's real name or a pseudonym will be used to credit the photographs. The form also acts as a backup to fully disclose the purpose and use of the photograph to both the photographer and the 'models'. This is particularly important if the photographs are likely to go on the internet or be used to advocate for a particular issue.

Activity 6.1 Ethical issues in a Photovoice project

Do you agree or disagree with the following statements?

1. It is possible to safeguard against all ethical dilemmas.
2. It is important to continually negotiate informed consent.
3. A Photovoice picture can be published in a newspaper.
4. 'Model' consent is required from an individual who appears in a photograph viewed from the back and who cannot be facially identified.

Feedback is available at the end of the chapter.

Workshop facilitation

The preceding section on ethics has underlined some of the skills that are required from a Photovoice facilitator. As Photovoice is about empowering participants to identify, represent, and enhance their community through photography, facilitators need to perform various roles. Facilitators need to be able to plan participatory workshops, promote equal participation in the workshops, and build a trusting and open environment for sharing (Rifkin and Pridmore, 2001). These roles require particular skills, knowledge, attitudes, and behaviours:

- knowledge of various participatory learning and action (PLA) tools and how to use them (see Chapter 5);
- knowledge of Photovoice, its aim, and objectives;
- an ability to work as part of a team;
- experience and skills in facilitating group discussions that enable everyone to participate, including children;
- the ability to ask questions effectively in a way that brings out local perspectives; and
- the ability to listen actively, both by using body language and facial expressions to show interest, and by analysing the information generated in the discussion on the spot to further spark discussion.

We have discussed these facilitation skills in greater detail in Chapter 5.

Delivering and facilitating Photovoice: 10 steps

So far, we have discussed some of the many things you need to consider before you start a Photovoice project. It may seem daunting at first, but please do not let this put you off. As explained earlier, there is no right or wrong way to implement Photovoice. Flexibility is important, not least so that you can tailor Photovoice to your context and target groups. This also gives you the chance to be creative and innovative, exploring new and different ways of using Photovoice. Although Photovoice projects can take different shapes and forms, there are some key elements and principles that would be good to follow. We will now outline 10 core steps for delivering and facilitating a Photovoice project, drawing on the experiences of a Photovoice project by Save the Children in Bangladesh (cf. Skovdal et al., 2014). Our aim is twofold: first, to provide you with inspiration for the planning of a Photovoice project; and second, to demystify the Photovoice process, giving you the confidence to believe that this is a tool you can use.

Step 1: Community sensitization and recruitment

In the spirit of accountability, an important first step in Photovoice is to sensitize the community where your Photovoice project will take place about your plans. Local community members need to be given relevant and clear information about the Photovoice project, including its intent, purpose, and scope. In addition to being accountable, there are a number of benefits from sensitizing the local community to a forthcoming Photovoice project. Firstly, it gives you an opportunity to introduce Photovoice to the wider community and get their authorization for participants to walk around in their community and take pictures. Secondly, the community can advise you on some of the ethical dilemmas of using Photovoice in this particular context. This may include discussions of what may be acceptable or unacceptable ways of taking photographs, and whether there are areas within the community that participants should avoid. Thirdly, it can provide you with an opportunity to identify participants in the project, either by recruiting participants from those who attend the community meeting (opportunistic sampling), or by having community members recommend and refer you to potential participants (snowball sampling).

The notion of 'community', of course, means different things in different contexts. Community can refer to anything from a geographical community to a group of people with shared interests or identity, or indeed a mix of these. You may not be able to gather the entire community, nor may this be necessary. If you anticipate that the participants will be moving around and taking pictures in a geographical community, a good starting point may be to reach out to local leaders in the community. Local leaders not only provide you with permission, but can advise you on who to invite to a community meeting about Photovoice. If, however, you are using Photovoice with a group of people in an organizational context, such as within a sports club, or in a hospital, you will need to reach out to people in the administration of these organizations.

Step 2: Introductions and establishing a safe social space

Once you have sensitized the community to the project, obtained permission from relevant authorities, and identified participants for the project, you are in a position to meet with the participants and get started. A first and important step is to introduce the participants to the project, providing them with all the relevant information they need to make an informed decision about whether they would like to continue with their participation. This involves a thorough introduction to Photovoice and the process you have planned and typically takes place in the first workshop that brings participants together. At this first workshop, participants and facilitators can also be introduced to each other. It is important that both participants and facilitators feel comfortable with each other and that a safe social space, based on mutual respect and rapport, is created for the Photovoice project in order to capture silent voices and hidden perspectives.

Establishing a safe social space where people are free to express themselves takes a bit of work. When you establish your facilitator team, you may want to include someone who has strong interpersonal skills and previous experience of facilitating group activities and fostering feelings of togetherness. This is particularly important if you are facilitating Photovoice with children. There are a number of exercises you can draw on to facilitate safe social spaces. Many of them seek to build trust and openness among group participants, as well as to nurture social skills and self-confidence. When you plan your activities, make sure that they are appropriate to the context, age, gender, and different abilities of your participants. Also choose activities that will develop interpersonal skills that will be relevant to the Photovoice project. For ideas and tips for rapport-building and icebreaker games, you can consult the 'A parrot on your shoulder?' resource developed by the International HIV/AIDS Alliance.[1]

Step 3: Formulating a research question

Once a safe and open environment has been created, you can start the process of helping the participants to think about issues that might be worth exploring using Photovoice. This is a process that has to be handled very carefully, both because the participants may have different interests, and because the project is funded and initiated by external change agents who have a particular interest. In an ideal world, both the external change agent (i.e. you and the organization you represent) and the participants would share a common agenda. However, this is rarely the case and you may find yourself facilitating a Photovoice project within the confines of the interests, values, and mandate of an organization or donor-funded programme. For example, if you facilitate a Photovoice project with funding from an education programme, this may limit the scope and determine the direction of your project, including the purpose of using Photovoice. For example, funding may dictate whether Photovoice should be used as a method to gather local voices about an issue (as part of a needs assessment, for instance) or a programme (perhaps as part of an evaluation).

Regardless of the agendas that may be at stake, it is important that all participants agree and recognize the value of the direction of the project and play an active role in refining, fine-tuning, and formulating a research question. It is important to be transparent about the scope of the project and its intended purpose. Although the scope may be limited, forcing the Photovoice project to look at a thematic area or with the purpose of evaluating a programme, there is still plenty of room for the Photovoice participants to take ownership of the project and refine the research question. Participatory methods (see Chapter 5) can be used to nudge the discussion of certain issues, which in turn can prompt the identification of knowledge gaps and help the participants recognize the importance of exploring certain issues through Photovoice. In other words, a facilitator needs to support a process whereby participants come to a consensus about the importance of studying a particular issue, and as a group agree on the research question.

In Chapter 2 we described in detail how you can go about formulating a research question. We explained that a good qualitative research question contains details about the issue that will be studied, where, and with whom. As such, a research question should not just specify what you are interested in studying; rather, it should help define the study and help set limits. Most importantly, it should be a question that can facilitate learning and generate insights into a topic, from a group of people in a particular location who are important to consider.

Here are three different examples of research questions for a Photovoice project:

- *What prevents men from using HIV services in Zimbabwe?*
  This research question implies that men in Zimbabwe are less likely to make use of HIV services compared with their female counterparts and

that it is important to find out why that is the case. Through Photo-voice, men can walk around the community and take pictures of some of the factors that prevent them from making use of HIV services. These pictures and accompanying stories can be used to inform the develop-ment of a programme looking to increase men's engagement with HIV services in Zimbabwe.

- *What do children perceive to be the most significant changes brought about by a cash transfer programme in western Kenya?*
  This research question could form part of an evaluation and reflects recognition of the importance of including children's perspectives. The question clarifies the topic (local perceptions and significant changes due to a cash transfer programme), who (children in communities tar-geted by the programme), and where (western Kenya) the study will take place.

- *How do programme staff characterize the internal and organizational factors that either inhibited or contributed to the successful implementation of a poverty reduction programme in Bangladesh?*
  Unlike the other two questions, which target community members, this question is interested in the views of staff involved with the imple-mentation of a programme. Akin to an after-action review, this research question invites programme staff to photographically capture lessons learned from programme successes and failures.

A research question can provide Photovoice participants with a sense of purpose. To operationalize the research question, and to provide the participants with a bit of guidance on how to answer the research question, it may be useful also to agree on a list of study objectives, which together can 'paint a picture' and offer some answers to the research question (see Chapter 2 for more detail).

Step 4: Speaking out through photography

Once a research question has been decided upon, it is time to discuss how best to answer this question by 'speaking out through photography' – capturing the issues of importance to the research question. One way to do this is to develop some notes or questions that can guide and focus the participants on issues of interest to the project. These guidance notes can be developed either by the project team or in close partnership with the project participants. The latter would be ideal, and so, if time and skills are available, it is recommended that you facilitate a process whereby the participants develop and agree on a set of questions that can guide their photography and storytelling so that the overall research question gets answered. If this is not possible, you can present small series of questions and invite the participants to either suggest changes or approve the guiding questions. Here are a couple of examples of questions that can guide the participants' photography.

If, for example, you are working with a group of disabled veterans in the UK and want to develop a programme that can help them cope with the new reality of being disabled, Photovoice can be used to explore the question: 'How do combat-injured British veterans cope with disability?' To answer this question in an exploratory way, guiding questions may include:

- What is your life like?
- What is good about your life?
- What makes you strong?
- What needs to change?

These general questions can help the veterans capture an array of factors that have an impact on their lives, both positively and negatively. Although these general guiding questions, when asked in the context of a clearly defined research question, may well be answered in relation to your thematic area and purpose, they enable the participants to go above and beyond what the project perceives to be relevant. This can be both a strength and a weakness.

If, for example, you work in the field of nutrition and maternal and child health and are looking to work with a group of malnourished women in India, Photovoice can be used to explore the question: 'What do Indian women perceive to be the main causes and effects of undernutrition during pregnancy and in the first two years of a child's life?' To answer this question in an exploratory way, guiding questions may include:

- What are 'good' and 'bad' foods for pregnant women and babies?
- What challenges do you face in accessing nutritious food?
- What are the causes and effects of these challenges?
- What helps you overcome some of these challenges?

When you develop the guiding questions, it is important that they do not predefine the issues, but are broad enough to allow the Photovoice participants to capture a range of factors they consider relevant. Once the guiding questions have been agreed upon by everyone involved in the project, arrangements can be made so that the participants have easy access to the questions during their fieldwork, for example by printing them on small stickers and attaching them to the back of the camera (if using disposable cameras).

Step 5: Introducing photography and the use of cameras

'Photography literacy' differs substantially across contexts and social groups. Whether you work in a context where older children and youth use camera phones to upload images on social media sites on a regular basis, or in a context where most children and adults have never held a camera in their hand, it is important that you tailor the Photovoice project to your participants. Photovoice is very adaptable and it is important that you recognize the 'photography literacy' and context of your participants and explore what opportunities this may give rise to. This may determine how you introduce Photovoice to your participants, the types of cameras to be used, and how photographs and stories are shared and communicated. Examples of types of cameras you might use include the following:

- *Disposable cameras* are inexpensive and may be useful if the security of the cameras cannot be assured. They are also useful in short-term projects where only a single roll of film is required. The drawback of disposable cameras is the picture quality, which tends to be inferior to that of other cameras. It is also important to note that it can be difficult to acquire disposable cameras in some developing country contexts.
- *Regular still cameras* share many of the same benefits of disposable cameras, but are easier to access. Regular still cameras also allow your participants to take several rolls of film.
- *Digital cameras* are more expensive but allow your participants to immediately review their pictures, supporting a process of reflection. This, coupled with the advances of digital photography, means that photographs taken with a digital camera tend to be of higher quality. If you plan to run a Photovoice project in another context, it is an investment worth considering.
- *Camera phones* share many of the same benefits of digital cameras and are readily available in some contexts. The benefit of using camera phones is that the participants almost always carry the camera around with them. It also means that you do not need to purchase cameras.

Irrespective of what camera is being used, a fourth step in implementing Photovoice is to facilitate workshops on photography. For example, a workshop can help the participants to:

- understand the different **functions of the camera**;
- know how to **use the camera** and take pictures – they may not know the benefits of looking through the lens or which button to press, or that some cameras need winding;
- be aware of key elements of **good photography** – such as what needs to be in the frame to capture the story, the composition of the picture, and holding the camera still – consider the role of light, lines, and movement, and make a deliberate choice about whether to take a landscape or a portrait photograph; and
- **practise** using the camera, both to learn from common mistakes and to explore different ways of taking 'good' pictures – to help the participants practise their photography skills you can prepare a 'picture treasure hunt', where you develop a list of items, shapes, colours, or feelings or expressions that participants are to capture through photography within a set period of time.

It is very important that the participants get an opportunity to discuss the power and ethics of camera use (see the section on ethical considerations). Such a discussion could be facilitated through the following questions:

- What is an acceptable way to approach someone to take their picture?
- Can you take pictures of other people without their knowledge?
- When would you not want to have your picture taken?
- Who might you wish to share the photographs with? And what might be the implications?

Such a discussion should lead to some 'ground rules' agreed by the Photovoice participants.

Step 6: Taking pictures

Once the Photovoice participants are motivated by the project's research question and feel equipped with guidance and skills on how to speak through photography, they are almost ready to enter the community with their cameras. However, before they go there must be an agreement on how long they have to take the pictures. Will they need half a day? A week? Two weeks? A month? Longer? If pictures are taken over a longer period, for example six months, will the participants meet on a regular basis – perhaps once a month – to deliberate and reflect on the photographs they have taken? Castleden and colleagues (2008) argue that such arrangements can lead to greater reflection and empowerment of the participants.

There is no single ideal duration. This very much depends on your approach and strategy. If the photographs serve the purpose of triangulating predefined themes, the pictures can possibly be taken in half a day. In most cases, however, the participants will need more time to capture the range of issues they would like to share with you and fellow Photovoice participants. If you are unsure, and not constrained by an institutional timeline, it is recommended that you ask the participants and get their opinion about how long they need to capture the 'issues at the heart of the project'.

Photovoice participants can adopt a variety of strategies to capture stories of interest to the project (Blackman and Fairey, 2007); this is related to 'speaking out through photography'. They can, for example:

- document their **own experiences** and life circumstances;
- develop a **photo documentary** of another child (a peer) or a family in which the Photovoice participants capture issues relevant to the project as they appear within a household;
- take the role of a **photojournalist** and walk around the community to capture the issues they find relevant to the project – they can do this either on their own or in groups, but the group strategy is useful if you have only a limited number of cameras;
- **stage a scenario** they want to show through photography – this may be a good option if the topic they want to capture is sensitive

and ethically problematic to capture 'in real life' (for example, sexual violence or drug use); and
- adopt a mixture of the above.

If Photovoice participants are unable to take a picture, either because the issue is sensitive or because they were unable to capture the issue within the given timeframe or season of the year, you can encourage participants to draw the situation.

Step 7: Story and caption development

The Photovoice participants are likely to return with a large number of photographs. If they were given regular still or disposable cameras, they may come back with rolls of film, ready to be developed. Equally, if they took photographs using digital cameras, they may come back with memory sticks or cards packed with digital photographs. Some of these photographs will be more relevant to the research question than others. You will therefore need to take the participants through a step-by-step process that systematically helps them identify the most interesting pictures and stories and those most relevant to the Photovoice project. Reflecting the work of Wang and Burris (1997) and Skovdal and colleagues (2009), you can adapt a version of the following process.

Ask the Photovoice participants to **choose six of their favourite photographs** that show something that is of relevance to the research question. These are the photographs they would like to include in the study. Again, here you can provide them with some guidance notes:

- General guidance notes: Choose six of your favourite photographs that show a mix of: 1) how you get by; 2) things you lack; 3) something or someone who is important to you.
- Guidance notes specific to a study on undernutrition: Choose six of your favourite photographs that show a mix of: 1) how undernutrition affects you; 2) causes of undernutrition; 3) something or someone that helps you access nutritious foods.

Once the participants have chosen the photographs they want to include in the study, you can provide them with the **opportunity to explain the significance of the photographs** they have chosen and their underlying meaning. This can be done in a number of different ways. Caroline Wang, the founder of Photovoice, has used the following two methods.

An easy and quick way of enabling participants to speak out on issues captured in their photographs is through writing. Reflection and story writing could be prompted by open-ended questions, such as:

- I want to share this photograph because...
- What's the real story this photograph tells?
- How does this story relate to your life and/or the lives of people in your community?

If any of your participants have inadequate literacy and writing skills, you can ask them to narrate their answers verbally and write the stories down for them. You can also facilitate group discussions or individual interviews, guided by the SHOWeD method (Wilson et al., 2007):

- What do you **S**ee here?
- What's really **H**appening here?
- How does this relate to **O**ur lives?
- **W**hy does this situation, concern, or strength exist?
- What can we **D**o about it?

These are just a couple of examples of how, in a structured and systematic way, you can facilitate reflection and support Photovoice participants to communicate the significance of their pictures and generate important qualitative data.

Step 8: Analysing stories and pictures

Traditionally, it is the researcher who carries out the analysis and interpretation of data. While there is still scope for the researcher to play a key role in the analysis and interpretation, for example by theorizing and relating emerging themes to the existing literature, it is the Photovoice participants who should identify those themes. In fact, Step 7, outlined above, constitutes an important analytical step in identifying key themes.

First, the process of selecting a handful of photographs encourages the participants to reflect on the significance of the photographs to the research question, and what they consider an important story to share. The participants effectively have the power and control to decide which photographs and stories they want to include, and which to exclude.

Second, the process of writing or narrating stories to accompany each of their chosen photographs ensures that the participants' interpretations of the images are brought to the fore. A number of commentators argue that image producers are the most appropriate people to interpret and communicate the meaning of their images – highlighting the importance of analysing images together with participant-generated descriptions (Campbell et al., 2010; Guillemin and Drew, 2010; Stanczak, 2007).

Each image and its accompanying description, whether written or spoken, represent qualitative data that can be thematically analysed. Many images are likely to relate to the same theme, but they can provide a different angle. As a researcher, you can either take these images and stories and group them together into higher-order themes, or facilitate a similar process with the participants, enabling them to identify the key themes emerging from the study. In Chapter 7, we describe in greater detail the process of condensing data into more interpretative themes. One way to facilitate this process relates to the next step: exhibition development. After the Photovoice participants have presented their images and stories to the rest of the group, you can ask them to identify the eight to 10 overarching themes that capture many of the emerging issues and that deserve a storyboard in an exhibition.

Step 9: Exhibition development

Disseminating and sharing the participants' images and stories is key to Photovoice – providing the participants with an all-important avenue and opportunity to voice their concerns and perspectives. To develop a strategy for showcasing the photographs and their accompanying reflections, a number of considerations will have to be covered (Blackman and Fairey, 2007). These include:

- being clear about who you are trying to reach – your **target audience**;
- being clear about how your target audience will be able to **access** your exhibition and how they will **react** to it;
- being clear about what **messages** you want to convey; and
- being clear about what **action** you are trying to prompt.

The target audience(s) will differ between contexts and will relate directly to your project goals. Examples of target audiences include those listed below:

- *Individuals in local communities*: Raising their awareness and understanding of the topic communicated, encouraging behaviour change.
- *Community leaders*: Helping them to understand what is important to their constituents and to get a better insight into their everyday lives and struggles.
- *Donors and the general public*: Improving awareness of the work of your organization.
- *Organizations and policy makers*: Informing them about what is important to your participants, in the hope that this can lead to policy change, new programmes, and the improved allocation of resources.

A Photovoice project can target a number of different audiences, but their ability to access the exhibition will differ. It is therefore important that you carefully consider what media are best suited for your target audiences. You can develop and share the photographs in many different ways. You could, for example:

- develop a set of **PowerPoint slides** where each slide contains a photograph and its reflection – the slides can be emailed around or used to present the findings in various forums;
- create a **video** and post it on various social media sites, including YouTube, showing snapshots of the photographs and their captions – you can find examples by searching 'Photovoice' on YouTube;
- take advantage of the various **social media** tools available for sharing pictures and ideas – internet sites such as Flickr, Prezi, SlideShare, Instagram, Pinterest, Facebook, and Twitter can all help to make voices heard;

- create **posters** that each convey a clear 'take-away' message – the posters could include photographs and their captions, and the Photovoice participants could glue pictures and their written reflections onto flipchart paper and exhibit their poster in a local community or religious building, for instance;
- create **leaflets** or **booklets** displaying the photographs and their captions – these resources can be shared on websites and in print;
- circulate a press statement or contact **media outlets**, making them aware of your project and asking them if they would be interested in featuring some of the images and their captions in print or in a slideshow on their website;
- develop and share one-page **policy briefs** that use images and their captions to summarize and communicate key messages from the Photovoice project;
- write an **academic article** giving details of the Photovoice process and key findings; and
- develop **exhibition** boards that clearly depict images and their captions.

Once it has been agreed with the Photovoice participants who to target, and how best to reach this audience, images and captions that should form part of the dissemination material can be identified. These images and stories should communicate their messages clearly and in a way that will encourage action. Some stories may be long and unsuitable for an exhibition or leaflet. If that is the case, you can, with the permission of the participant(s), shorten or extract parts of their reflections. It is also important that material that is sensitive or could put the photographer, or those who appear in the photograph, in any danger is not exhibited (Skovdal et al., 2014).

Step 10: Going public

One of the last steps is to make your dissemination material available to your target audience. How you go public depends on your primary medium. Through some media, such as social media, your exhibition material will go public the moment you upload it. For other media, such as posters and exhibition boards, you will have to distribute the posters or mount the boards. Whichever medium you use, you may wish to consider the following tips and ideas about going public:

- You can help **organize a meeting** and invite key stakeholders (your target audience) to come and have a look at the photographs and their accompanying reflections.
- You can help **organize a workshop** where your audiences, made up of both key stakeholders and the Photovoice participants, discuss the images and use the findings of the project as a platform to discuss and develop a plan of action for change.

- You can work with **key stakeholders to distribute** your marketing or advocacy material, whether it is leaflets, books, PowerPoint slides, in print or electronically.
- If possible, when you go public, try to **pitch and relate** the Photovoice material to other activities. For example, you could pitch your project and its messages to an international day (such as a day during the Child Rights Week, International Women's Day, or World AIDS Day), the publication of a high-level report, or a current and public debate. This, of course, depends on your topic and what other activities are happening.

Summary

This chapter has introduced you to a participant-generated visual methodology called Photovoice. It has underlined that a key characteristic of Photovoice is to give voice to community members, enabling them to learn from each other, reflect on their circumstances, and share their perspectives with more powerful actors. In many respects, Photovoice is not merely a research method but an approach to research that requires recognition of the moral imperative that drives the social justice goals of the method. At a practical level, the chapter has offered some more concrete guidance on how you can plan and design a Photovoice project, including 10 simple steps to deliver and facilitate a Photovoice project.

Endnote

1. This resource is available from the Save the Children Resource Centre at <http://resourcecentre.savethechildren.se/library/parrot-your-shoulder-guide-working-orphans-and-vulnerable-children> [accessed 29 July 2015].

References

Blackman, A., & Fairey, R. (2007) *The PhotoVoice Manual: A Guide to Designing and Running Participatory Photography Projects*, London: PhotoVoice, <www.photovoice.org/wp-content/uploads/2014/09/PV_Manual.pdf> [accessed 29 July 2015].

Campbell, C., Skovdal, M., Mupambireyi, Z. and Gregson, S. (2010) 'Exploring children's stigmatisation of AIDS-affected children in Zimbabwe through drawings and stories', *Social Science and Medicine* 71 (5): 975–85.

Carlson, E., Engebretson, J. and Chamberlain, R. (2006) 'Photovoice as a social process of critical consciousness', *Qualitative Health Research* 16 (6): 836–52.

Castleden, H., Garvin, T. and First Nation, H. (2008) 'Modifying Photovoice for community-based participatory indigenous research', *Social Science and Medicine* 66 (6): 1393–405.

Downey, L., Ireson, C. and Scutchfield, F. (2009) 'The use of Photovoice as a method of facilitating deliberation', *Health Promotion Practice* 10 (3): 419–27.

Duffy, L. (2011) '"Step-by-step we are stronger": women's empowerment through Photovoice', *Journal of Community Health Nursing* 28 (2): 105–16, doi: 10.1080/07370016.2011.564070.

Fournier, B., Bridge, A., Pritchard Kennedy, A., Alibhai, A. and Konde-Lule, J. (2014) 'Hear our voices: a Photovoice project with children who are orphaned and living with HIV in a Ugandan group home', *Children and Youth Services Review* 45: 55–63.

Freire, P. (1973) *Education for Critical Consciousness*, New York NY: Seabury Press.

Graziano, K. J. (2004) 'Oppression and resiliency in a post-apartheid South Africa: unheard voices of black gay men and lesbians', *Cultural Diversity and Ethnic Minority Psychology* 10 (3): 302.

Guillemin, M. and Drew, S. (2010) 'Questions of process in participant-generated visual methodologies', *Visual Studies* 25 (2): 175–88.

Harley, A. (2012) 'Picturing reality: power, ethics, and politics in using Photovoice', *International Journal of Qualitative Methods* 11 (4): 320–39.

Kramer, L., Schwartz, P., Cheadle, A. and Rauzon, S. (2013) 'Using Photovoice as a participatory evaluation tool in Kaiser Permanente's community health initiative', *Health Promotion Practice* 14 (5): 686–94, doi: 10.1177/1524839912463232.

Pies, C. and Parthasarathy, P. (2007) 'Photovoice: giving local health departments a new perspective on community health issues', *Contra Costa Health Services* 1–8.

Poudrier, J. and Mac-Lean, R. T. (2009) '"We've fallen into the cracks": Aboriginal women's experiences with breast cancer through Photovoice', *Nursing Inquiry* 16 (4): 306–17.

Rifkin, S. and Pridmore, P. (2001) *Partners in Planning: Information, Participation and Empowerment*, London: TALC and Macmillan Education.

Russinova, Z., Rogers, E. S., Gagne, C., Bloch, P., Drake, K. M. and Mueser, K. T. (2014) 'A randomized controlled trial of a peer-run antistigma Photovoice intervention', *Psychiatric Services* 65 (2): 242–6.

Short, R. (2006) 'New ways of preventing HIV infection: thinking simply, simply thinking', *Philosophical Transactions of the Royal Society B: Biological Sciences* 361 (1469): 811–20.

Skovdal, M. (2011) 'Picturing the coping strategies of caregiving children in western Kenya: from images to action', *American Journal of Public Health* 101 (3): 452.

Skovdal, M., Newton, J. and Rumi, S. (2014) *Photovoice Guidance: 10 Simple Steps to Involve Children in Needs Assessments*. Dhaka: Save the Children Bangladesh, <http://bangladesh.savethechildren.net/sites/bangladesh.savethechildren.net/files/library/Photovoice_needs_assessment_guidelines_full_report_0.pdf> [accessed 29 July 2015].

Skovdal, M., Ogutu, V., Aoro, C. and Campbell, C. (2009) 'Young carers as social actors: coping strategies of children caring for ailing or ageing guardians in western Kenya', *Social Science and Medicine* 69 (4): 587–95.

Stack, R., Magill, C. and McDonagh, K. (2004) 'Engaging youth through Photovoice', *Health Promotion Practice* 5 (1): 49–58.

Stanczak, G. C. (2007) *Visual Research Methods: Image, Society, and Representation*, London: SAGE Publications.

Tanjasiri, S. P., Lew, R., Kuratani, D. G., Wong, M. and Fu, L. (2011) 'Using Photovoice to assess and promote environmental approaches to tobacco control in AAPI communities', *Health Promotion Practice* 12 (5): 654–65.

Teti, M., Pichon, L., Kabel, A., Farnan, R. and Binson, D. (2013) 'Taking pictures to take control: Photovoice as a tool to facilitate empowerment among poor and racial/ethnic minority women with HIV', *Journal of the Association of Nurses in AIDS Care* 24 (6): 539–53, doi: http://dx.doi.org/10.1016/j.jana.2013.05.001.

Vaughan, C. (2014) 'Participatory research with youth: idealising safe social spaces or building transformative links in difficult environments?', *Journal of Health Psychology* 19 (1): 184–92.

Wang, C. and Burris, M. (1997) 'Photovoice: Concept, Methodology, and Use for Participatory Needs Assessment', *Health Education and Behaviour* 24 (3): 369–87.

Wang, C. and Pies, C. (2004) 'Family, maternal, and child health through Photovoice', *Maternal and Child Health Journal* 8 (2): 95–102.

Wang, C. and Redwood-Jones, Y. (2001) 'Photovoice ethics: perspectives from Flint Photovoice', *Health Education and Behaviour* 28 (5): 560–72.

Wang, C., Yi, W., Tao, Z. and Carovano, K. (1998) 'Photovoice as a participatory health promotion strategy', *Health Promotion International* 13 (1): 75–86.

Wilson, N., Dasho, S., Martin, A., Wallerstein, N., Wang, C. and Minkler, M. (2007) 'Engaging young adolescents in social action through Photovoice – The Youth Empowerment Strategies (YES!) project', *Journal of Early Adolescence* 27 (2): 241–61.

Feedback on activities

Feedback on Activity 6.1 Ethical issues in a Photovoice project

1. No, it is not possible to guard against all ethical dilemmas. But it is the responsibility of the researcher to make sure that many have been considered and every plausible effort to mitigate risks has been exhausted.
2. Yes, ethical dilemmas evolve and participant motivations change. For example, it is important to remind the participants of their rights to withdraw throughout the project.
3. Yes and no, it depends on the circumstances. If the photographer and the person (or people) who appears on the photograph have agreed for it to be used for this purpose, then yes. If they do not know that the picture is going to be used for this purpose, then no.
4. Yes and no. This scenario is in a grey zone and whether 'model' consent is required has to be negotiated with people from the local community, or with a national research ethics committee.

CHAPTER 7
Analysing qualitative data

Abstract

Qualitative methods often generate heaps of data and it can be difficult to work out what exactly needs to be done with all this information in order to construct and present a story, or an argument that is based on qualitative evidence. While there is no single formula or procedure to analyse qualitative data, there are some guiding principles and approaches that can help you get started. This chapter introduces you to some of those guiding principles and presents step-by-step guidance on two concrete and commonly used strategies for analysing qualitative data. One strategy falls under the category of 'thematic analysis', and the other relates to the analysis and presentation of 'case studies'. Depending on your study, you may be inspired to use one of these approaches. The approaches are not mutually exclusive, and you may see the potential to draw on elements from both. We end the chapter by discussing the use of computer-assisted qualitative data analysis software (CAQDAS).

Keywords: Qualitative research; qualitative analysis; thematic analysis; case study analysis; CAQDAS

Learning objectives

After reading this chapter, you will be able to:

- prepare data for analysis;
- conduct a thematic analysis; and
- present and analytically discuss case studies.

Key terms (definitions)

- *Code*: A descriptive or conceptual label that is assigned to sections of data (for example, a text segment of an interview transcript, or a section of a photograph). The process of assigning these 'codes' is referred to as 'coding'.
- *Coding*: The indexing of a data set through the application of codes from a coding framework.
- *Coding framework*: A list of descriptive codes that have been systematically generated to capture the content of the data.

http://dx.doi.org/10.3362/9781780448534.007

- *Data*: Information that has been collected, generated, and captured with the purpose of developing evidence around a topic.
- *Data analysis*: The process through which data, whether quantitative or qualitative, is reduced to produce a coherent interpretation.

Introduction

In some ways it is misleading for us to place the qualitative data analysis chapter at the end of the book. It leaves the impression that this is a distinct stage in the research process, something you do once the data has been generated. However, this is not the case. Analysis takes places throughout the research process. Your research question reflects an analytical interest, which in turn shapes the questions that you pose to your participants. As you conduct interviews, or generate data through other methods, you automatically process the information communicated to you. The impressions you are developing are likely to then influence the questions you ask in subsequent data collection activities, and help you 'see' the emerging story. If you take field notes, or keep a research diary, you are making choices about what is interesting and relevant and what is not. While these processes are first and foremost meant to facilitate data generation, they simultaneously involve a degree of analytic filtering and mark the beginning of your qualitative data analysis.

As such, the so-called qualitative data analysis stage is really more about organizing and indexing the heaps of data that have been generated in such a way that patterns and relationships emerge (Mason, 2002). In some respects, you could call this stage of the research process 'categorizing and indexing data'. It is a process that reorganizes your data and helps you 'reduce' or 'condense' it into manageable pieces, while simultaneously constructing a story or argument. How you break up, categorize, and index the data involves the same kind of analytic filtering as when you generate data.

The point we are trying to make here is that interpretation and analysis are infused into all stages of the research project and reflect your analytic interests (Mason, 2002). By the time you get to 'qualitative data analysis' as a research stage, you have already made some headway in the interpretation and analysis of the data. The process of organizing and indexing your data is, in many ways, merely an extension and acceleration of those thought processes. It is, however, at this stage that the story or argument of your research really takes shape, and where new and exciting insights begin to emerge.

Some of you may ask yourselves: Why go through this long and time-consuming process of categorizing, indexing, and interpreting data when you can just write up general impressions after the interviews? Interviewing and speaking to programme stakeholders is always a good thing. In some cases it may be perfectly fine for you to write down your impressions and key messages emerging from your interviews. However, in doing so you are making it difficult for readers of your report to: 1) judge whether those key messages also reflect the perspectives of your informants; 2) decide whether they agree with your interpretations of what was being said. In adopting a 'research approach', you both commit to transparency around how you reduce and summarize your data, and give yourself time and space to carefully interrogate the data. Taking time to interrogate data may open your eyes to new perspectives and interpretations, giving your study more depth. It may help you see nuances and complexity as well as the role of context in shaping what is being said. By carefully categorizing, indexing, and interpreting your data, you signal openness to surprise and a willingness to learn something new. Approaching the analysis of data in a way that is transparent, systematic, and open to surprise is key to being able to claim rigour (Gaskell and Bauer, 2000), something that is increasingly required of those engaged with monitoring, evaluation, accountability, and learning (MEAL). A risk of not using this approach to qualitative data analysis is misinterpretation of data, which in turn may lead to poor programme development and reduced programme effectiveness. It is the aim of this chapter to equip development practitioners with the skills and confidence to adopt a research approach in the analysis of qualitative data, enabling them to demonstrate rigour in their reporting of qualitative evidence.

Getting started with qualitative data analysis

The overall aim of qualitative data analysis is to reduce vast amounts of data so as to summarize key messages and emerging stories. Before you can start the process of reducing your data, you need to: 1) capture and prepare your data for analysis; 2) consider and be aware of the 'analytical gaze' guiding your study.

Data preparation

To start the qualitative data analysis process you need data. This may sound obvious, but what is not immediately clear is what qualitative data looks like. This lack of clarity can be explained by the fact that qualitative data can take many forms. Although it is possible to categorize, index, and interpret data made up of still or moving images and sound, in this chapter we will focus on text-based data. Text-based data is the most common form of data used in qualitative analysis, and can be easily analysed with the two strategies we introduce later in this chapter. Alternative forms of data can also be subjected to a thematic or case study analysis, but we focus here on text for the sake of simplicity. Once you understand the principles, you will be able to apply the methods more widely. There are two things you need to do in order to prepare your data for qualitative analysis:

- *Capture and record your data*: Data only becomes data once it has been captured and recorded. It is therefore important that you write down your reflections (see the section on writing field notes in Chapter 4), digitally record interviews (see 'Step 4: Conduct the interview' in Chapter 3), and take pictures when possible or relevant. All of these recording activities help you generate data that is tangible and able to be categorized and indexed.

• *Transcribe your data*: Some of your data may be generated textually. For example, you may have taken some notes from informal conversations with programme beneficiaries, or invited children to write essays about their experiences of a programme. Some of your data may be on audio recordings. For example, you may have digitally recorded a series of interviews or kept an audio diary. Other data may be recorded on video. For example, you may have videotaped a workshop with children producing a body map (see Chapter 5). Although you can analyse data in raw textual, audio, or video formats, it is easier to process data that has been transcribed into a text-based format. Also, the process of transcription, often seen as tedious, offers an important analytical opportunity. Not only will it carefully introduce you to every spoken word, it will connect you to the participants in a number of other ways. The tone of their voice, pauses, and other non-verbal communication, evident in an audio or video file, can help you better understand the experiences and perspectives communicated by the participants. Text-based data is also easier to store and access for further use. Table 7.1 provides step-by-step guidance on how to prepare a transcript, while Figure 7.1 includes an extract of a transcript.

Table 7.1 Steps and guidelines to prepare a transcript

Step	How to...
1	Open a Word document.
2	At the top of the page, include information about the data generation activity. This might include: • **type** of qualitative method used (e.g. in-depth interview or focus group discussion) • **where** the data generation took place • **when** the method was used (date and time of day) • **who*** participated in the data generation activity, including demographics (e.g. age, gender, and role) and type of informant (e.g. service user or provider) • **who** moderated the data generation activity • **time** spent on the data generation activity • **transcription** and/or **translation** details (names and dates) • If you have many transcripts, you may wish provide each one with a **transcript code** for easy recognition. If you conducted an in-depth interview (IDI) with a key informant (KI) in London (LO), the transcript code could read: LO-KI-IDI-1.
3	Use the remainder of the first page to include details about the context of the data generation activity. This may include: • the **physical setting** of the data generation activity (e.g. locality, comfort, and noise) • **reactions** of the participants(s) to the activity (e.g. to the audio recording) • the **dynamics** observed • **impressions** about the informant(s) and the data generation activity (e.g. did the informant(s) feel comfortable and free to talk?)

4   Word for word, write down exactly what is being said.
- Differentiate between speakers by recording their speech in a new paragraph.
- Use the real name of the moderator and write down his or her speech in bold.
- Use either initials, numbers, or names* to identify the informant(s).

5   Number each line consecutively (in Word, go to page layout and select continuous line numbers).

6   Add page numbers.

* To protect the identity of the informant(s), it is recommended that you do not use the real names of your informants on transcripts but instead use pseudonyms. You can link pseudonyms to the informants' real names in a separate document that is kept in a secure location.

1	**Transcript Code:**	NU-UG-IDI-2
2	**Date of interview:**	16/01/2015
3	**Moderator(s):**	Tom Thomson
4	**Type of interview:**	In-depth Interview
5	**Transcriber:**	Jacquie Smith
6	**Date of transcription:**	20/01/2015
7	**Interview location:**	Motyambo, western Uganda
8	**Length of interview:**	57 minutes
9	**Interviewee(s):**	Jack, age 39, male
10	**Type of informant:**	Nurse at a rural health clinic

11
12   **Comments about the context:**
13   The interview was conducted in a meeting room of the Motyambo health clinic. Jack is a head
14   nurse and agreed to participate in the study following our letter of invitation. The interview was
15   delayed by 35 minutes as he needed to assist another nurse. The interview took place a Monday
16   afternoon and the room was comfortable, neither too hot nor too cold. I brought us a soda each
17   and biscuits, which he seemed to enjoy. We sat next to each other in comfortable chairs. The
18   interview was only interrupted twice when Jack received text messages that he had to reply to.
19   Jack was used to being interviewed and had no problem with me recording our conversation. Jack
20   seemed confident and had a lot of interesting things to say about men's use of HIV services. He
21   draws on 4 years of experience as a head nurse.
22
23   - Interview start -
24   **Tom: What makes men different with regards to HIV service use?**
25   Jack: Men do not value their health until they become seriously ill... they have this 'I don't care
26   attitude'. They think that they are strong and resilient and not as weak as women. Some quickly
27   give up their HIV treatment because they are not patient or see the hospitals as a place for women,
28   not men.
29   **Tom: so men have a problem?**
30   Jack: Generally fewer men than women are enrolled onto our HIV treatment programme. Women
31   generally do not have a problem coming to the hospital as well as getting tested for HIV, men have
32   this tendency of feeling embarrassed by their being HIV positive... so they don't want to come and
33   get tested at all, they feel exposed, somehow to them it brings a sense that they are being exposed
34   for sleeping around.
35   **Tom: next question...**

Figure 7.1 Extract of a transcript

If you have audio recordings of 10 interviews, you should end up with 10 Word documents, each of which represents one participant's interview. If you are not carrying out the study yourself, but have recruited a consultant or employed research assistants, you ought to train and request them to prepare transcripts.

Your 'analytical gaze'

Key to the research approach in qualitative MEAL activities is acknowledging and recognizing your 'analytical gaze'. This is the way you look at and filter your data, in order to categorize, index, and organize your material so that a few key findings emerge. All researchers have an analytical gaze. Broadly speaking, the analytical gaze refers to your interests and the way these interests affect your decisions to speak to certain groups of people, the questions you ask them, and the way you categorize and index your data in order to answer your research question.

You can think of the analytical gaze as a pair of spectacles, whose lenses constitute your area of interest. The lenses guide you to generate and look at specific types of information and knowledge. The analytical gaze gives your study a focus and helps you categorize and index your data. It can be more or less theory driven. Examples of analytical gazes relevant to the field of development are listed below:

- Local **understandings, constructions**, and **social representations** of a phenomenon or programme.
- People's **perceptions** and **experiences** of an issue, their needs, or a programme.
- Local **responses, acceptability**, and **feasibility** of a programme.
- **Meanings** people attach to certain experiences, relationships or life events.
- **Social processes** and **contextual factors** (for example, social norms, values, behaviours, and cultural practices) that marginalize a group of people or have an impact on a programme.
- Local **agency** and responses in mitigating poverty and the marginalization of vulnerable populations.
- The role of **social recognition** and **identity** in helping people living with HIV cope with **stigma**.
- The **relationship** between stakeholders involved in the implementation of a programme.
- **Pathways** to health or the programme's success.
- The **causes** and **effects** of a social issue.
- The role of **social norms** and **social networks** in marginalizing a social group.

Many experienced academic researchers – who, of course, also have analytical gazes guiding their research – tend to draw on theories from the social sciences to articulate their interests further. If you are familiar with any theories that can help you demonstrate, explore, or explain the complex social processes that you are studying, please do not hesitate to bring these into your study.

How you then go about indexing and organizing your data – guided by your analytical gaze – can be more or less driven by predefined ideas. In other words, if you already know what kind of story you want or expect to tell, you can develop categories in advance and use these categories to index data relevant to test and tell your story. This approach has its foundations in quantitative research and is often considered ill-suited to qualitative research. While it is possible to index and organize qualitative data using entirely predefined categories, this undermines the exploratory potential of qualitative research. More common in the qualitative research approach is openness to new, changing, and complex stories. You may develop some predefined categories to index your data, inspired by your analytical gaze, but you should be open to changing these categories and adding new and emerging ones. For example, you may have conducted a study that set out to investigate local experiences of a programme. As you organize and index your data, you realize that the data generated largely relates to how context shapes local experiences. This encourages you to change your analytical gaze and to explore the role of context in shaping possibilities for or barriers to programme impact. In this example, your analytical gaze changed from a focus on 'local experiences' to 'role of context'. The qualitative research approach encourages you to let the data speak, and to adapt your analytical gaze accordingly.

Your interests, or analytical gaze, play an important role in guiding the research process and in shaping the findings of your study. It is therefore important to be aware of your analytical gaze before you start the analysis and to be explicit about it when writing up your findings (see Chapter 8). Often, your research questions indicate what your analytical gaze is. But just as your analytical gaze can change, depending on the data generated, so can your research question. For example, it is not uncommon for qualitative researchers to amend their research question to reflect the dynamic and emerging nature of their data.

Qualitative data analysis strategies

So far, we have discussed qualitative analysis as a process of categorizing, indexing, and organizing qualitative data. In this section we will outline two concrete, but different, strategies to 'slice up' (Mason, 2002) data in ways that can help you interrogate and understand emerging stories. The first one is thematic analysis, which typically involves breaking up all your qualitative data and dividing it into themes. In other words, it is a strategy that encourages you to identify information across and between different sources of data.

This way you can easily retrieve information about a theme and gain an overview of some of the key issues evident in the data. Case study analysis, on the other hand, typically involves analysing the data within its context. Here, you bring cases together, describe and analyse interwoven parts, and present an in-depth and holistic picture of the case(s). We will start by presenting a step-by-step guide to thematic analysis.

Thematic analysis

Thematic analysis is one of the more common strategies for analysing qualitative data. Thematic analysis allows you to index and organize your data into themes, with the aim of unpacking a story within the data. Inspired by Attride-Stirling's (2001) thematic network analysis, we present 13 steps to thematic analysis.

Step 1: Get familiar with the data.   Read and re-read your data (field notes and diaries, transcripts, etc.) and then read it all one more time. Take plenty of notes of your thoughts and ideas as they develop during the reading. Write a summary for each of your transcripts or data sources.

Step 2: Make a start on your coding framework.   Once you have read your transcripts you will have some idea about emerging themes in your data. This awareness, combined with your analytical gaze, can help you make a start in developing categories – what we will henceforth call 'codes' – that can help you index your data. This process is called 'coding'. A code contains a label that summarizes a descriptive and primary theme relevant to portions of your data. The codes you develop will begin to form and shape your coding framework, which is essentially a list of codes.

Do not attempt to develop all your codes at this early stage. Some of the codes you develop at this step may be too broad, while others may be too narrow. You therefore need to be prepared to change them later on. Your coding framework will always be a work in progress.

Step 3: Begin to code your data.   The coding stage involves indexing the qualitative data by applying codes.

- Every time you read a sentence or paragraph of textual data, you need to think about whether you can apply one of your existing codes or need to develop a new code to capture the meaning of that portion of data.
- You can code manually or using a computer program. One way to do it manually is to write the codes in the margins of your textual data, or to write your codes in a word-processing document or Excel spreadsheet, and simply copy and paste text segments into the table under the relevant code. We discuss the possibilities of computer-assisted qualitative data analysis software at the end of this chapter.

- Continue to apply and develop your list of codes until all of your data has been coded. You do not need to code every single word within a transcript. Perhaps the interviewer and interviewee are talking about the weather or the neighbour's dog at the start of the interview. This is irrelevant to the study and can be left out. However, take care not to leave out information that on the face of it seems irrelevant to the study. Sometimes the unexpected and seemingly irrelevant information is key to understanding the issue being studied.

Activity 7.1 Coding your data

This exercise will provide you with an example of coding and highlight the importance of refining codes.

Here is an example of data:

'This is a photo which I took of my uniform. I want to share this photo because it is the only uniform I own, it is torn and is the one I wear when going to school.'

Figure 7.2 Picture taken by a study participant

What descriptive label (i.e. code) would you apply to describe the primary theme of this text and photo?

Feedback is available at the end of the chapter.

Step 4: Finalize your list of codes.   The meaning you attach to a code can easily change over time as you progress with the coding of your transcripts. Once all the data has been coded, we recommend that you revisit each code and make sure that the text segments within the codes still relate to the primary theme that your descriptive coding label refers to. You can refine your list of codes in different ways:

- *Merge codes*: As you read through the text segments within your codes, you may discover that a few codes relate to the same primary theme, and contain only a few text segments. If that is the case, you can merge the codes together into a single code, bringing together all the related text segments.
- *Split codes*: You may also find that some of your codes contain a large number of text segments, and are perhaps too broad to illustrate variations within this primary theme. To ensure that this variation is captured and considered in the analysis, you can split up the code by creating new and more detailed codes, and cut and paste the relevant text segments into the new codes.
- *Re-name codes*: You may also realize that the meaning of a code has changed over time, requiring you to re-name the code so that it captures the essence of the text segments.

This iterative process of refining codes can be long and slow. There is no rule about how many codes you need. This depends entirely on the scale of your study. However, it would not be unrealistic for small, medium, or large studies to have around 50, 100, or 150 codes respectively (plus or minus 20 codes). If you develop a list of 200 codes for a small study of around 10 interviews, it is likely that your codes are too detailed and each one contains only a few text segments. In this case, it may be possible to merge some of the codes. On the other hand, if you end up with a list of 35 codes after having coded 75 interview transcripts, it is likely that you have coded too broadly, and your codes contain a large number of text segments that illustrate variations on a topic. In this case, it may be possible for you to split up some of your codes. Try to find a balance so that each code, or primary theme, refers to a single idea, yet is broad enough to be illustrated by several text segments.

Step 5: Identify secondary themes. When you are happy with your list of codes, each of which contains text segments that describe a common, salient, and primary theme relating to aspects of your data, you are ready to explore how the codes relate to each other. This requires you to have a good understanding of each code and a bird's-eye view. To identify secondary themes, we suggest you do the following:

- Write your codes on small pieces of paper. If you coded manually, you can write the codes on Post-it notes, one code per note. If you coded using a computer, you can print your list of codes and cut them out so that you have small pieces of paper, each with a code label written on it. It is recommended that you print the code list with a minimum font size of 16 and with plenty of spacing between the codes.
- Spread the codes out on a large table (Step 1 in Table 7.2) and assemble them into thematic groupings. You need to cluster codes that refer to the same theme together (Step 2 in Table 7.2). When you look down at your codes, you may see two to four codes that relate to each other. Bring them together and think of a label that summarizes and interprets the

Table 7.2 Five steps to develop a thematic network from codes or primary themes

Step	How to...	Illustration
1	Place your codes (primary themes) on a table. To illustrate the steps of identifying secondary themes, we draw on a small selection of codes from a study on orphaned and vulnerable children in East Africa. Please note: you are likely to have many more codes than the illustration suggests.	
2	Cluster your codes together so that they relate to each other. The top left cluster of codes relates to orphaned children looking poor. The top right cluster relates to orphaned children being bullied. The bottom cluster relates to the education of orphaned children.	
3	Identify a secondary theme for each of your cluster of codes. The secondary theme should encapsulate and interpret the meaning of the cluster of codes. Write the theme on a piece of paper and place it on top of your cluster of codes. The secondary themes should reflect your interpretation of the primary themes and can be informed by your analytical gaze.	

(Continued)

Table 7.2 (Continued)

Step	How to...	Illustration
4	Look at your primary and secondary themes in each grouping and think about how they relate to each other. Develop a label that describes the essence of the story that emerges from your themes. The story emerging from this example could be about how poverty-related stigma affects children's education.	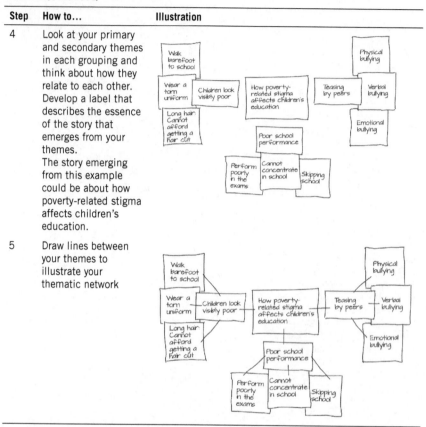
5	Draw lines between your themes to illustrate your thematic network	

story told by the cluster of codes. Your analytical gaze may well inform the label and the way you cluster the codes. Write the label on a new piece of paper and place it on top of the cluster of codes (Step 3 in Table 7.2). This label makes up your secondary theme.

Step 6: Identify tertiary theme(s). Look at your primary and secondary themes in each grouping and think about how they relate to each other. Group them under a tertiary theme. If you have a small number of related secondary themes, you can try to think of a word, concept, or sentence that captures the essence of the story being told through all of your secondary themes (see Step 4 in Table 7.2). If you have a number of secondary themes, you can explore how they connect and relate to each other, and organize them under two or three different higher-order and interpretive tertiary themes.

Step 7: Illustrate your thematic network.   At this stage of the analysis you have condensed your data set to themes at three different levels, going from de-scriptive primary themes through to more interpretive secondary and tertiary themes. A story is emerging. To illustrate your thematic network, and the emerging story, you can draw lines that connect your primary, secondary, and tertiary themes (see Step 5 in Table 7.2).

Step 8: Describe the themes.   For each of your secondary and tertiary themes, write a short summary that describes the story emerging from each theme. For example, a summary of the secondary theme 'Poverty – children look visibly poor', could talk about how some orphaned children living in poverty in the particular context of the study are unable to go to the hairdressers or buy a pair of shoes or a new uniform, and that this means that some orphaned children look different from other children.

Step 9: Verify and refine the thematic network.   At this stage, Attride-Stirling (2001) recommends that you return to your transcripts and double-check that summaries (from Step 8) and the overall story emerging from the thematic network reflect the 'raw' data. This also gives you the opportunity to actively seek out instances that appear to contradict the story emerging from your thematic network analysis, and to use these 'deviant' cases to modify and nu-ance your story (Seale, 1999). Following this, you may decide to change the wording and formulation of some of your themes.

Step 10: Use the thematic network(s) to interrogate and analyse your data.   The thematic network or networks do not constitute the analysis per se; they are merely tools to assist with the analysis (Attride-Stirling, 2001). You can use the thematic network in combination with your summaries (Step 8) to explore differences, similarities, and contradictions in the emerging story between locations (for example, communities, organizations, countries), in-terviewee categories (gender, age, service user or provider), and type of data collection method (participant observation, interview, focus group discus-sions, Photovoice).

If you have a large data set and find that, for example, men and women describe a phenomenon very differently from each other, you may need to develop codes and secondary and tertiary themes that are unique to each gender. This will result in two thematic networks: one for men and one for women. The two thematic networks will then illustrate similarities and differences in how men and women view and describe the phenomenon being studied.

At this step, it is important that you write down all of your analytical observations and think about how they contribute to answering your research question.

Step 11: Participant follow-up or feedback. If you are still in contact with your participants, at this stage of your analysis you can decide whether it would be helpful to meet up with some of them again. This would be beneficial for two reasons:

- *Follow-up*: If your analysis is raising more questions than answers, or if you want to follow up on surprising themes emerging from the analysis, it would be helpful for you to conduct follow-up interviews with some of your participants. In a follow-up interview you can get clarity on specific themes emerging from your analysis and explore particular themes in more depth.
- *Feedback*: If your analysis is revealing a story, or multiple stories, you can arrange one-to-one or group meetings with some of your participants and share with them some of your summaries (Step 8), thematic networks (Step 9), and key analytical points (Step 10). By doing this, you can get feedback on the accuracy and relevance of your findings. This exercise may also provide you with further information, which you can incorporate into your analysis (as you can from follow-up interviews).

Step 12: Present your findings. Use the thematic network(s) to make explicit the patterns emerging from your exploration. You can do this by letting the findings section of your report be driven by the structure of your thematic network(s). Take the thematic network in Table 7.2 as an example. The report may be entitled *How Poverty-related Stigma Affects the Education of Orphaned and Vulnerable Children*. The findings section may then have three headings that reflect and connect your secondary themes: 1) 'In contexts of poverty some orphaned and vulnerable children look visibly poor'; 2) 'Orphaned and vulnerable children looking poor are subject to hurtful teasing by their peers'; 3) 'Teasing and bullying impacts on the education of orphaned and vulnerable children'.

Under each of the three headings, you can then present the relevant primary themes. For instance, in the section called 'In contexts of poverty some orphaned and vulnerable children look visibly poor', you can present your findings and analysis of the three primary themes 'Walk barefoot to school', 'Wear a torn uniform', and 'Long hair: Cannot afford getting a haircut'. If you have a lot of data and analysis to present, you can develop subheadings that reflect the categorization of your primary themes (see Box 7.1).

If you structure the findings section according to your thematic network, you will be able to draw on your summaries (Step 8) and analytical points (Step 10) to identify data (quotes, pictures, or participant observation notes) that is relevant to the thematic findings you are presenting. The data should not stand alone, but be used actively as evidence to substantiate an argument or claim, to illustrate an analytical point, to provide further depth and understanding of an issue, and to give voice to your participants (see Box 7.1). In other words, you need to add your interpretation of the data and highlight

---

**Box 7.1 Example of how a thematic network can guide
the structure of your presentation of findings**

Findings: How poverty-related stigma affects the education of orphaned and vulnerable children [tertiary theme]

1. In contexts of poverty some orphaned and vulnerable children look visibly poor [secondary theme]

Walk barefoot to school [primary theme]
[Insert text and quotes under each primary theme]
Wear a torn uniform [primary theme]
For some of the orphaned and vulnerable children, poverty manifested itself in their school uniforms. Some children, and their families, were simply unable to replace old and torn uniforms, requiring some children to attend school wearing torn uniforms [analytical point].
'This is a photo which I took of my uniform. I want to share this photo because it is the only uniform I own, it is torn and is the one I wear when going to school.' [transcript quotation supporting an analytical point]
Long hair: Cannot afford getting a haircut [primary theme]

2. Orphaned and vulnerable children looking poor are subject to teasing by their peers [secondary theme]

Physical bullying [primary theme]
Verbal bullying [primary theme]
'I feel embarrassed when I put on this torn uniform because parts of my body get exposed. Some children utter bad words about me.' [transcript quotation]
Emotional bullying [primary theme]

3. Teasing impacts on the education of orphaned and vulnerable children [secondary theme]

Skipping school [primary theme]
Cannot concentrate in school [primary theme]
'This makes me sad and sometimes makes me not to want to come to school. Because of the embarrassment that my torn uniform causes me, and the teasing by other children, affects my concentration in school.' [transcript quotation]
Perform poorly in the exams [primary theme]

---

surprises and contradictions as well as consistencies, as you alternate between discussing and presenting data.

Step 13: Discuss your findings. An important final step in the analysis of qualitative data is to discuss your findings. You can do this in a separate section in your report, or integrate it into your findings section. Irrespective of how you incorporate the discussion, we recommend that it includes the following elements:

- Discuss how your findings shed light on your research question(s). Help the reader understand how your findings answer the research question, as well as the nuances and complexity that the study has brought out. Remember: if your findings do not address your original research question, you are allowed to tweak it so that it matches your emerging findings. However, you will need to declare this in the report.

- Discuss how significant themes emerging from your study relate to the wider empirical literature. Help the reader understand how your findings corroborate or contradict studies conducted elsewhere. If your findings differ from what others have found, discuss how and why this might be. Please note that it is perfectly OK if your findings contradict existing findings in the empirical literature.
- If your study was driven by theory, you can discuss how your findings support, develop, or contradict existing ideas within the theoretical literature.
- Discuss the implications of your findings. In what ways do your findings support, challenge, or problematize existing policy or practice? By asking yourself this question you can help the reader answer the 'So what?' question of your study.

Although we have added the discussion of research findings as a final step in qualitative data analysis, it is advised that you return to the literature throughout the research process and continually engage with it to sharpen your analytical gaze and better understand the themes emerging from the analysis.

We have now presented 13 steps towards thematic analysis, and, with help from Attride-Stirling (2001), we have illustrated how this process for indexing data into thematic areas can be aided by thematic networks. The very nature of qualitative research means that each qualitative study is different, making it virtually impossible to develop and apply step-by-step guidance. It is therefore important that you do not consider the 13 steps outlined above as the 'right' way to conduct a thematic analysis, but that you continually think about how these steps highlight principles that would be relevant to analysing your data.

Thematic analysis is good for researchers who require a systematic overview of their data and are looking for those overarching stories that dominate the data. However, if you do not wish to break up your data into slices, but believe that themes, issues, and topics should be understood and carefully interpreted in context, you may prefer case study analysis.

Case study analysis

Case study analysis is another common method for analysing qualitative data. It is a qualitative analysis approach that encourages you to interrogate themes within a bounded system (a 'case') or multiple bounded systems ('cases'), using detailed data from multiple sources (Creswell, 2012). So, rather than taking portions of your data and indexing them using a code, free from their broader context, case study analysis encourages you to explore issues holistically and within their context, using 'thick description' (which means contextual information) to develop in-depth and detailed understandings of interwoven parts of your data set (Mason, 2002). It can help you paint a detailed picture of a situation, or a programme, and makes case study analysis particularly helpful in answering 'how' and 'why' questions in the context of MEAL. Although analysing themes in context is not unique to case study research, it is a feature that guides much of the case study analysis approach. It should be said that case study analysis is not just a method of analysis; it is intrinsically linked to an approach to research (case study research). The best examples of case study analysis draw on data that was generated with an appreciation of 'thick description' and that comes from many different sources but has a clearly defined system or 'case'.

As with any qualitative data analysis, your analytical gaze plays a key role in guiding what you are looking at when conducting a case study analysis. In addition to clarity with regard to your analytical gaze, you need to consider the following parameters:

- **What is the purpose of your analysis?** Yin (2003) discusses a number of different potential purposes for case study analysis. These include the following:
    a. *Explanatory*: An explanatory case study analysis seeks to understand and explain why and how different themes are linked and interwoven. If, for example, a boy talks in an interview about how his torn uniform makes him look visibly poor, encouraging other children in school to tease him, which in turn discourages him from attending school, an explanatory case study analysis approach would interrogate the causal link between looking poor, teasing, and education. In the context of MEAL, the explanatory case study approach can be used to explore how a programme or intervention led to particular outcomes.
    b. *Exploratory*: An exploratory case study analysis approach seeks to explore and observe an issue, phenomenon, or programme with the intention of generating an in-depth understanding of key factors and processes influencing the situation being studied. If, for example, you are in the process of developing a programme to combat poverty-related stigma, an exploratory case study analysis can help you map out the manifestations of stigma in a particular context. An exploratory case study analysis could also be used for needs assessments, exploring the needs of individuals within a bounded system.
    c. *Descriptive*: A descriptive case study analysis approach seeks to chart a case in great detail. This involves developing 'thick description' of the case, describing the socio-economic and cultural context, actors, programmes, and other influences of daily life.
- **How do you define the 'case' to be analysed?** Clarity around the scope of your 'case' is important. The case constitutes your unit of analysis and determines who you should recruit to participate in the study. Your research question is likely to give you some answers about the scope of your case. It should specify whether the focus of your study is to analyse an individual, a family, a community, an organization, a geographical location, or a particular process.

- **Are you analysing single or multiple cases?** You also need to determine whether you are analysing a single case or multiple cases, or a mix of both. Let us say that you want to analyse children's education outcomes. You could then either focus on a single school (a single case), or you could compare and contrast the education outcomes of two different schools (multiple cases). Even if you focus on a single school, you can conduct multiple case studies of individuals within the school environment (for example, teachers, students, and school management staff). This way, you are conducting a study of both a single case (the school) and multiple cases (individual actors within the school). Having multiple cases allows you to identify similarities and differences between the cases.

Once you are clear about the parameters of your case study analysis, and aware of your analytical gaze, you are ready to interrogate your case study or case studies. To help you with this, we propose the following six steps.

Step 1: Examine and understand the context of the case study.   A case and real-life events do not exist in a vacuum, but are shaped by broader socio-economic, cultural, historical, and geopolitical factors. Before you start developing and analysing your case study, you need to familiarize yourself with the broader context of the case(s). This would involve a lot of reading and having conversations with people who have background knowledge of the context of your case.

Step 2: Get familiar with the data.   Read and re-read your data (field notes and diaries, transcripts, etc.) and then read it all once more. Take plenty of notes of your thoughts and ideas as they develop during the reading.

Step 3: Begin to code your data.   Once you have developed and familiarized yourself with the repository of information about a case, you can code the data. This is much like the process described for thematic analysis. To help capture interconnections within the case, you can develop a coding framework that takes into consideration the following elements:

- *About*: The who, what, where, and when of the case.
- *Actions*: Practices, events, crises, problems within the case, and the phenomenon being studied.
- *Appraisal*: The meaning and significance ascribed to the actions.
- *After-effects*: Implications, outcomes. and solutions to the actions.

The focus of your coding will depend on your analytical gaze. If we take the example from before, and assume your analytical gaze to be the processes through which poverty-related stigma manifests itself within a school (the case), 'about' codes relating to the context may include details on poverty, the school environment, pupils, teachers, and parents. 'Action' codes may be 'cannot afford to buy a new uniform', 'cannot afford to get a haircut', 'some children look visibly poor' and 'teasing by peers' – each of which represent a crisis, event, practice, or problem. An 'appraisal' code relates to the significance of the actions, and may include 'children feeling stigmatized' or 'sadness'. An 'after-effect' code, which relates to the implications of this, may be 'children skipping school'.

Step 4: Develop a detailed description of the case.   Use your coding framework to structure your case summary. Start off by giving some context to the case (about), describe the phenomenon being studied (actions, crises, and practices), account for the meaning and significance that people, organizations, or communities ascribe to the phenomenon (appraisal), and end with a description of the implications, outcomes, and proposed solutions to the phenomenon studied (after-effects).

The case summary is likely to be long and detailed, providing a holistic overview of the case in relation to your topic. It should allow you to explore the interconnections between the context, actions, appraisals, and after-effects, offering holistic explanations of the processes and practices studied. In other words, as you write this description, you need to explore the role of contextual factors in influencing the explanations and processes.

Continuing with the example above, your detailed description can focus on explanations of processes and practices that contribute to poverty-related stigma within the school. Depending on your data, your description may go something like this: 'Poverty means some children in this case study are unable to replace their torn uniforms, which means they look visibly poor and get teased by their peers. This makes them feel stigmatized and sad, which in turn encourages them to skip school.'

This is a very crude description, but gives you an idea of how you can structure your summary, and use the process of writing as an opportunity to explore, analyse, and underline interconnections and explanations.

Step 5: Comparing cases.   If you have more than one case, and if the coding revealed similar themes, you can advance your analysis by comparing the cases, looking for similarities and differences across your codes (Creswell, 2012). But, in addition to comparing descriptive similarities and differences, you can compare the different explanations and processes that arise from your case studies (Mason, 2002). One way to do this is to condense and chart your summaries into a table. The chart depicted in Table 7.3 encourages you to compare more than one action across two cases. You will have to decide how many actions you want to compare.

Step 6: Present and discuss your findings.   There is no single right way to report on a case study analysis (Merriam, 1988). The way you decide to present your analysis will depend on the purpose of your case study analysis (exploratory, explanatory, or descriptive, for instance), how you have defined the scope of the case, and whether the case is single, multiple, or a mix (for example,

Table 7.3 Example of a case study comparison chart

Focus elements	Case 1		Case 2	
About	The who, what, where, and when of case 1		The who, what, where, and when of case 2	
Actions	Practice, event, crisis, problem	Practice, event, crisis, problem	Practice, event, crisis, problem	Practice, event, crisis, problem
Appraisal	Meaning and significance	Meaning and significance	Meaning and significance	Meaning and significance
After-effects	Implications, outcomes, and solutions	Implications, outcomes, and solutions	Implications, outcomes, and solutions	Implications, outcomes, and solutions

multiple cases within a single case study) (Yin, 2003). Although you have a lot of flexibility to present the findings of your case study in a way that makes sense to your particular analysis, it is generally recommended that you start off by providing plenty of detail about the case study and its context (about). You can then proceed to present the issues being studied (including actions, appraisal, and after-effects), and discuss the explanations and processes your analysis has uncovered.

We have now presented two ways for you to interrogate your data. We have presented them as two distinct approaches to qualitative data analysis, but often researchers are inspired by elements of both. For example, one might conduct a thematic analysis, but continually examine emerging themes in their broader context (i.e. with a case). Equally, one may conduct a case study analysis, yet thematically code the data within the case. It is therefore difficult to fully separate the two approaches. While you are welcome to follow the step-by-step guidance presented above, and to align yourself with a particular approach, it is also OK to deviate from, and change, the process to suit your research aim and data. What is important is that you document your analytical procedure.

Both approaches are time consuming and may seem tedious at first. In many ways, qualitative data analysis is cumbersome, and not everyone has the patience to go through the process. If you work under strict deadlines or resource constraints, you may even be inclined to skip a few steps. We would discourage this for no other reason than that the process makes you thoroughly familiar with the data, and can help you document how you unravel the mass of textual data and make sense of others' sense-making. By following and documenting a process, you can convince the readers of your research report that the findings did not emerge from intuition, but are based on an interrogation of your analytical gaze and the perspectives of your participants.

We hope to have debunked the myth that qualitative data analysis is simpler and easier than quantitative analysis. The flexibility and fluidity of qualitative data analysis are bewildering to many people working in MEAL, who are often accustomed to more clearly defined plans and procedures for data analysis. Nonetheless, we hope to have introduced a balanced account of qualitative data analysis, both explaining procedural steps and highlighting the importance of your 'analytical gaze' in guiding the process.

As we discussed earlier, these processes can be usefully aided by computer-assisted qualitative data analysis software (CAQDAS), particularly if you have a large data set. We will now discuss possibilities and challenges for using CAQDAS.

Computer-assisted qualitative data analysis software

Computer-assisted qualitative data analysis software (CAQDAS) has grown in popularity since the 1980s (Kelle, 2000). There are numerous programs you can choose from, and they all share the same aim: namely, to help qualitative researchers manage and analyse their data in a way that is thorough, transparent, time saving, and easily shared with colleagues. This is particularly the case if you have large amounts of data, or multiple forms of data, including interview and focus group discussion transcripts, field notes, literature, videos, photographs, blogs, and social media updates (Mason, 2002). It is important to note that CAQDAS programs do not do the analysis for you, as is the case with statistical analysis software in quantitative research. It is you, the researcher, who: 1) organizes the data within the software; 2) codes the data; 3) decides what queries to run in order to explore patterns. We will describe these three functionalities in a little more detail.

Information management

A key feature of CAQDAS is its capacity to manage large amounts of information. Most CAQDAS allows you to import a variety of files, including audio, video, still images, documents, and Excel spreadsheets. Some programs, like NVivo, also enable you to import websites and social media content, for example from Twitter, Facebook or LinkedIn. This allows you to bring all the relevant research information together in a single program. How you organize and use this information within the program is up to you. You can, for example, import both literature and data into the program, which means it can be used both for a literature review and the interrogation of data. Aside from helping you manage vast amounts of data, a benefit of bringing all the relevant information together in one program is that you can more readily share the project with colleagues, helping them understand your research.

Code and retrieve

Perhaps the most common use of CAQDAS is to aid the coding process, which is typical of thematic analysis. Within CAQDAS, you can develop codes: these are little thematic containers that can be used to index the data imported to the

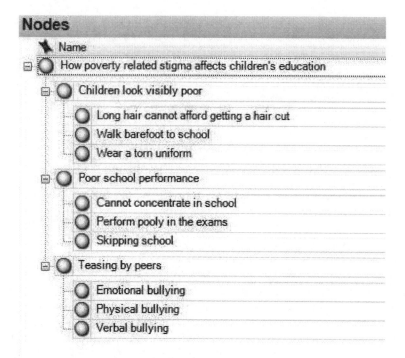

Figure 7.3 Primary, secondary and tertiary themes as they appear in NVivo

program. The codes can be developed in advance and applied, or simply created during the process of going through your data. Most CAQDAS programs allow you to organize your codes, further aiding the thematic analysis process described earlier. Some CAQDAS, such as NVivo, enable you to cluster codes together into higher-order themes, creating a coding and thematic structure similar to that illustrated in Table 7.2. Figure 7.3 shows how, within NVivo, researchers can organize codes into higher-order themes. Using the same themes that emerged from Table 7.2, Figure 7.3 illustrates how the codes, or primary themes 'Long hair: cannot afford getting a hair-cut', 'Walk barefoot to school', and 'Wear a torn uniform' have been clustered under a secondary theme called 'Children look visibly poor'. The three secondary themes have in turn been clustered under the tertiary theme 'How poverty-related stigma affects children's education'.

A benefit of CAQDAS is that, once you have coded your data and would like to retrieve information about a topic, you can do so through a click of a button. In most CAQDAS, you would simply have to double-click on a code, and all the information you have indexed with this code will immediately appear, whether it is text, a sound bite, a clip from a video, or the corner of a still image. If, for example, you have coded different text segments from a series of transcripts as 'wear a torn uniform', you can quickly retrieve all the information that relates to the topic of children wearing torn uniforms. You can then easily compare and contrast what is being said about this topic.

Exploring patterns

CAQDAS programs have different search or query functionalities to help you explore patterns. Some basic search functions include 'word frequencies' and 'text searches'. Word frequency searches can provide you with an overview of which words appear most frequently in your literature or data. This can provide you with some ideas of what themes appear in your material. Text searches allow you to search and explore the context of particular words. If, for example, your analytical gaze draws your attention to the issue of 'teasing', you can do a search on the word 'tease' and obtain information about how 'tease' appears in your data set. You then have the option of indexing this information into new or existing codes (such as 'emotional bullying', 'physical bullying', or 'verbal bullying').

For those with a little more experience in using CAQDAS, it is possible to run queries that enable you to compare and contrast qualitative responses according to particular variables, such as age, gender, occupation, community, and so forth. For example, a query could be used to explore how boys and girls talk differently or similarly about the topic 'wearing a torn uninform'. While such queries can help explore patterns within large data sets, they follow a logic common to quantitative analysis, and may not necessarily be appropriate to all qualitative studies (Mason, 2002). If you are conducting an exploratory study, for example, you may not necessarily look for patterns, but instead seek to map out a broad spectrum of views and perspectives.

What CAQDAS program should you use?

In Chapter 2, we explained that NVivo and ATLAS.ti are two of the most commonly used subscription-based software.[1] Both programs are fairly sophisticated and have many different functions that can help you manage and analyse large amounts of data. They are updated regularly with new functionalities. There are free and open-source alternatives, such as CATMA for Windows, Macintosh and Linux, TAMS Analyzer for Macintosh, and Coding Analysis Toolkit (CAT), which is web-based.[2] If your organization has access to subscription-based software, you may as well choose either NVivo or ATLAS.ti. If not, you are likely to find that any of the freely accessible programs are perfectly adequate for the sort of analysis you are trying to do.

Summary

This chapter has introduced you to some key principles behind qualitative data analysis. It has underlined that analysis is not a single event, or something you do after data collection. Instead, qualitative analysis is a continuous activity that starts the moment you form a research question. Every decision you make in the research process, or question you ask a participant, is shaped by what we call your 'analytical gaze', an interest that provides your study with a focus. This, coupled with your background (gender, age, previous experience on the topic, and so on), makes you, the researcher, a key instrument in the analysis process. Your analytical gaze also plays a role in helping you decide which strategy to use to systematically condense your data into a few key findings. We have presented two commonly used strategies for systematically interrogating qualitative data. One is thematic analysis, which allows you to slice up, identify, and explore themes across your data set. We also presented case study analysis, a strategy used to explore how themes within a case relate to each other. The two strategies serve slightly different purposes. Thematic analysis is good to provide you with a broad-brush overview of key themes within a data set. Case study analysis is well suited to understand how and why something works in a particular way within a case. Having said that, researchers often draw on elements from both strategies. What is important is that you approach your data systematically and take time to carefully interrogate the different themes emerging within your data and understand their interconnections.

Endnotes

1. NVivo is available at <www.qsrinternational.com/> and ATLAS.ti at <http://atlasti.com/> [both accessed 24 July 2015].
2. CATMA is available at <www.catma.de>, TAMS Analyzer for Macintosh <http://tamsys.sourceforge.net> and CAT at <http://cat.ucsur.pitt.edu/> [all accessed 24 July 2015].

References

Attride-Stirling, J. (2001) 'Thematic networks: an analytic tool for qualitative research', *Qualitative Research* 1 (3): 385–405.

Creswell, J. W. (2012) *Qualitative Inquiry and Research Design: Choosing Among Five Approaches*, London: SAGE Publications.

Gaskell, G. and Bauer, M. W. (2000) 'Towards public accountability: beyond sampling, reliability and validity', in M. W. Bauer and G. Gaskell (eds), *Qualitative Researching with Text, Image and Sound*, pp. 336–50, London: SAGE Publications.

Kelle, U. (2000) 'Computer-assisted analysis: coding and indexing', in M. W. Bauer and G. Gaskell (eds), *Qualitative Researching with Text, Image and Sound*, pp. 282–98, London: SAGE Publications.

Mason, J. (2002) *Qualitative Researching*, London: SAGE Publications.

Merriam, S. B. (1988) *Case Study Research in Education: A Qualitative Approach*, San Francisco CA: Jossey-Bass.

Seale, C. (1999) 'Quality in qualitative research', *Qualitative Inquiry* 5 (4): 465–78.

Yin, R. K. (2003) *Case Study Research: Design and Methods*, 3rd edn, Thousand Oaks CA: SAGE Publications.

Feedback on activities

Feedback on Activity 7.1 Coding your data

There is no right or wrong answer. You may suggest 'torn uniform', or 'children look visibly poor', or 'poverty'. These three codes are all correct, depending on your data set. If poverty is a dominant theme that is described in many different ways, poverty is likely to be too broad a code. You would simply have too much data lumped together under the code of poverty. Equally, if children talk about some of the different ways they look poor (for example, walking to school barefoot, or unable to get a haircut), then the 'children look visibly poor' code may also be too broad, and the code 'torn uniform' would be a more suitable code for a primary theme. It is difficult to know whether a code label is too broad, too narrow, or just perfect, until everything has been coded – which highlights the need for you to continually refine your codes.

CHAPTER 8

Writing a research report

Abstract

This chapter sets out the key concerns in writing up development research for a variety of different audiences, and provides practical tips for such writing. The research report is the most common output of a piece of development research. The primary concern of this chapter is to outline the structure of a research report and to clarify which material belongs within each section. Writing for the public and for peer review are also discussed. For community, public, and policy-making audiences, the chapter suggests that brief texts and more active dissemination efforts such as video or workshops are useful. In writing for peer-reviewed journals or other academic forums, such as conferences, the 'contribution to the literature' is the most important concern, and guidance on how to determine this is given.

Keywords: Qualitative research; report; executive summary; peer-reviewed article; writing

Learning objectives

After reading this chapter, you will be able to:

- distinguish different types of research outputs, their audiences and characteristics;
- structure a research report;
- ensure that each section of your research report covers the essentials; and
- present qualitative research findings.

Key terms (definitions)

- *Executive summary*: The condensed account of a research project, which conveys the important messages, in accessible, brief text.
- *Research report*: The full account of the research conducted, with sections including introduction, methods, findings, limitations, and recommendations.
- *Peer review*: The process through which academic articles are given a quality check by experts in the field, thereby increasing the credibility of the research.
- *Dissemination*: The communication of research findings through a variety of means, including write-ups, video, and participatory activities.

http://dx.doi.org/10.3362/9781780448534.008

Introduction

Applied development research is typically written up in the form of a report. The report explains the rationale and methods upon which the research was based, details the findings of the research, and leads to a conclusion and a set of recommendations that typically target policy and practice. The report provides new knowledge on the settings, projects, communities, and people studied. It also sets out key messages in the form of conclusions and recommendations.

While a report is often the primary means of disseminating development research, researchers often bemoan the phenomenon of crates of unread reports gathering dust somewhere in the corners of NGO offices. Other dissemination strategies are also often advisable. Sending a 40-page report to a policy maker or a community activist is not likely to be the most effective way of communicating research findings! Policy makers work with very short 'briefing papers'. Frontline workers and community members are rarely interested in reading about research as an abstract set of findings, but they *are* interested in findings that have significance and implications for their own lives and work. Peer-reviewed and more academic journal articles have a much more formal set of requirements of the authors, and of the content and structure of the report. In sum, the most important point in writing up research is to think of your audience, and to adapt your write-up and your dissemination strategies to their needs (Nutley et al., 2002; Cornish and Honeywell, 2015). Table 8.1 compares the important characteristics of different kinds of research outputs.

Structuring a development research report

The 'report' is the primary format in which your research is likely to be written up. It is an important format. It has sufficient space to allow you to properly document the research that backs up the conclusions you draw. Blogs, briefing papers, or workshop activities might be 'spin-offs' that extract the key messages, or which identify provocative aspects worth further discussion. But they do not allow the space or format to provide evidence for your claims. The process of developing the analysis, ensuring that you have quotations and examples to back up your claims, and writing up the report all contribute to the thinking process that allows you to develop new understandings and meaningful, grounded 'take-home messages' from the research. In other words, much of the thinking about research is done in the process of writing a good report.

This section focuses on the structure of a development research report, and what should be covered in each section, to ensure that all of the essential components are included. While each report, of course, looks different, and has different headings and subheadings, there are some standard expectations of what needs to be included. These standards are the focus here. Table 8.2 summarizes the sections of a development research report, and the essential components of each section. In what follows, we expand on each section in turn.

Table 8.1 Comparing different types of research output

Type of output	Audiences	Purposes	Key features
Research report	Colleagues Practitioners in other NGOs Donors Policy makers	• Planning • Learning • Evaluation • Accountability	• Clear account of methods and findings • Makes recommendations
Peer-reviewed journal article	Academics Policy makers Development workers	• To add a novel contribution to the literature • To establish the credibility of the research or intervention	• Engages with current literature and theory • Makes an explicit argument in relation to literature • Methodological rigour important
Policy briefing	Policy makers	• To inform policy makers • To influence policy	• Brief (1–2 pages) • Clear take-home messages
Blog	Public development workers	• Thought leadership • Building networks and connections	• Accessible and interesting • Timely • Offers an opinion
Dissemination to communities	Affected communities	• To seek feedback on the validity of findings • To offer feedback to the community • Engagement • Accountability	• Active and engaging (e.g. workshop, training) • Focused on community needs and interests

Executive summary

The executive summary is the most important section of the whole report. Many readers will not find time to read the whole report, but will want to know what it contains. The executive summary is your chance to convey, quickly and briefly, your top 'take-home messages'. It should convey the essence of the report. This means that you need to take a 'big picture' view of your research, so that, rather than a list of perhaps individually interesting but disconnected findings, the executive summary has a clear direction and narrative. The research was conducted purposefully, in order to answer some research questions, and in order to shed light on a particular humanitarian or development problem or intervention. The executive summary reflects those purposes, so that the reader gains a new understanding of the issues in relation to those problems, and comes away with a clear sense of the 'take-home messages'.

The executive summary needs to stand alone, so that a reader can make sense of it without having to go on to read the full report. It communicates the main points from each section of the report, but without using subheadings. This means that it needs to explain why the research was conducted and

Table 8.2 How to structure a development research report

Section heading	Purpose	What to include
Executive summary	• To communicate the essence of the report to a reader with little time, in less than 2 pages of very short paragraphs • To be read as a stand-alone piece • To be very focused on 'take-home messages'	• Why the research was conducted • What methods were used • Main findings • Conclusions • Recommendations
Introduction	• To explain the purpose of the study • To set the context	• Your 'analytical gaze' • The purpose of the study • Context • What is already known • Gaps or limitations in the literature • Aims or research questions
Methods	• To document the methods on which the research claims are based, covering:	• Research design • Research ethics
	• Data collection	• Setting and selection of sites • Sample and recruitment • Tools or instruments • Procedure
	• Data analysis	• Type of analysis • Process of analysis
Findings	• To set out your analysis of the main findings • To provide evidence for that analysis using examples of primary data	• Subheadings to organize the findings into different areas • Analytical statements about what the research has found • Evidence drawn from the primary data
Discussion and conclusion	• To establish the answer to the 'So what?' question	• Summary of key findings • Discussion of findings in relation to the literature (do they support, contradict, or build on existing evidence?) • Commentary on the significance and/or implications of the findings ('So what?' for policy and practice) • Limitations and reflexivity • Recommendations (for policy and practice)
Annex or appendix	• To document important details that do not fit into the flow of the text • To provide transparency	• Any useful information about the conduct of the research • Copies of research tools • Further details on the sample • Full coding frame

mention the methods used, in order to set the context. Then the bulk of the space will be given over to the main findings. In the executive summary, the findings are presented without examples or evidence (unlike in the body of the report). At the end, the conclusions and recommendations are presented.

The style of the executive summary is direct and brief. It should run to around two pages, and be structured with very brief paragraphs (perhaps two sentences each), and/or bullet points – to make it easy to navigate.

Checklist: Your executive summary

- Runs to no more than three pages.
- Contains short paragraphs (no more than three to five lines).
- Starts a new paragraph for each new point.
- Is a stand-alone document.
- Presents only the essential points of the research.
- Concludes with clear recommendations and/or 'take-home messages'.

Having emphasized the importance of the executive summary, it is also important to understand that a good executive summary cannot be written without having first written a solid report. The executive summary needs to reflect substantial engagement with a large body of empirical data – so that there are new findings to report. It also needs to reflect deep analytical thinking about the findings, which lead the authors to be able to make substantial and actionable recommendations. Writing the full report requires us to find the right language for our aims and our contributions. It forces us to state our findings in a way that we can evidence with data and that forms a meaningful narrative in response to the research questions.

So, the executive summary is the section that should be written last, but it should not be rushed. It should be written at the end of the writing process so that it can reflect all of the thinking work that has been required to produce the full-length report. The risk of leaving it until the end is that it is often hurried to meet a deadline. Remember that the executive summary is the section of the report most likely to be read, especially by senior-level people with decision-making power. Therefore, it should be well structured, to the point, and clearly written. It should highlight the most important points of the document, including key findings and recommendations.

Introduction

The introduction sets the scene for your study. By the time the reader finishes the introduction, he or she should understand the purpose of the study and why it is being conducted. The introduction may or may not use subheadings. Even if you do not use these headings, it is useful to think in terms of covering: the 'analytical gaze'; the purpose of the study; the context; what is already known and what the gaps are; and the research questions.

Activity 8.1 Write an executive summary

Jejeebhoy and colleagues (2013) present a very well researched and written report on norms and experiences regarding gender-based violence in India, which is available here: <http://r4d.dfid.gov.uk/pdf/outputs/ORIE/Qualitative_report_Formative_Study_VAWG_ Bihar_DFID_India.pdf> [accessed 24 July 2015].

This excellent report has no executive summary.

Write an executive summary for the report.

The executive summary will not have subheadings, but you might use the structure outlined below as guidance for the flow:

- context of gender-based violence in India (one or two paragraphs);
- aims or purpose of the study (one paragraph);
- methods used (one paragraph);
- main findings (several brief paragraphs, one for each main finding);
- recommendations (a separate paragraph or bullet point for each recommendation).

Feedback is available at the end of the chapter.

To orient the reader, early on in the introduction it is important to indicate your 'analytical gaze' (see Chapter 7). What is the focus of your study? Is it a study about local knowledge regarding a particular topic? Or a study of the local feasibility of a particular programme? Perhaps it is an evaluation looking at pathways to programme success or failure. Whatever your 'analytical gaze', it is an important part of the context of the study, and should be stated clearly early on.

The purpose of the study is the reason why you needed to conduct it. Explain the development problem that is faced, and the reason why primary research may be useful to shed new light on that problem.

Establishing the context means providing the reader with sufficient information about the setting of the research to enable them to make sense of it. This should include key information about the country or context, and background statistics about the issue within the country or context (for example, what is known about rates of gender-based violence; or nutritional status; or girls' school attendance; or whatever are the key dimensions of the issue at hand).

Summing up what is known is achieved through your literature review. Before conducting new primary research, it is important to know what has already been researched, studied, and documented about the subject matter. A brief literature review of papers that have similar goals will help to set the context, and will also enable you to illustrate or justify the need for this piece of research you are presenting.

On the basis of the literature review – and particularly after identifying what has already been studied in your topic area, and what gaps there are in the evidence base – you can make a statement about the particular niche or area that your study can fill.

Finally, every report needs a statement of the aims of the research; this is often linked to the original research questions. The research questions are the link between your research interests and the research you carry out, and so they play a crucial role in the logic of the report. They reflect your analytical gaze and narrow that gaze by turning it into a set of questions that you can answer by gathering and analysing data. Getting the phrasing right is important. (See Chapter 2 for a further discussion of research aims.) Having identified the development problem that will be addressed, as well as the gaps in the literature, the aims and questions should emerge as an appropriate response to those problems and gaps. They also open the door to a discussion of the methods, as it is through the methods that your study proposes to offer answers to the research questions.

Methods

The methods section often gets relatively little attention in development reports, because the findings are deemed more important and interesting than the methods through which those findings were reached. Authors, and indeed readers, are impatient to get to the substance of the report, and so, often, they give the bare minimum of space and detail to the methods. Sometimes the methods are discussed as part of the introduction.

To boost the quality of development research in general, we recommend describing the methods in sufficient detail for the reader to understand what exactly you did in conducting the research. Documenting the methodology is also important to allow for a replication or similar study to be designed and carried out at a later date. A detailed methods section also enables the reader to form their own view of how rigorous, convincing, and generalizable your study may be, and thus how much weight to give to the findings and interpretation. Of course, given all we have said about focusing on your audience, you must write your reports in the way your audience expects, and not drown them in methodological detail for the sake of scientific rigour. So, again, the first principle is to follow the norms of your field, to ensure that your readers get what they expect.

Ideally, to provide a comprehensive account of the methods used, a development report's methods section would include details on the following topics. These are the same topics that should be covered in the methods section of an article being prepared for an academic or peer-reviewed journal.

Research design. In addition to specifying that you have conducted a qualitative study, you also need to briefly identify and explain the sort of study you are reporting. Is it an interview study? A Photovoice study? Is it a piece of participatory action research? Is it a case study of an intervention? A formative evaluation? An exploratory study? A few sentences defining and elaborating the type of study are needed, because not all readers will be familiar with the methodological language that you use.

Research ethics. Research must follow established research ethics principles, which should be documented in the report. This section should state which ethical principles were followed and whether or not the research was approved by an independent research ethics committee. It should discuss any potentially ethically challenging or controversial aspects of the study, as well as the safeguards employed to ensure that the study was ethical. If the research involved children, it is especially important to outline child protection policies and practices that were followed. Any risks of harm to participants should be discussed carefully. Typically, the processes used to ensure informed consent should be detailed, as well as means of ensuring confidentiality.

Selection of site. The choice of a geographical site – such as a village, an informal settlement, or a district – or an institution such as a school, or an NGO, or a refugee camp is a key methodological decision. It is important to document how and why you chose the particular location for recruiting research participants. You should include some background details of the site, and you should comment on to what extent it may be typical or unique, or it otherwise compares to other settings in the country.

Sample and recruitment. Narrowing in from the selection of a site, you then construct your sample (see Chapter 2). Your definition of your target group is important. Who was eligible to take part in your study? Did you divide your sample into different groups (such as male/female, or service users/service providers)? Recruitment is the process through which you practically access the site and identify possible research participants, inform them about the research, and invite them to take part. For example, you might recruit research participants through 'gatekeepers'. These are groups of people (community leaders, health clinic managers, or social workers within an organization, for instance) who mediate contact between the researcher and research participants. This process should also be documented, as well as challenges you faced in accessing the site and recruiting research participants.

Data collection tools. How did you go about collecting your data? What tools informed your data collection? Did you use a topic guide, and, if so, what were the main areas covered? How did you guide your observations? If it was a participatory study, what data did you capture and how did you record that data? This section also needs to give details of who administered the data collection tools, with particular attention given to their background and experience. A local researcher who speaks the local language is likely to generate different responses from research participants compared with an external researcher who works through an interpreter.

Procedure. What was the process that research participants experienced and that you used in order to collect the data? For example, if you used an interview study, where were the interviews carried out, and how long did they last? Were participants offered an honorarium or other reward in compensation for their participation? If you used a Photovoice study, what were the instructions given to participants?

Data analysis. This section explains how you moved from your hundreds of pages of transcripts, or dozens of photographs and essays, to your final subheadings, themes, and analysis, which are covered in the pages that follow. This section should identify the type of analysis conducted and explain the main steps taken in conducting that analysis. Did you, for example, conduct a thematic analysis or a case study analysis, as detailed in Chapter 7? It needs to convince the reader that a systematic process was applied to the data set as a whole, so that the resulting main themes and claims emerge from a sustained engagement with the data set and are not simply a personal and impressionistic take on what can be seen in the data.

Findings

This section comprises the main body of the report and will be its longest section. It presents the results of your data analysis in such a way as to answer the research questions.

In quantitative studies, the results (findings) section is often relatively brief, with a longer section discussing and interpreting the findings. In qualitative studies, the findings section is often the longest section of the report. Qualitative findings can be summarized, but the summary is not sufficient on its own. Because qualitative research aims to convey what a particular setting, intervention, or social problem is like, in all its variety and complexity, it is necessary to allow sufficient space to develop and illustrate a picture of the whole.

Structuring the findings section. The findings section will need to be broken down into chapters, or sub-sections, to give a sense of logical order. It can be useful to return to the research questions at the start of the findings section, and to organize the findings so that they respond to the research questions. Introduce the findings section with a statement about its structure, so that the reader understands the structure and what to expect of each section. How to present your analysis is also discussed in Chapter 7; Box 7.1 shows an example of how to structure a findings section.

The topic of each subheading will be elaborated and explored, in the author's own words. For example, in a study conducted by Save the Children (2011), assessing children's psychological needs in the aftermath of flooding in Pakistan, the authors organized their qualitative findings in terms of types of stressors identified in the data. Their analysis of observation and interview data identified: psycho-physiological stressors (e.g. water noises); information stressors (e.g. where to go); emotional stressors (e.g. fear of death); and social stressors (e.g. missing friends). These different types of stressors are used as subheadings to organize the presentation of the qualitative findings.

In a study about stigma and support for people living with HIV/AIDS in Khartoum, Christian Aid (2008) reported its findings regarding the forms of stigma in terms of six main categories: stigma within families; self-stigma;

stigma within the community; stigma and faith-based groups; stigma in the workplace; and stigma in the media. A subsequent section reported on the impact of stigma, dividing it up in terms of four subheadings: psycho-social impact; gender, HIV, and stigma; economic impact; and voluntary testing.

These examples show that the structure of the findings section can be quite simple and straightforward, serving to put things in the same category into the same section, and to make sensible distinctions within the data.

Using qualitative material within the report. Within your chosen structure, the text that you write should describe the main findings under each heading, and illustrate those findings with excerpts from the qualitative material. These might be example quotations from interviews, photographs from a Photovoice project, or excerpts of field note data.

Qualitative material can play a variety of possible roles in the report:

- providing facts from key informants;
- bringing local experience to life;
- revealing different points of view;
- illustrating your argument;
- providing case studies.

Excerpts of data should be chosen to exemplify the key themes. They put flesh on the bones of your statement of the findings, giving readers an insight into what these issues mean to the research participants.

Typically, each excerpt of data is reported along with some minimal details about the context of data collection (for example, important demographics of an interviewee, such as gender or age group). These details help the reader to contextualize the excerpt.

You should avoid including too many quotes. Participants' voices do not simply 'speak for themselves'. The role of the researcher is to present an analysis: that is, an interpretation that goes beyond the individual voices, to offer a synthesis of those voices. A long series of quotations is bewildering to the reader, who does not know what he or she is supposed to take from that list. It is the author's role to present the reader with an analysis that synthesizes the data as a whole, and to illustrate their analysis with one or two quotes for each main point.

Quotes should be chosen carefully so that it is clear how they back up or elaborate the point that they are supposed to illustrate. The beginning and end of the quote should be selected with care, to make it as meaningful as possible. If the beginning is at all ambiguous, some introductory words might be needed to contextualize the quote.

Discussion and conclusions

In the conclusions section, you draw together the threads of the research to come to your 'take-home messages'. Based on your primary research, you

---

Box 8.1 Reporting findings on stigma among people living with HIV in Khartoum

In the previous section, we outlined the structure of findings of the Christian Aid report on stigma among people living with HIV (PLHIV) in Khartoum. The first section of findings reported on 'Forms of stigma', and the first form of stigma identified was 'stigma within families'.

Here is an example of how to write up qualitative findings and illustrate those findings with quotes, taken from the Christian Aid report (2008: 5).

Stigma within families

A sense of social belonging, based on family and community ties, is a very strongly apparent characteristic of Sudanese culture, and the opinions, judgements, and attitudes of kin and social peers are exceptionally important. When someone falls ill, families are usually the first and the main caregivers, providing care and moral and financial support for PLHIV. Family members with HIV seek support and acceptance, and look for compassion and empathy, from their families first.

'I told my family about the result, and that I'm HIV-positive...they treated me very well...They took care of me...they stood by my side and sympathized with me...there is no problem.'
    PLHIV18, female, age 48

Sadly, however, not all families respond positively. People with HIV often first encounter stigma and prejudice at home. More than two-thirds of PLHIV interviewed for this report have been discriminated against, stigmatized, condemned and isolated by close family members. Families frequently turn their backs on those diagnosed with HIV, as one participant describes:

'I'm stigmatized...I'm invisible now...my family abandoned me and left me here alone...I really...really don't know what to do...really...what crime I did? Nobody come and visit...they forgot I exist...My brothers always blame me...and they believe I'm bad...They said I've disgraced the entire family.'
    PLHIV38, male, age 37

Wrong perceptions about HIV transmission and the fear of becoming infected increase the segregation, rejection, and harassments which led many of the people interviewed in this study to cut off completely any contact with their families:

'All of them [all of the family] are not accepting...They are not yet aware of the disease... they believe it can be transmitted by other ways...I mean by meetings...talking...and things like that...I don't live with them anymore...'
    PLHIV30, male, age 43

---

are now in a position to offer your statement of what you have found in answer to your research question, the significance of those findings, and recommendations.

Summary and significance. The first step, especially if the findings section is long, is to sum up your main findings as you see them. What answer have you provided to your research questions?

In addition, you may comment on the significance of those findings. Why are they important findings? What new light do they shed on the development problem of interest? Refer back to the literature. In what ways do the findings support, contradict, or build on the findings reported by other researchers?

Limitations. Like the methods section, discussions of limitations are not always prioritized in development reports. No author likes to undermine their own work, or draw attention to flaws. But every method has strengths and weaknesses and every study has some limits to the conclusions that it can support. In identifying limitations, you will not want to completely undermine your study, but to show that you understand these strengths and weaknesses.

But a discussion of limitations is important for establishing the scientific rigour of a report, as it also is in the methods section. A discussion of limitations helps the reader identify the degree of generalizability and applicability of a study. It helps the reader be aware of possible gaps or pitfalls. A discussion of reflexivity can be useful in this section (see Chapter 2). Reflexivity refers to the researcher documenting their own reflections on how their particular position (gender, role, how the research is seen by the community, and so forth) and their conduct of the research (for example, how they secured access, their preconceptions) may have influenced the course of that research. It is important to demonstrate critical awareness of the strengths, limitations, and applicability of the study.

As well as discussing the limitations, authors can also identify how they sought to overcome or compensate for them. They can also identify alternative options for future research, which might go beyond the particular limitations of the given study.

The discussion of limitations should not deeply undermine the study. It should rather set the boundaries for what can be concluded. If you have followed the guidance in this book, and have taken reasonable and justifiable decisions at each step, then the resulting study will certainly be of some value. The purpose of discussing the limitations is to pin down that value, and to exercise caution and avoid making overly grand claims about the results.

Recommendations. Policy-making readers of development reports will be interested in the question: What should be done? Recommendations can be given for particular interventions, for policies, and for further research (depending on the purpose of your report). Recommendations are often presented in bullet points.

The recommendations given in the report should clearly build on the findings of the research. They should not be general recommendations that could be made simply on the basis of current common sense, or existing literature, or a general philosophical approach to development. The recommendations in a research report should all be specific recommendations that are founded on the findings of the research and that are justified by reference to the research.

Recommendations are prescriptions for action. Even more than the report itself, recommendations need to be oriented to their audiences. This means that they need to match the tools and possibilities open to the policy-making, practitioner, or researcher audiences to whom they are addressed. To understand the avenues of action open to those groups, and thus to write realistic recommendations, it is a good idea to have a dialogue with representatives of the groups to which you wish to make your recommendations. Presenting your research findings to programme managers or policy makers may result in them seeing avenues for action that you had never anticipated. Not doing so risks the author making unrealistic recommendations. In other words, consultation with relevant parties is a helpful step before drafting the recommendations.

The next step for your recommendations is for programme managers to consider them and develop an action plan. The report is part of the cycle of development and improvement of programmes. Keeping that in mind helps you focus your recommendations.

Annex

The annex is the final section of the report. It is not a part of the main text but is a place to store important documentation that is too detailed to fit in the flow of the main body of the report. It can often be seen as a more detailed or technical extension to the methods section. Archiving important methodological details in the annex allows for transparency and replicability of the research.

Copies of the tools or instruments used to conduct the research are often available in the annex. Topic guides for interviews or workshop plans for participatory research exercises, for example, would be useful documents to include in an annex. If a thematic analysis has been undertaken, a detailed coding frame can be informative here. If you wish to give more details of your sample, the annex may be the right place to do so (but be careful to preserve anonymity and confidentiality). Sometimes examples of the primary data (such as interview transcripts, photographs, or field notes) are documented in the annex.

Writing for the public

Communicating your development research to affected communities, to research participants, and to a wider public contributes to the interest in 'downward accountability'. In recognition of the contribution that individual research participants, or gatekeeper organizations, have made to your research, it is typical to offer them an appropriate form of feedback.

Communication to audiences for whom research is not an everyday occurrence calls for brevity, clarity, and active engagement. Written materials should be short (perhaps two pages) and written in everyday language. Methods sections are probably not appropriate. The messages should be very clear, and their significance in relation to public concerns should be evident. Diagrams or photographs can be useful visual aids, and videos are an alternative and accessible means of communication (see Box 8.2).

Overall, active engagement with relevant communities is most likely to be productive (Cornish and Honeywell, 2015). Handing out leaflets is

---

Box 8.2 Alternative means of communicating research to the public

Video

The Bangladesh Reality Check (described in more detail in Chapter 4) created videos to convey the experiences of the researchers. These simple videos documented what was observed at the start of the project, and again towards the end of the project. They illustrated what had changed, and brought the reports to life. They can be viewed here: <http://reality-check-approach.com/reality-checks/bangladesh/bangladesh-reality-check-2007-2012/> [accessed 24 July 2015].

Workshops

'Dissemination as intervention' is an approach outlined by Campbell et al. (2012). After their qualitative research identified a range of barriers to tackling HIV/AIDS, they devised a set of participatory workshops, designed not only to disseminate their work but also to intervene by starting a critical dialogue about the issues. For community members, active processes such as workshops are often more successful that written reports as means of disseminating research.

---

unlikely to produce a significant change in public understanding or action. The most promising dissemination methods are ones that engage people actively in a discussion of the issues, to facilitate the development of new understanding and action in relation to the issues. For example, Sandercock and Attili (2012) created a film documenting a community conflict, screened it at community venues, and after the screenings offered post-viewing dialogues, which brought together diverse groups of people to discuss the film and its implications. Others use workshops, which might involve brief presentations of findings, as a stimulus to group discussions and action planning (see Box 8.2).

Writing for peer-reviewed publication

Peer review is a means of providing a quality check to a piece of research. As a result, publication in peer-reviewed literature is often considered to offer credibility to a research project, suggesting that it is more serious, more objective, and more worthy of attention than a report that has not undergone peer review.

Peer review, in this context, usually means that at least two experts in the field read the manuscript, make a recommendation as to its acceptability, and give constructive criticism to guide a rewrite of the manuscript before publication. Typically, the names of authors and of reviewers are hidden from each other, so that the peer review process is 'blind'. This is done so that the reviewers operate as independent experts. Increasingly, and especially with online open-access publishing, the names of authors and reviewers are made known to each other. This is done on the assumption that reviewers will be more responsible and constructive if they are accountable (by virtue of their name being visible).

Box 8.3 Is my research suitable for peer-reviewed publication?

Does it identify a contribution to the literature?
  Does it engage with literature and theory?
  Are the methods employed with sufficient rigour?
  Has the analysis revealed something surprising or new?
  Have I discussed reflexivity and limitations?
  Do I make a conclusion that goes beyond the immediate study to link back to the literature?

Academic journals are the main type of outlet using peer review. Many books also use some form of peer review, but because their processes are less clear than those of academic peer-reviewed journals, book chapters are often perceived as less credible than articles published in such journals.

Box 8.3 presents a series of questions to ask yourself about your research, to test whether a revised version may be suitable for submission to a peer-reviewed journal. There are two main criteria for the acceptance of peer-reviewed articles: firstly, that they make a justified contribution to the literature; and secondly, that they are methodologically rigorous. These are elaborated in the following section.

Writing for peer-reviewed publication, just like writing for communities or policy makers, requires careful attention to the audience, their expectations, and their preferred writing style. The style takes time to learn. Knowledge of the literature takes time to develop. And writing with the precision and focus required for peer-reviewed articles is very demanding, typically requiring several drafts to produce a submittable paper. In order to write for peer review, an author needs to have dedicated time to do so. For all of these reasons, it is usually very helpful to have a co-author who habitually writes for peer review – someone who can help steer the paper through the process and ensure that it is of sufficient quality to be submitted.

'Contribution to the literature'

The defining feature of articles for peer-reviewed publication is that they must make a contribution to the scholarly literature. This means that peer-reviewed articles need to:

- review the literature in their area;
- provide an analysis of their material that adds something new to that literature; and
- make an explicit statement (at the end of the abstract and in the conclusion) about what this study adds to the literature.

Some peer-reviewed journals require authors to write bullet points summarizing 'what is already known about the topic' and 'what this study adds'. They ask for this in order to help the authors to be crystal clear in their understanding and their statement of their contribution to the literature.

Box 8.4 'What this study adds'

Lindsay Stark and co-authors (2010) published a paper entitled 'Measuring violence against women amidst war and displacement in northern Uganda using the "neighborhood method"' in the *Journal of Epidemiology and Community Health*. The paper sets out a new method – the 'neighbourhood method' – for estimating the rate of violence against women. To summarize the contribution to the literature, and in accordance with the journal's requirements, the paper includes the following summary.

What is already known on this subject

- Violence against women has major impacts on physical, sexual, behavioral and mental health.
- Gender-based violence is widely considered to be more common – and its reporting less common – in the context of complex humanitarian emergencies.
- Reliable estimates of incidence in such contexts are rare given the methodological challenges in conflict-affected settings.

What this study adds

- This study indicates that gender-based violence – particularly violence perpetrated by an intimate partner – is commonplace in post-conflict Uganda.
- The data suggest that fewer than one in ten incidents of such violence are formally reported, indicating that such formal reports are an unreliable basis to estimate current exposure and develop programming responses.
- The paper illustrates an innovative methodology – the 'neighborhood method' – for estimating the incidence of gender-based violence and other human right violations.

Source: Stark et al. (2010: 1060).

Activity 8.2 'What this study adds'

Think about a recent piece of research you have been involved in. If you have not done research recently, think about an intervention or other project you have actively engaged in. Imagine you want to write up the research or experience. To help you figure out the 'contribution to the literature', draft two or three bullet points for the two questions. What is already known on this topic:

-
-
-

What this study adds:

-
-
-

Even if your target journal does not require bullet points on 'what this study adds', it is a useful exercise to try to write them. Your abstract should state explicitly what your study adds, and your conclusion should sum up your contribution.

Summary

Reports should always be written with the audience in mind. Development reports provide a comprehensive account of the research study. There is a standard structure, which should be followed, to help readers navigate the report. Brief and active forms of dissemination are often more useful for achieving impact. Articles for peer review are judged on whether they make a novel contribution to the literature.

References

Campbell, C., Nair, Y., Maimane, S., Sibiya, Z. and Gibbs, A. (2012) '"Dissemination as intervention": building local HIV competence through the report back of research findings to a South African rural community', *Antipode* 44 (3): 702–24.

Christian Aid (2008) *Condemned, Invisible and Isolated: Stigma and Support for People Living with HIV in Khartoum*, London: Christian Aid, <www.christianaid.org.uk/images/stigmatisation.pdf> [accessed 24 July 2015].

Cornish, F. and Honeywell, S. (2016) 'Disseminating qualitative research: from clarity of writing to collaborative action', in N. King and J. Brooks (eds), *Applied Qualitative Research in Psychology*, Basingstoke: Palgrave Macmillan.

Jejeebhoy, S. J., Santhya, K. G. and Sabarwal, S. (2013) *Gender-based Violence: A Qualitative Exploration of Norms, Experiences and Positive Deviance*, New Delhi: Population Council, <http://r4d.dfid.gov.uk/pdf/outputs/ORIE/Qualitative_report_Formative_Study_VAWG_Bihar_DFID_India.pdf> [accessed 24 July 2015].

Nutley, S., Davies, H. and Walter, I. (2002) *Evidence-based Policy and Practice: Cross Sector Lessons from the UK*, Working paper 9, St Andrews: Research Unit for Research Utilisation, University of St Andrews, <www.kcl.ac.uk/sspp/departments/politicaleconomy/research/cep/pubs/papers/assets/wp9b.pdf> [accessed 24 July 2015].

Sandercock, L. and Attili, G. (2012) 'Unsettling a settler society: film, phronesis and collaborative planning in small-town Canada', in B. Flyvbjerg, T. Landman and S. Schram (eds), *Real Social Science: Applied Phronesis*, Cambridge: Cambridge University Press.

Save the Children (2011) *Psychological Assessment Report: Psychosocial Problems and Needs of Children in Flood Affected Areas in Pakistan*, London: Save the Children, <www.savethechildren.org/atf/cf/%7B9DEF2EBE-10AE-432C-9BD0-DF91D2EBA74A%7D/pakistan-psychological-assessment-2011.pdf> [accessed 24 July 2015].

Stark, L., Roberts, L., Wheaton, M. I. A., Acham, A., Boothby, N. and Ager, A. (2010) 'Measuring violence against women amidst war and displacement in northern Uganda using the "neighborhood method"', *Journal of Epidemiology and Community Health* 64 (12): 1056–61.

Further reading

Becker, H. S. (1986) *Writing for Social Scientists: How to Start and Finish Your Thesis, Book or Article*, 2nd edn, Chicago IL: Chicago University Press.

Jack, S. (2006) 'Utility of qualitative research findings in evidence-based public health practice', *Public Health Nursing* 23 (3): 277–83.

Sandelowski, M. and Leeman, J. (2012) 'Writing useable qualitative health research findings', *Qualitative Health Research* 22 (10): 1404–13.

Feedback on activities

Feedback on Activity 8.1 Write an executive summary

Executive summary

Despite national policy commitments to eliminating violence against women and girls, one in three Indian women has experienced physical or sexual violence, with an even higher rate (56 per cent) in Bihar (International Institute for Population Sciences and Macro International, 2007).

The Population Council undertook formative research in the district of Patna to better understand the norms and experiences of girls, boys, women, and men regarding the acceptability of physical, emotional, and sexual violence against women. The study also explored factors that may be associated with 'positive deviance': that is, the characteristics and motivations of non-violent men. Additionally, it explored participants' awareness of relevant programmes and entitlements.

The study was conducted in rural areas of Patna district, and comprised three components. A total of 21 focus group discussions were held with unmarried youth aged 15–25, and married women and men aged 15–50, addressing experiences and perceptions of violence against women, and of possible help-seeking. A survey of married women and their husbands (n=118) investigated experiences of violence. In-depth interviews (n=32) with violent and non-violent husbands investigated men's characteristics, motivations, and attitudes regarding violence against their wives.

Participants expressed traditional notions of masculinity, describing a 'real man' as providing for the family, educating his children, and conducting himself respectably within the village. While most participants agreed that a 'real' man would not perpetrate violence against his wife, many agreed that if disobeyed or provoked, a 'real' man should indeed 'control' or perpetrate violence against his wife. A 'good husband' was described as not abusing alcohol or perpetrating violence. Descriptions of a 'real woman' were brief, gendered, and centred around caring roles, serving her husband, and obeying him.

Most girls maintained that violence was never justified, and advocated verbal resolution of conflict. Boys argued that violence was an appropriate way of responding to a perceived transgression by women or girls. Among adult married people (both men and women), a minority viewed violence as unacceptable, with the others suggesting that it was acceptable under certain conditions. Forced sex outside marital relationships was generally defined as violence, but no participant agreed that forced sex within marriage constituted rape.

Unmarried participants considered violence against girls to be quite common, including sexual harassment by boys and men in public places, parental restrictions on movement and behaviour, and physical punishment by relatives. Home and school were considered the only safe spaces for girls. Girls would rarely report or act on such violence, particularly if the perpetrator was a family member.

According to married participants, violence perpetrated by husbands against wives was common. A gender difference was evident, in that marital violence was reported more frequently by women than by men.

According to women participants, violence perpetrated by members of the marital family other than the husband was common and frequent. Men were less likely to agree that marital family members were perpetrators of violence.

The most commonly reported response to marital violence was silence and toleration, particularly in the case of sexual violence. Informal support from family members, friends, and neighbours was more likely to be sought than formal sources of support such as panchayat, police, or courts. Fear of negative consequences such as further violence, or being thrown out of their home, discouraged reporting of violence. Families and friends were described as not necessarily being supportive. Participants were ambivalent about whether the authorities should be more proactive, with some arguing that violence was a family matter, and others arguing that panchayat and police involvement were necessary.

Non-violent husbands shared many characteristics with violent ones, but consumed less alcohol, and had more equal gender role attitudes. They valued peace and marital harmony. Violent husbands justified their violent behaviour with reference to traditional notions of masculinity and recognized that they were criticized within their community for their violence.

Participants reported that there were no programmes available in their villages to counter violence against women, and recommended four programme directions: reducing misuse of alcohol and other drugs; economically empowering women; changing gender norms; and raising awareness of women's rights and legal options.

The report leads to recommendations for multipronged programmatic action among young and adult populations, both women and men, as well as in schools, at health facilities, and among other service providers.

For the prevention of violence against women, the report recommends: programmes to empower women, to break their social isolation, and increase their economic opportunities; programmes for men and women that challenge traditional gender norms; addressing men's alcohol misuse; building adolescents' life skills and egalitarian gender norms; and encouraging parents to socialize their children in gender-egalitarian ways.

For care and support, the report recommends: efforts to identify, screen, and counsel women at risk of violence; and the publicizing and strengthening of help facilities.

Glossary

Accountability

The means by which people and organizations are held responsible for their actions by having to account for them to other people.

Bias

A tendency to yield one outcome more frequently than others, often as a result of showing an unfair tendency to select some people or locations over others.

Code

A descriptive or conceptual label that is assigned to sections of data (for example, a text segment of an interview transcript, or a section of a photograph). The process of assigning these 'codes' is referred to as 'coding'.

Coding

The indexing of a data set through the application of codes from a coding framework.

Coding framework

A list of descriptive codes that have been systematically generated to capture the content of the data.

Community

A group of people who have something in common. This may include living in the same geographical area or sharing common attitudes, interests, or lifestyles.

Community-based participatory research

An approach to research that enables participants to gather information, reflect upon it, and use this as an opportunity to instigate some level of action.

http://dx.doi.org/10.3362/9781780448534.001

Community participation

A process (and approach) whereby community members assume a level of responsibility and become agents for their own health and development.

Data

Information that has been collected, generated, and captured with the purpose of developing evidence around a topic.

Data analysis

The process through which data, whether quantitative or qualitative, is reduced to produce a coherent interpretation.

Dissemination

The communication of research findings through a variety of means, including write-ups, video, and participatory activities.

Duty bearer

'Duty bearers are those actors who have a particular obligation or responsibility to respect, promote and realize human rights and to abstain from human rights violations. The term is most commonly used to refer to State actors, but non-State actors can also be considered duty bearers' (UNICEF).

Ethnography

A type of study that presents an overall picture of a community, its culture, context, and practices. Multiple methods may be used, usually including participant observation.

Evidence

The available body of facts or information indicating whether a belief or proposition is true or valid.

Executive summary

The condensed account of a research project, which conveys the important messages in accessible, brief text.

Field notes

Also called a 'field diary', field notes are the record of participant observation data, written up by the researcher, usually daily.

Findings

Summaries, impressions, or conclusions reached after an examination or investigation of data.

Focus group discussion

A discussion among four to eight participants, facilitated by a researcher, generating data on the research topic through peer discussions.

Formative evaluation

An early examination of an active programme with the aim of identifying areas for improvement in its design and performance.

Generalizability

The ability to make statements and draw conclusions that can have a general application.

In-depth interview

A one-to-one conversation between researcher and participant, providing information on the participant's point of view.

Individual interview

A structured one-to-one conversation between researcher and participant, generating information on the participant's point of view on a topic.

Mixed method research

Intentionally integrating or combining qualitative and quantitative methods to draw on the strengths of each in answering a research question.

Participant observation

A data collection method in which the researcher learns about the daily lives and broader context of a community by spending time observing and participating in community life.

Participatory learning and action

A collection of methods and approaches used in action research that enable diverse groups and individuals to learn, work, and act together in a cooperative manner, to focus on issues of joint concern, identify challenges, and generate positive responses in a collaborative and democratic manner.

Peer review

The process through which academic articles are given a quality check by experts in the field, thereby increasing the credibility of the research.

Photovoice

A methodology that enables people to identify, represent, and enhance their community and life circumstances through photography.

Programme cycle

The process and sequence in which a programme develops from start to finish.

Qualitative research

A method of inquiry that takes as a starting point the belief that there are benefits to exploring, unpacking, and describing social meanings and perceptions of an issue or a programme.

Reality check

A specific development of participant observation methodology for the purposes of evaluation, in which researchers live with families to understand the impact of a programme in their everyday lives.

Reflexivity

A critical awareness of how the particular position, expectations, and role taken up by the participant observer may have affected the field, research participants, and data.

Research

To study something systematically, gathering and reporting on detailed and accurate information.

Research question

The question that the research will answer.

Research report

The full account of the research conducted, with sections including introduction, methods, findings, limitations, and recommendations.

Study design

The approach and methodological procedure adopted to explore a research question.

Study protocol

A document that describes the study design and operating features of a study.

Topic guide

The researcher's list of issues and questions guiding the conduct of the interview or focus group.

Triangulation

A comparison of a number of different data sources and methods to confirm your findings. For example, you could compare the perspectives of teachers, students, and parents on the quality of schooling. Triangulation can bring strength to your conclusions or identify areas for further work.

Save the Children

Save the Children works in more than 120 countries to save children's lives, keep children safe and help them learn. Established in the United Kingdom in 1919, today Save the Children helps millions of children around the world through long-term development programmes, through emergency responses to conflicts and other disasters, and through promoting children's rights.